THE MAN IN THE MIRROR

JOHN BELFIELD M.I.T.

MAPLE
PUBLISHERS

The Man In The Mirror

Author: John Belfield M.I.T.

Copyright © 2024 John Belfield M.I.T.

The right of John Belfield M.I.T. to be identified as author of this work has been asserted by the author in accordance with section 77 and 78 of the Copyright, Designs and Patents Act 1988.

ISBN 978-1-83538-436-7 (Paperback)
      978-1-83538-437-4 (E-Book)

Cover Design by Getcovers

Book Layout by:
    White Magic Studios
    www.whitemagicstudios.co.uk

Published by:
    Maple Publishers
    Fairbourne Drive, Atterbury,
    Milton Keynes,
    MK10 9RG, UK
    www.maplepublishers.com

The views expressed in this work are solely those of the author and do not reflect the opinions of Publishers, and the Publisher hereby disclaims any responsibility for them. This book should not be used as a substitute for the advice of a competent authority, admitted or authorized to advise on the subjects covered.

CONTENTS

INTRODUCTION 07

CHAPTER ONE: *The Early Years* 08

CHAPTER TWO: *Changes* 20

CHAPTER THREE: *Summer Away in Spain* 23

CHAPTER FOUR: *Student of the Year* 28

CHAPTER FIVE: *The Beatles/Rolling Stones* 31

CHAPTER SIX: *And Then I Found London* 36

CHAPTER SEVEN: *Connecting with the South* 40

CHAPTER EIGHT: *Styling Both Men and Women* 44

CHAPTER NINE: *Christie's Path Labs and Trichology* 47

CHAPTER TEN: *Japan Universal Championships* 56

CHAPTER ELEVEN: *Almost an Astronaut* 61

CHAPTER TWELVE: *1971 - Hair Raising Luxembourg* 68

CHAPTER THIRTEEN: *One of Britain's Super Salons* 72

CHAPTER FOURTEEN: *Missed Opportunity* 76

CHAPTER FIFTEEN: *Going for Gold* 80

CHAPTER SIXTEEN: *The First Hairdresser to Have a Minder!* 87

CHAPTER SEVENTEEN: *It's Like a Rest Home for Retired Hairdressers* 96

CHAPTER EIGHTEEN: *The Science of Hair on Our Doorstep* 99

CHAPTER NINETEEN: *Going Hungry in Paris* 103

CHAPTER TWENTY: *Dodgy Hairdryers and Drunken Staff* 108

CHAPTER TWENTY-ONE: *A Sad Loss – A time to Remember* 113

CHAPTER TWENTY-TWO: *Cheating Germans !* 120

CHAPTER TWENTY-THREE: *Alcohol in the Workplace* 130

CHAPTER TWENTY-FOUR: *An Unexpected Japanese Visitor* 133

CHAPTER TWENTY-FIVE: *Pickled Herring and Gun Boats* 137

CHAPTER TWENTY-SIX: *Retirement for Dad and the Door to Dave Cooke* 142

CHAPTER TWENTY-SEVEN: *Alan Hudson Opening the New Salon* 152

CHAPTER TWENTY-EIGHT: *New York, New York* 158

CHAPTER TWENTY-NINE: *Sharing a Room with Trevor Mitchell* 164

CHAPTER THIRTY: *Policing the Salon Front Door on Match Days* 170

CHAPTER THIRTY-ONE: *The Start of Photography* 175

CHAPTER THIRTY-TWO: *Candles, Wine, Sue* 180

CHAPTER THIRTY-THREE: *The Beginning & End of Travers Belfield Design Ltd* 186

CHAPTER THIRTY-FOUR: *Fire Down Below* 193

CHAPTER THIRTY-FIVE: *New York Once More* 198

CHAPTER THIRTY-SIX: *Flying Concorde* 203

CHAPTER THIRTY-SEVEN: *Judging in Paris* 208

CHAPTER THIRTY-EIGHT: *All Roads Lead to Vegas* 214

CHAPTER THIRTY-NINE: *Las Vegas World Championships 1984* 226

CHAPTER FORTY: *Well-Earned Vacation Gone Sideways* 235

CHAPTER FORTY-ONE: *A Move from Hanley* 238

CHAPTER FORTY-TWO: *A Haunted Salon and Challenging Clients* 245

CHAPTER FORTY-THREE: *John Belfield Product Range* 251

CHAPTER FORTY-FOUR: *1986 - My Last World Championship in Verona Italy* 256

CHAPTER FORTY-FIVE: *Hannah & Harrison Arrive* 261

CHAPTER FORTY-SIX: *Suspicious Times* 266

CHAPTER FORTY-SEVEN: *From Bad to Worse* 274

CHAPTER FORTY-EIGHT: *Ireland, Here I Come* 281

CHAPTER FORTY-NINE: *Delivering an NVQ to a Fourteen-Year-Old Still at School* 288

CHAPTER FIFTY: *Celebrating Ninety Years in Business with Boxer Frank Bruno* 293

CHAPTER FIFTY-ONE: *Diagnosed with Advanced Prostate Cancer* 300

INTRODUCTION

My grandfather, Ralph Belfield, opened his barber shop in Liverpool Road, Stoke, in 1908. Born in Silverdale, he was one of a family of five—two girls and three boys.

When they were older, all three sons had their own shops: Frank in Burslem, Jack in Fenton, and my grandfather, Ralph, in Stoke. It's odd that all of them became barbers. I'm not sure of the reasons why.

But it was at 58 Liverpool Road, Stoke, where my grandfather's shop was, and it was there where my father, Joseph, or Joe, as he was known, was born on February 2, 1911, and later his sister Doris.

So, our family history in hairdressing began at 58 Liverpool Road in 1908 and has so far spanned four generations over more than a century. It began, of course, with Ralph, followed by my dad Joseph, and then me John, and now Jonathan, my son.

My dad had his own shop in Wolfe Street, Stoke until the Second World War broke out in 1939. He served in the Royal Artillery in Belgium, but when he came back from the war five years on, his business had gone, the premises in use as a retail shop by someone else. So, he returned to Liverpool Road, working for his father Ralph. It was here that I started hairdressing after leaving school on July 27, 1962.

CHAPTER ONE

The Early Years

I was born on June 1, 1947. It was the same date my parents, Joseph and Marjorie, were married, some three years earlier. By this time, my family was housed in temporary, prefabricated accommodations, known as prefabs, in Trent Vale.

So, Marcel Close, Trent Vale, became my first home until I was five. I lived with my parents, my older brother Stuart, and our Alsatian Rusty. I don't have many memories of living there, but I do remember Rusty biting the postman one day and we had to have him put down.

Mum worked at a furniture store opposite my granddad's shop, and it was there where my mum and dad first met. I suppose back then, people connected by simply being more active in the proximity of each other's workplace. There weren't cars back then, only walking to and from the nearest bus stop. By the time I was five years old, we had moved over the main road (the A34) to a three-bedroom house in a cul-de-sac called Bramley Place on a new council estate. It was from there that I started school at Oakhill Primary when I was five, later moving to Oakhill Secondary School.

I left there at fifteen. The old prefabs we'd lived in previously were eventually demolished, and the land became part of the Michelin Tyre Company site.

The Man in the Mirror

I remember my first day at primary school. I recall sitting in a sand pit with a lad named Phillip Berry. I cried my eyes out, thinking that at the end of the day it was done. No more school! Or so I thought. Little did I realize it was to take up the next ten years of my life.

My dad had three jobs when I was little. He worked with his father Ralph in the barbershop on Liverpool Road on Tuesday and Friday. He also did haircutting for patients and shaving at the Royal Infirmary in Hartshill, not far from the shop, and on Saturday nights, he went to Manchester, where he parcelled Sunday papers for *Robinson's*, a newspaper wholesaler in Burslem. He worked all night, returning at five a.m. on Sunday morning, and then delivered to all the local newsagents. Dad was a well-known character among the newsagents.

My grandfather's shop also sold newspapers, and he had a small delivery round in Stoke and Oakhill. He sold cigarettes, as well as fireworks when they were in season. Looking back now, I realize how hard it was for my parents then, and I wonder how they both managed to do all the work they did.

Dad was also a church warden at St Andrew's on Hartshill Bank, not far from the hospital and the shop. Sunday was a busy day, as there was an eight a.m. 'spoken' Eucharist service, a nine-thirty a.m. sung Eucharist, with morning worship at eleven a.m. and Evensong at six-thirty p.m. Dad was also a chorister for most of his life, seventy-eight years or more, so being involved in the church was a big part of his routine.

At the end of the 1950s, St Andrew's Church closed, and Dad then joined the Minster Church of St Peter Ad Vincula in Stoke. It was here, at the age of ten, that I joined the church as a choir boy and later became an altar server and a bell ringer.

In those days, I never looked back, asking, 'Why did I commit my Sundays at church so much'. It just evolved over time. So many people went to church then, and their social life also revolved around it. The bonus, as far as church was concerned, was when weddings were held on Saturday afternoons and the choir was required. I got half-a crown for doing it, which was quite a lot of money in those days. As an added bonus, we often played football around the back of the vestry.

Sunday lunch was spent listening to the radio. First to air was the BBC's Forces network for listeners' requests, followed by Jimmy Clitheroe and Round the Horne with Kenneth Horne. It was the same every Sunday.

Family holidays were spent in either Blackpool or Rhyl in my younger days. You were thought to be a bit better off if you went to Blackpool rather than Rhyl. Needless to say, we went to Rhyl. We would go during the Potters' Fortnight, or Wakes Weeks, as they were known. But we didn't go as a family. I went with my mum and older brother on the train with most of the rest of Stoke-on-Trent.

Stoke station was always packed with families doing the same thing. We shared a caravan with Auntie Doris and Uncle Eric on a site in Towyn, near Rhyl. Dad would come over on the Thursday of the second week and then go back with us on the Saturday. Dad never had a full holiday with us as a family, although that changed when Uncle Eric got a car and let Dad use it to drive over to us on the weekend. On these occasions, Dad used to join the choir at the parish church in Rhyl town centre. He always found time to go to church and for choir singing, even away on holiday.

But Uncle Eric's car wasn't the most reliable of vehicles, and I remember many occasions when it broke down before we got to Rhyl and we'd be hours stuck on the roadside. Some holiday!

The caravan we stayed in was small. It had gaslights and a gas stove, with no electricity like caravans of today. We had to walk down a field to portable loos if we needed a toilet.

The main part of the holiday was joining up with other kids, and we'd play football in the middle of the field every day, as all the caravans were situated around the perimeter of the field. There was an amusement arcade at the entrance to the site, though we had no money to play in the arcade, but it was the 'hub', and we would make friends there for the holiday.

Having an older brother meant that anything he grew out of would be handed down to me. It wasn't rocket science to see he was the family favourite, particularly with Doris and Eric, but it was how family life was. He got a new bike for Christmas and I got an old frame done up by my Uncle Tony (my Mum's brother). We did get to a point where there wasn't much difference in our sizes in clothes, but Stuart got the new ones and I got the hand-me-downs.

Back then, we had a bath once a week. My brother always went in first, and I had his bathwater after. I hated it! The only thing that really got to me wasn't to do with my older brother—although I was a bit miffed when he got piano lessons and I didn't—it was being the last boy in my class to still be wearing short trousers. All my school mates got long trousers and I was still in short trousers, with my underpants hanging below the level of my trouser legs!

I suppose I drifted through my early years at school, particularly junior school.

When it came to the town swimming gala, it was just my brother and me competing for the school. We usually won our races; not because we were that good but because back then, most kids couldn't swim. I can't even remember not being able to swim. Our family life outside of school revolved around swimming. My Dad played water polo for Stoke Swimming Club, and Club night was Wednesday evenings. On Tuesday evenings, Dad had his own club night, which included Stoke Boat Club, with their kayaks and canoes in the pool, too. Dad used to have me demonstrate how to turn a kayak over submerged and then right itself again, all good fun. Then, on Mondays and Fridays, my Mum had her own swimming club at the Blurton School pool. I was never out of the water!

Our swimming master at Oakhill Junior School was Derek Taylor, a geography teacher and the guy who started COSACSS (City of Stoke-on-Trent Swimming Club). He didn't have a swimming background, but he saw an opportunity to create a schools' swimming section, mainly on the back of me and my brother doing so well in all the schools' galas, then he took the credit for our school's success.

Dad was also secretary of the North Midlands Swimming Association and a member of the Staffordshire County ASA. I saw Derek Taylor at my granddad's barber's shop more times than I had hot dinners. He'd be finding out as much information as he could about swimming in the North Midlands. I believe that without my dad's help, Derek Taylor and COSACSS would never have happened.

After the war, competitive swimming in the North Midlands gained international influence from my dad, for during his time stationed in Belgium, he played water polo for Antwerp Swimming Club. I know it may sound crazy now, but he did create that influence in the region. He kept that connection for more than fifty years after the war.

I took him to Dover fifty years later in 1995 so he could cross the English Channel to be met in Ostend by the last remaining member of the team he played in during the war. Their reunion lasted four days. Then I drove back to Dover to pick him up. He was well made up!

We also billeted some Belgium swimmers who took part in the 1948 London Olympics. Back then, they made their own way to this country to compete.

So, with his international water polo experience from his time during the war, Dad introduced the continental style of water polo to the Northern Counties ASA as a coach. He had trials for the national team but never made the cut. However, he did change the way water polo was played in England back then.

During those early years at Oakhill Junior School, pupils used to go to Stoke Baths once a week for swimming lessons, but because my brother and I could swim, we weren't allowed to go. So, when it came to the town swimming galas, my brother and I were the only swimmers from Oakhill school. We had to swim in all the races. It used to really annoy my dad because, as a family, he felt the school took advantage of us when it suited but not when it came to weekly swimming lessons for us.

I was pleased when my brother passed his 11-plus exam and moved to Longton High School. He had a reputation for fighting a lot, which didn't help my time at junior school level, and because of this, our family didn't have the best of reputations at Oakhill Junior School. Even back in those early days, I didn't get on with my brother. I never looked up to him, nor did I enjoy his company. He didn't like me back then, and he doesn't like me now. Looking back as I write this, in today's terms, I suppose I saw him as a bully. Whether that was the case for others, I wouldn't like to comment, but that's how I saw him.

Being two-and-a- half years younger made a big difference when he got to sixteen and me at thirteen and a half. On one occasion, when we were practicing water polo at Stoke Swimming Club, I was on the opposite side to him and dis-possessed him of the ball. He just turned around and hit me, and I mean *HIT* me. That's something I will never forget. I didn't understand the anger he had toward me, as would most of the players back then too.

Junior school was okay. I got on with it, but I have no major memories that stand out from my time there. I was rather quiet and shy at that age, and though I wasn't the best in my class, I wasn't the worst, either. I had no real challenge to achieve. Homework and end of term exams in my day meant studying the night before or at breakfast on the morning of the exam.

As I've said earlier, we moved when I was five to a new council estate away from the prefabs, as did all the prefab families like us. Britain in the 1950s saw the country rebuilding after the war. Our council estate had many families resettling. In fact, the whole estate was like a new village. All of us were in similar circumstances.

Dad went back to barbering in his father's shop, having lost his salon in Wolfe Street, Stoke after being away from it for so long because of the war. Mum worked as a wage clerk at the AA (Automobile Association) offices in Stoke. She was known as the woman who was always in a rush. Wherever she went, to and from the bus, on her way to and from work, she was always in a hurry. She usually got home by five-fifty p.m. on the dot.

The Man in the Mirror

I walked home from school every day, and our back door was always unlocked. Our house wasn't the only one with an unlocked back door, but burglaries were non-existent back then. We just didn't need a door key.

In the summer, we played hopscotch in the street outside our house till Mum got home from work. In the winter, I had to light a coal fire. That was something else. *Old Sentinel* newspapers were made into sticks to start the fire, and I had to carry the coal from a coalhouse in the entry by the side of the house. It was dirty and dusty and had an outside toilet.

In order for me to get the fire going, I put a shovel vertical against the fireplace with a large sheet of newspaper against it to create a draft to get the fire started. I had to be careful, because once the fire got going, so did the paper against the shovel. If the paper caught fire too, I'd chuck it on the fire quick and all was well. How the house never caught fire, God only knows, but that was how it was every winter's day after school. So, by the time mum got home, we had a warmish house and a back boiler behind the fire knocking out some warm water.

Dad was never home at those times, and we never had tea at the table as a family, only on Sunday lunch after church and before Evensong. I didn't see any of this as anything but normal. It was how life was back then, and it hasn't created any baggage in my life, as some people might claim today.

During the summer holidays, we were left to ourselves. My brother did his thing, and I joined my school friends and did the same. Mum and Dad went to work. I wasn't left or abandoned, just left to look after myself, as were all my other school friends. We played down the Lyme Brook, jumping across at the narrow parts, and if we felt adventurous, we'd try our luck getting into Trentham Gardens. My Dad knew one of the blokes on the gates, so we'd say: 'I'm Joe Belfield's son'. If we got the right bloke, we'd get in. Otherwise, we got our collars felt and ran off back home, hoping we didn't get found out. That was summer.

You know, I can't remember it raining, only the good days.

We also tried our luck getting a swim at Stoke Baths. Same system for getting in. 'I'm Joe Belfield's son'... Well, the baths superintendent was a man named Norman Gifford. He was a loud, miserable bloke, but he had a kind side. The problem was which side he'd be when we tried to get in. Stoke Baths was a fair bike ride from where we lived. I don't know why we bothered; apart from the fact we had no money. If we got in, it was bedlam, and you had to change in a cubicle with at least two others!

Health and safety was unheard of then. There were no poolside attendants, nothing. Kids were climbing on top of the cabins, jumping in the pool, and landing on people in the water. Yeh, bedlam it was!

Senior school was an extension of the same. I got on with it. Classes were graded A, B, or C. I was in the A stream; not brilliant at anything but not bad at any of my subjects either.

We had a great sports master, Mr Cookson. I engaged in all the sports and became the school swim captain, not the fastest but the best at all of the strokes. We had the best school swim team in the area and, individually, I made it to county level as a back stroker. When I look back, Mr Cookson was having his best time as a sports master.

It could have been coincidence, but when we all left the school, he retired at the same time. He was a great teacher. We all went the extra mile for him, and he did for all of us too. His ethos toward work has stayed with me throughout my working life.

From the age of twelve, I began going to the shop in Liverpool Road after school or straight from Burslem baths after city schools' swimming training. Friday evenings were the nights when we had the once-a-week customers in for a shave, most of them from the Salvation Army Hostel, which was in the back street behind the salon.

But there was always one constant denominator. It was pay day for other customers, so they'd have been gambling in the bookmakers', then the pub, and then down to our barbershop for a weekly shave before going home with whatever money they had left. These were blokes who never told their wives what they really earned. They were the same ones every week with a full week's growth of beard—dirty buggers, they were. Most of them had their own shaving mug at the shop, so it was a face wash and shave, courtesy of me, the lather boy. There's a skill in lathering up a thick growth of beard, softening up the stubble with a badger bristle brush dipped in boiling water from the little tub in the back kitchen. I added Shavellow shaving soap, which was a professional brand of shaving soap used back then for the softening process, and I lifted the beard hair with a rotary action, repeating dipping into the boiling water for a good five minutes so that my Dad, with his mega-sharp, hollow ground razor could get really, really close to the face for an extremely smooth, refreshing, and, for some, sobering shave.

I learned how to strop a razor to bring up the blade to sharpness again, learning the same process on a stone, and all for nine pence (old money). The odd customer would buy ten Woodbines and, occasionally, 'something for the weekend'—if they had enough left from the bookies. The only time I ever got a tip was at Christmas, and it was from one guy named Jimmy Burns. He was a typical Friday night regular, but he always remembered to tip me three pence at Christmas. It was my only tip, as I recall. The customers who did have a few bob never tipped. They never really noticed me. I was just part of the crap, dingy furniture.

By eight-thirty p.m. I was emptying the shaving slops out of the bucket under the sink (no drains) and cleaning and mopping an uneven tiled floor, where the mop water would lie in puddles. Everything had dirt on it, be it clay from the pot banks or coal from the pits. I had no pay, either, so if that's what they call 'baggage' for a twelve-year-old in today's terms, then I've got plenty of it!

Then off I'd go to home to Trent Vale. I'd cycle home in the summer; otherwise, I went on the bus.

Saturday, it was much of the same. The shop opened at eight a.m. If I had football for school, then I'd go down to the shop after that.

During the summer months when there was no football, it was an eight a.m. start. We had more hair cutting in the mix on Saturdays. Dad would have me run the clippers up and around each head in a U shape. I did this with hand clippers in the early days and later with posh electric ones. Then Dad would taper out each clipper line I'd put in and then move on to the next customer.

It was like a production line, either up the head with the clippers or down to the back kitchen, boiling the kettle to fill a shaving mug for the next shave lather-up. Oh, and I had to sweep up and keep an eye on the bucket under the sink, which needed regular emptying of slops down the grid in the yard at the back of the shop.

In the winter months, I was allowed some time off on my Saturday mornings if I had a school football match to play. After that, it was down to the shop to help Dad. If Stoke City had a home game, the salon was quiet while the match was on, so Dad would let me go to the match. Kick-off back then was three-fifteen p.m., so ten minutes before, I would run down to the Victoria Ground for the game. But I needed to leave ten minutes before the end because the shop was mega busy with customers coming in after the game had finished. It was solid right up to closing time around eight-ish. Dad would catch a couple of hours sleep before going to his Saturday night job, on what I knew as the paper trains. As I said earlier, he worked for Robinson's in Burslem, whose workers would collect and parcel the Sunday newspapers for all the local newsagents and deliver them around five a.m. before each newsagent opened. Then Dad would get a few more hours sleep before going to church at ten a.m. That was the start of each Sunday.

CHAPTER TWO

Changes

I was about ten when my grandfather died. My grandmother had passed when I was very young, so I barely recall her. There wasn't much of a social life for families back then. My only memory of them both was working and living at the shop on Liverpool Road. My Auntie Doris, Dad's sister, and her husband, Uncle Eric, also lived above the shop. Eric was a bus driver for the PMT, a local bus company, and Doris worked at Wooldridge's Butcher's in the centre of Stoke.

When my grandad died, some issues developed, or more probably evolved, between my dad, Doris, and Eric. Looking back now, I can understand it. I was a bit in the way, the reason being that Eric fancied doing barbering and connecting with the business. So, when Dad was on his Tuesday and Friday days at Royal Infirmary, Eric was having a go at cutting hair. Dad was furious when he came back one day and found Eric cutting a customer's hair.

I think Doris and Eric felt I was 'in the way' of Eric's ambitions for joining the business, although it was years later before it really registered with me because I always felt my brother was number one in their eyes. I suppose from their point of view, I was in the way, and they did live over the shop, too.

There was more friction to come. The shop takings paid all the bills, the rates, and electricity, plus whatever else needed to be paid, so it meant Doris and Eric had no overhead because they lived above the shop, the shop paid for all the bills. But Dad wasn't about to subsidize their outgoings. Also, around this time, I was biking down to the shop from school for my lunch, and I got the tail end of most of the arguments. Aunty Doris would get back to the shop for her lunch around the same time as I did, so, if there were no customers in the shop, she would turn the lights off to save money, I think Dad was asking for some sort of contribution toward these bills. It wasn't a happy period, and from that time on, I felt resentment from both Doris and Eric. They saw me as next in line to the business and not Eric, and that stayed with me as I got older.

When I eventually left school and started working in the shop, Doris and Eric were still living above it, sharing the back room and kitchen downstairs behind the salon and the outside toilet in the backyard. If anyone needed a bath, people went to the communal baths at the rear of Stoke Baths. In fact, all the local swimming pools in the area had rows of personal baths at the back of the premises. People didn't have a bathroom in the traditional terraced properties. Bathrooms came with the new builds and council houses.

The Potteries in the 1950s was a community rebuilding itself after the war. The population was a big, industrial mixture of pottery workers, miners, steelworkers from Shelton Bar, and just up from Stoke was the 'new money' from the Michelin Tyre Factory in the West End area of the town.

Senior school came and went. I enjoyed woodwork, metal work, free hand art, and technical drawing. Maths was okay, so long as the maths teacher was sober. The first lesson after lunch, he would openly go to the cupboard by his desk and have a drink. I could never understand what he was saying, his words were so slurred.

Science, too, was a good subject for me. It covered an awful lot of topics. After talking to our young hairdressing apprentices over the years, I believe my education covered far more on my subjects than the generation of today.

There was always one teacher you never got on with, and, for me, it was my geography teacher. His method of teaching and keeping us in order came right at the beginning of the class, which was to give one of us the cane. That way, the class was silenced with fear. And the one who usually got the cane was me. It probably wasn't always me, but that's how it felt.

"Belfield, get out here," he would say.

"Why me, sir?"

"Shut up, boy. Hand out." *WHACK. WHACK.*

You could hear a pin drop in the class. The only time I ever spoke to him after that was on the last day of leaving school. I stood by the school gates and, as he stopped his car to drive out, I leaned forward and shouted a load of abuse at him. Boy, did I feel good. He just looked at me and drove off, but he knew. It took a lot for me to do that, but I felt better for it. With The tirade I unleashed, you wouldn't think I was a quiet shy boy, but believe me, I was!

CHAPTER THREE

Summer Away in Spain

It wasn't long before I got into the competition side of barbering. At least there was job satisfaction in pursuing that side of the trade, and my ambition was to have the standards of Jimmy O'Neil and Albert Hartland.

I got to know a few of the regular competitors, and my questions would be, "Where did you get those brushes?" And the same for combs, too, particularly because your comb was the most important tool for a hairdresser. Even today, when visiting hairdressing exhibitions, I'll always come away buying combs; they became an obsession, I filed the teeth down, sharpened them, and broke every other tooth out, creating my own style of comb. Some of my combs had teeth as sharp as razors, but they went through hair like a dream.

And so the word 'hairdressing' started to have a meaning, i.e., hair dressing! I started to understand how important the comb and the method of being able to dress hair was. Yes, back then, the better you dressed hair, the better the hairdresser you were, adding all this up. A French Razor cut resulted in beautifully dressed hair, usually with no more than two to three inches, and it was my perfect haircut, known as a sculpture cut—the classic of all men's haircuts back then.

I practiced every minute of every day. I called on all the techniques

I'd seen from the demonstrations my dad had taken me to, and yes, practice does make perfect, but it takes hours, days, weeks, and months to get to that standard, that ultimate haircut! Barbering today is a doddle—try doing it on some guy who's just come off a factory with a head full of dust, and the dust is so thick you can't get your comb through the hair and you breathe it in, because that's how it was and not how it is now, and then cut with a pair of hand clippers, too! Nobody had their hair washed, and I think in some cases, the only time they had a face wash was when they had a weekly shave.

I became known as the guy who could razor cut hair. Yeah, me and my French razors, and the new kids on the block wanted me to razor cut their hair. Everything was French—French was the fashion; it had a MAGIC ring to it.

The two main haircuts that I practiced and practiced on were the classic sculpture cut and the crew cut, because those two haircuts had every technical craftsmanship skill in doing them. Luckily, I had two reliable models and friends to practice on. For my classic sculpture cut, my model was my school friend Keith Bridget, and my crew cut model was a guy who worked at the front desk at Hanley police station. His name was Phil Maskery, and we became and still are very good friends. I wouldn't be the hairdresser I am today without the support of Keith and phil. They sat for me patiently for hours and hours, weeks and weeks, months and months, year in and year out.

Phil still comes to the salon over fifty years on and is probably one of our longest serving clients. Okay, you're wondering if he still as a full head of hair, which is something I can claim because of the way I've always looked after his hair, although he thinks it's all down to him. Well he can have his opinion, and that's mine!

I never practiced during working hours, I needed to put money in the till, and that was the order of the day, so all my practice was done after hours. Many late hours of the night, you could drive past our salon and the lights would still be on, and I would still be there, practicing away. It's weird saying this because that wasn't me when I was at school. Yes, swimming and football were okay, and everything else was alright, but as I started to grow up, I felt all my school friends had moved on. My brother was at high school and my cousin also, and there I was, a bit of a joke as far as they and my friends were concerned, and it got to me. It really got to me. I never let it show, but deep down, I had something to prove, and thanks to them, it gave me the vision that I hadn't had at that age, but once I did, I wasn't going to get left behind, even if I was a joke in their eyes. It may be a part of growing up, but at that age, it was a big thing for me. They made me feel that if you didn't go to high school and you ended up in your dad's barbershop, you didn't have anything going for you that they would have any interest in still having anything to do with you.

Manchester and the guys in my college course became my friends. My school mates were doing their thing, and with me working on Saturdays, it meant there was no time for me to take Saturdays off, while all my school friends didn't work on Saturdays. So, for no other reason, my social circle of friends became some of the guys I played football with in the half holiday league on Thursday afternoons. I made friends in the Potteries and District Sunday morning league, playing for a team called Albion, and I still saw all those at Stoke Swimming Club, many of whom I still see today.

So, the guys on my hairdressing course in Manchester became my social friends, at the age of sixteen going on seventeen. Back then, annual holidays were just two summer weeks a year, and this particular summer, I had my first holiday away from my family.

Ginger, one of the guy's on my course, my first real friend who wasn't from Stoke. It sounds daft now, but in 1963, Bolton was miles away from Stoke. He had two male 'friends' in Bolton who owned a café, they were an item, if ya see what I mean, but really nice people, and they were driving down to Pampalona in Spain for the Bull running festival. They had two spare seats in their car and were doing it on the cheap, i.e., camping.

So, off I went, me and Ginger in the back of their car, all the way down through the west side of France, stopping over a couple of times on the way. The first main stay was at San Sebastion in Northern Spain. It could have been anywhere, to be honest, as I was so made up with being away in another country, it might as well been Timbuctoo!

To add to the adventure, it's best said that camping on this holiday was me and Ginger in a tent six feet in length. We just about fit in it, nothing else, no stove for cooking, just a place to sleep.

We finally arrived, and after three days in the back of a car, we soon made ourselves known, and we went straight down onto the beach. The only problem was it was after midnight, just the two of us, and in the sea we ran, just in our underpants. It was one of those moments you re-live for years to come—off with our clothes and a good hundred- metre run into the sea! Who was going to be first!

We both ran straight in, diving into the waves. We really thought we were the only ones on the entire beach, until two policemen with their guns out turned up. We'd no idea it was against the law to be on the beach after midnight, let alone going in the sea.

My first brush with the law!

Fortunately, we only got a caution. Mum and Dad would have gone nuts if they knew, though that wasn't the only thing they'd have gone nuts about on this holiday!

After a couple of days, we moved on to the next location for our trip. This was for the festival in Pampalona for a whole week, but still camping on the cheap.

I didn't bother to find out much about what this festival entailed, but I soon discovered they run the bulls through a shuttered street at six a.m. every morning to prepare for an afternoon of bull fighting—the main event of the festival. Only, the real main event was that you ran in front of a herd of angry bulls down to the arena. You have a few minutes start on the bulls, that's fine, except they could run a lot quicker than most of us running in front of 'em. As the thunder of bulls running behind you got louder, the only escape was to jump up and claw up the shutters, hoping one didn't gore you.

I never made it to the arena before those bulls!

After three days and nights of fiesta partying with a group of Spanish lads, I went back to our tent, only to find a Canadian couple sleeping in it, thinking it was abandoned. Boy, what a week!

I managed to get back home in one piece, but I'd had an unbelievable time.

CHAPTER FOUR

Student of the Year

Back at the salon, I picked up where I left off before my Spanish holiday, spending as much time as I could practicing. Not just everyday stuff but also competition hair styles, and I went to as many hair demonstrations and competitions as I could, mainly in Manchester or Birmingham. Dad would take me, or I'd go on the train, but one way or another, I got there.

Hairdressing competitions was the big thing in those days. The British Championships was the ultimate event of the year, and from this came the British Hairdressing Team selection for the World and European Championships—this was my goal! To make the British Team. After my second year at Hollings College, I was "Student of the Year" in 1965. It seems a bigger thing saying it now than it did back then. In fact, I ended up student of the year again in '67.

I fitted in well with college life, even though it was still one day on Monday, doing my City & Guilds in Men's and Ladies Hairdressing, then an afternoon and evening on Tuesday on a Trichology Course.

I was incredibly fortunate in 1966 to be invited to go to the World Championships in Italy. I suppose some of the well-known competition workers were starting to notice me, I can only assume that's why I was invited.

So, off to Milan I went as a helper to the men's team. This was an amazing experience for me, watching a world championship for the first time.

Thirty-two countries competed in men's hairdressing and ladies' hairdressing, and the weekend flowed really well, the main events taking place on Sunday and Monday and the parade of nations and results taking place on Tuesday.

On Tuesday at lunchtime, Albert Hartland, the team manager, came to me and invited me to dress all the models' hair for the parade of nations that evening, I was really excited, what an opportunity! So, I spent all that afternoon preparing the models for that evening. Little did I realise that my contribution gave the men's team the afternoon off to drink in the bar. But I learned something, and it stayed with me to this day. When the team manager came back to check that all the hair looked good, he'd allowed me to use his tools and saw that his equipment I'd been using hadn't been put back exactly as I found it.

He became annoyed and turned to me and said, "Boy, when you use my tools and equipment, you put it all back exactly how you found it."

I was really upset at that time, as he was my hero, and I thought that I'd had a really good weekend doing all he'd asked me to do, and here I was, finishing it on a low note.

I attended the parade of nations with the team, and it was a wonderfully moving occasion, but I couldn't get out of my mind the telling off I'd had a few hours before. That telling off was carried forward for the rest of my career, as I treated my tools and equipment with care, as they were such a big part of my life, and I didn't like anyone touching them or using them. If they did and didn't put them back, boy, was I angry.

In the end, neither of our teams' ladies or men placed in the championships, and as usual, it was either the French or the Italians who won. That was the way was back the—they were so advanced in the hairdressing and fashion world.

The other things that weekend the blew me away was the exhibition, the stands, the shows, and the people walking around. I felt really out of place, as I had no style to me. I was sure nobody saw me as a hairdresser. I suppose I never have looked like a hairdresser, or certainly not the image the clients and people expected to see from a male hairdresser.

All that was about to change, as music was the biggest single fashion influence to happen, and it affected everyone. And I, like everyone else joined in. I grew my hair, the short back and sides was quickly a thing of the past, though the local branch of the National Hairdressers Federation blamed me for a downturn in their barbershops. In fact, it was debated whether we should be thrown out of the federation because of it.

The Man in the Mirror

CHAPTER FIVE

The Beatles/Rolling Stones

I saw the Beatles at Trentham Gardens in 64. I say saw because there was that much screaming going on, I never heard them sing a note the entire evening. Three thousand people packed into the ballroom at Trentham Gardens, and at the end of the night, we just heaped up broken chairs and tables where people had been standing on them to get a better view. The same thing happened when I went to see the Rolling Stones at the Gaumont in Hanley. It was a great occasion, but the same outcome—never heard a single thing but screaming all night. Funny really, as I still came away thinking they were brilliant.

And so I left my buddy Holly and Eddie Cochran Era of the late 50s. In the 60s, which we all now know, the Beatles, the Stones, Elvis, plus the fashion with Mod's & Rockers it was an amazing decade. Twiggy, the mini skirt, and Mini Cars too!

With *Vogue*, David Bailey, and of course Vidal Sassoon cutting Mary Quant's hair in 65, Cut and Blow had arrived, and I was all for it.

Who and whatever you were into created part of your personality—everything was visual, or your style of music projected your image. Mods & Rockers for example, or the Elvis hairstyle carried on from the end of the 50s. I remember having an Elvis quaff before

I left school, I used to comb it in with soap and then let it dry; it was rock solid. That was until I went swimming, and when diving in, I left a trail of bubbles behind me.

If I had to pick one hairstyle from that era, it would have to be Elvis. People wore that look from the late 50s all the way through the 60s, and for some it stayed with them and they never changed, as long as they had hair, that is. Blowing in Elvis quaffs from 63 onward put our barbershop on the map—we were the first in the area, and all from watching that guy from Australia at a hairdressing demonstration in 1958 blowing waves in a bloke's hair. So, the term Blow Wave came from Men's Hairdressing originally, it entered our pricelist as soon as we could afford to buy a blow wave type of hand dryer.

And we have to add in Bob Dylan! It extended your music influence by a mile, and from 66 onward, I was a big fan. Even now, it's still there, and I might as well get it out now—I played the harmonica, though not so much Blowin' in the Wind, more of She'll be Coming 'Round the Mountain!

The year 1966 was a big one, not just for me going to the World Hairdressing Championships in Milan, but it was the year we won the Word Cup at Football!

It was the first Saturday of Potter's Holidays, and Stoke was like a ghost town, apart from the railway station, which was always rammed with families going on holiday. But by lunchtime, the salon was completed empty. You couldn't have gone out on the street and dragged somebody in because there was nobody anywhere to be seen. You could have had a game of footie right outside in the middle of Liverpool Rd.

Dad and I borrowed an old B/W tele off Uncle Eric, who was a dab hand with electric plugs—he used matchsticks! So long as we didn't move the TV off the kitchen table in the back living room, we were fine.

Throughout the entire game, we never had one client in, not one! That meant we would likely be staying open later that evening with the hope we might make up for it.

To think that England's hero of the day, hat trick goal scorer Geoff Hurst, would one day be playing for Stoke City, and me and Dave (Arry) Roberts and Barry Adams would be playing Tennis on Geoff's tennis court at his house in Beech. Amazing!

I was now starting my Advanced City & Guilds course on Mondays, plus continuing on a Tuesday afternoon from four p.m. until nine p.m., with my three year course in Trichology. Dad encouraged me to go for it; he believed "learn as much as you can while you can." I enrolled for it, but you had to sit for a test, not quite an exam. This was a new beginning for me, not just an extension to my hairdressing but a good catch up on my missed opportunity of an education at Oakhill School.

There'd been no real encouragement from my parents to have a go and do better, except at sport, that was. It was always, "Get down the shop un help your dad."

The course was for three years, the first year was an O Level standard in Human Biology, Physics, and Inorganic Chemistry. The second year was to an A Level standard in Human Biology, Physics, and Organic Chemistry. The third year was a Study of Maladies Peculiar to the Hair & Scalp, an outline in Materia Medica & Pharmacy three times a month in the Path Labs at Christies, three times a month at Withington General Hospital physiotherapy Department, and a hundred hours at the Institute of Trichology Hair & Scalp Hospital in Brixton London.

So, Mondays were college days, Tuesday evenings were Trichology studies, and my only afternoon off was Thursday, and that was football in the half holiday league, playing for Lewis's store, which, don't get me wrong, I enjoyed it, apart from the fact that were we useless! Then Hanley Baths in the evening with Stoke Swimming club. It made for a busy week, a busy life.

We were only were able to use Stoke Baths in the summer up to October, then it closed and we used Hanley baths in the winter, which was crap, as the water was like a sauna, and there was so much steam you couldn't see one end of the pool from the other, not much good for water polo practice, but, I suppose, better than nothing.

Early '67 was mainly the same. We went back to Stoke Baths at Easter on a Wednesday night for water polo, and I'd passed my driving test the previous October, so I bought my first car, a Triumph TR2, an old knackered sports car I'd spent all my £120-00 savings on, but it managed to take me to Manchester twice a week instead of the train.

Well, the car lasted until the summer. It was a Monday lunchtime, the sun was shining, I'd had the roof off, and a couple of my mates were sat on the back of the car, posing, as we returned from a spin, ready for the afternoon session.

One of the guys on the back of the car said, "Johnny (that's what they all called me), if ya turn the ignition off and pump the accelerator a couple of time, then turn the ignition on again, ya get a real BANG out of the back of the exhaust from the ignited petrol fumes, yeah that will get us noticed!"

Well, the stunt backfired in more ways than one. The car went with a *BANG* alright, flames not only came out of the back of the exhaust, the flame's came up through the centre consol, the car caught fire, and the exhaust fell of as well. I was the biggest laughingstock in front of all the students going back in after lunch. That got me noticed alright, what a wally! And it ended the ownership of my first car! Fortunately, it was coming up to the end of the summer term, so I had quite a few weeks to recover my embarrassment and sort some wheels out by September, hoping nobody remembered me from the incident.

CHAPTER SIX

And Then I Found London

In 1967, I entered the Golden Scissors hairdressing competition at the Europa Hotel in Grosnenor Square in London, right next door to the American Embassy.

It was a Sunday afternoon, and Mum and Dad came with me. I was quite nervous, as London was like another planet—all the best of everything was there... through the eyes of someone from up North. I thought the Manchester lot were on a different living level to me, but London, well, this was well up the ladder, and that American Embassy just blew me away. America, here I was.

It felt that for the first time it actually was such a country, and I was getting the feeling that I was close to it. Call it weird, but that's how it felt, and I was going to be telling all the customers that I'd seen the American Embassy. That was more important than competing in the Golden Scissors in my eyes.

Well, the competition went better than I expected. Once I got going, my nerves settled, and by the end, when I looked at everyone else's work, I thought I might be in with a chance. Well, at least a place. I'd of settle for third if it was offered. But wait for it, third place was called out, not me. Then second place was called out, again not me. I was preparing for a disappointment when—In first place, John Belfield!

I was right made up, and so was my model Keith and my Mum and Dad. Winner of the Golden Scissors!

There were a lot of people coming up to me, saying congratulations. It was an amazing feeling, and there was £25 prize money too. Well at least it helped toward the cost, and I always gave Keith something if we won money.

Then a man came toward me and said, "Excuse me (in a deep, Southern accent), are you coming back next year?'

"Sorry, who are you?" I asked.

"I'm Trevor Mitchell. I came in second, so," he repeated himself, "are you coming back next year?"

I thought he was going to have a go at me, ya know the bad looser approach, So I said, "I don't know, why?"

And he looked straight at me and said, "Because I'm going to win it next year." He smiled at me, and it was a warm smile. I relaxed and shook his hand. "I'm from Southampton," he told me, then made some nice comments about my work, and from this conversation, we exchanged phone numbers. This was to be the beginning of our friendship, which continued and grew throughout both our careers, and lasting over fifty years until he passed away in the summer of 2020.

The name Trevor Mitchell, MITCH! will feature a lot throughout this book.

I should say, he did go back the next year and won the competition, and if you're from the Southampton area, Mitch always advertised himself as Trevor Mitchell International—Winner of the Golden

Scissors. From this win, there was a connection with London, and I went back and did another event in Shoredich Town Hall and won that competition too. Joe Baker, who played for Arsenal, presented me with my prize. I'm including this now because years later, Mitch was responsible for recruiting a cast of extras as hairdressers for a new film that was coming out in 2002 called *Blow Dry*, and most of the scenes were shot in a then defunct Shoreditch Town Hall. But during the four days I was there, the extras cast was surprised that I'd actually won a competition there. That was a dent in some of their egos, all wanting to be centre stage in the film, but more on that later.

Another person at those two competitions who had an early influence on my progress was a man named Robert James. he approached me to join a group of guys he was mentoring for future international competitions. He had an amazing new range of men's products coming out called Magic Form. These product were by far better than anything else that was out there and was aimed at men. He obviously realised getting a group of up and coming hairdressers training together and using these products was a great way of establishing them in the men's trade.

Unfortunately there weren't enough forward thinking hairdressers in the men's industry to get them off the ground. Had he done it five years on in the mid-seventies, they would have taken off. Also, the retail side of the men's side of products was aimed more toward hair loss rather than styling, but for blow drying, Magic Form lotion worked brilliantly on women's hair too, a lot better than my home made FIXIT product for blow drying. However, there were only a few of us mixing it up, doing ladies' and men's hairdressing, as the trade was very much either one or the other, and most hairdressers couldn't see the changes coming.

CHAPTER SEVEN

Connecting with the South

Robert James was a bit of an edgy sort of character. He was an excellent hairdresser, but where his salon was in Soho, it left you wondering a bit after you'd been down there a few times. But his wife Dee was a barrister, a lovely lady who somehow balanced out everything that looked a bit iffy and improved Robert's credibility with all of us. It was a big learning curve for me, as London was something I needed time to adjust to.

Robert had an assistant named Brian Hamell who could see there was a gap between the northern hairdressers and the London based ones. He originated from Ireland he could see we needed a connection, and he helped fill the north/south gap that existed.

I'm only talking about ten or so of us. Some came in and others left; it was a changing group. In my opinion, they couldn't see a bigger picture; those who didn't stay only wanted a quick improvement on their standards. But for me, the hairdressing quality that Robert brought to the table was right up my alley. The rest of it probably improved my ability to see life from a less narrow perspective.

From Stoke to where I was at that time was a huge adjustment for me. If I had to single out my adjustment between North and South, I would have to say that my training time on Sundays at Robert's

Salon in Soho was right up there, and from a different perspective, in Manchester, there was a guy named Roy Chritchley who was well-known around Manchester City Centre, and to be honest I was highly impressed with Roy. He had a Lancashire style to his personality, and we really connected. I learnt a lot about life in a city like Manchester, and his assistant Tom, who was as camp as they come. Between those two salons, Robert's in Soho with a working girl over the top of his salon, and Roy's Salon, with Tom and his outrageous personality, I was beginning to have a broader view on life outside of Stoke!

Back at 58 Liverpool Rd, our original Salon since 1908, Dad had ideas of expanding. We only had two chairs and one naff sink with a bucket under it for a drain, even though we had fixed the place up some. Doris and Eric were still living there, so the back room and kitchen were shared, which wasn't ideal, even the electricity was on one shared meter. In fairness to them, the salon was now busier than it had ever been, and so it was time to move on for all. Doris and Eric moved to a bungalow in Hanford, on the south side or the Potteries, and the salon moved to an empty shop premises slightly lower down on the opposite side, number 81 Liverpool road. I'm not sure where the money came from, some from the sale of 58, plus I'm sure Uncle Roger had an involvement in it in some way, because he always had a free haircut and so did his son, also named Roger.

This shop gave us five working positions, each with a front wash basin, a very traditional-looking barbershop. We had two extra staff, Alan and Tony, where Alan had trained with us at the old salon, and Tony had trained at his uncle's salon in Silverdale he had a good personality, our clients quickly warming to him.

Our reputation was growing in the area, and our salon was becoming the place to go to. I think it's a fair assessment to say we were the first salon, certainly in North Staff's, to change from a Barbershop to a men's hairstyling salon. But this still wasn't enough.

It was just the beginning of a new era, both for me and all those who worked for us at this salon. Our product range changed, too, out with the old traditional Brylcream and Bay Rum, in with Robert James's products Magic Form, and a shampoo cut & blow was on the pricelist, which was totally unheard of back then. We hadn't gone unisex just yet, but we were rammed with clients every day, and it was easier to recruit staff too. People wanted to work and be trained by us, or more accurately—me!

It was a fantastic period in my life, as Dad was still doing his older clients, even shaving too, but there was a new generation of customers coming in, and the cars parking outside the salon became expensive looking.

We kept our philosophy the same; a family business was our brand, although we didn't have any business acumen to create a brand, it just evolved from where it began all those years ago.

I was now well into my Trichology course, as I'd completed my advanced City & Guilds in Hairdressing.

Competition work started to have a much stronger fashion look to it, and during 68/69, I started using more vibrant colours for the modern trend styles, and I was the first anywhere to use curling irons, too. These irons gave a more textured wave than just blow waving. Some criticized me, saying this was too effeminate, but I was moving on toward mixing my work up with techniques for ladies' and men's hairstyling.

I started to grow my hair out long, it was more trendy, an individual look, much to the annoyance of the local Hairdressers Federation. Dad was on the local and area branch of the federation, so he was getting plenty of stick from the older members saying I was ruining the men's trade. They even threatened to chuck us out if I didn't toe the line. Well, I wasn't going to live in the past—either I did hairdressing the way I wanted it to be or I would move on and do something else.

CHAPTER EIGHT

Styling Both Men and Women

My long hair was layered with a styled look to it, and guys were coming in asking if they could have a haircut like mine. Our salon was the only place to get a long, layered, haircut... and you know what's coming next. One or two women started walking in, asking for a long, layered haircut just like mine.

And so, by the beginning of 69, we converted the upstairs room into a "hair boutique". Trendy clothes shops were opening up, using the title Boutique, and so I wanted this room upstairs to be a "Hair Boutique", only this was my space. I wanted an appointment system, and you had to have your hair shampooed, too. No one was doing appointments, but it was *my* space, and it was either you made a reservation, or you could stay downstairs and use the salon as normal. I got so much stick for the "must have your hair shampooed", but that was my rule. I also introduced perming. This was crazy, really, and a bit too far for some, but I had a perm trolley full of perm curlers right by the shampoo area, so every person that came upstairs could see it.

So, ya know what coming now...

"John what's them rollers for?"

"Well, some of the looks we are doing need an extra bit of movement!"

"Blokes don't have curlers in their hair, do they?"

"Yes, up here they do if I think it's needed to give them the look they're asking for."

Well, that got the tongues wagging all over town! It's funny, really, because more people who seemed to criticize, the more people wanted to come.

I took on an apprentice to work with me upstairs, a young fella named Paul Santrian. He was a real mixture of fashion. Bear in mind, this was 69, he had a hairstyle that I could only describe as a "busby hat". He was stick thin with spray on clothes, most of which he'd bought from women's clothes shops, including his shoes. He had the look, and it worked well for the image and brand I was trying to create. As camp as he looked, he wasn't, in fact; just the opposite! He worked hard when he felt like turning in for work, being very unreliable, and I tolerated him as much as I could. But he got the door shown to him in the end. When there's only two of you and your other half doesn't turn up and your appointment book is full, it's a big problem. Reliability is a must in hairdressing, and he just didn't get it!

I didn't set out to copy anyone, but what Roy Chritchley and camp "Tom" his assistant was doing in Manchester, I was in Stoke doing something similar. To be honest, I looked up to Roy; he was more mature and outgoing than me, and his personality was big City. But I had the hairdressing ability he wanted, and so we connected and stayed that way for years. I was always in his shop after college, and though he and Tom lasted a lot longer than me and Paul, I was up and running, and my shop was a lot busier than his. I don't know why, but it was to the point where we had a queue of guys all the time trying to get in, and mixed in with them were women, which added to the atmosphere. Plus, playing some heavy music, it was amazing.

We opened at eight a.m., with no closing time, it was never before nine and usually around ten p.m. when we finally finished. And at the end of the day, there was a smell of perm solution lingering in the air. I knew an up-and-coming artist, Sue Hardacre (married name), and she painted our front widows. I gave her free rein to do it her way, and it just added to our already psychedelic décor.

Sue stayed as a client and still is a client and a very good friend.

That upstairs salon was my space in hairdressing, with so much going on. Clients who became regular customers are still clients today. And if any of you are reading this, THANK YOU!

I don't know how I fitted it all in, Manchester twice a week, water polo Wednesday evenings, football Thursday afternoons and Sunday mornings, and studying for my Trichology course, too. All this formed me into the way of life I know—I never saw it as anything other than that, and still do.

CHAPTER NINE

Christie's Path Labs and Trichology

Each year seemed to add something new, and '68 and '69 were no exception.

My Trichology course was going into its final stages. Tuesday evenings were now three times a month at Withington General Physiotherapy departments, learning the practical uses and methods of infrared and ultraviolet light, plus galvanism and faradism, motor points, and the manipulation of muscle and nerve using electrical methods, and of course the one which I still use today; "Hi Frequency."

It may be dated, but it still has its place in treatments of some hair loss and hair thinning conditions. After that was three months in the path labs at Christie's, histological sectioning and staining slides, and a whole lot of culturing using blood agar and a whole variety of different antibiotics and drugs to see which were the most effective in the samples that we were culturing.

TB was the biggest fear in samples coming into the lab, and as it was explained to me, there was nothing normal in the samples that ended up in there. Well, that was inside Christie's, outside was a very strong smell of mice and rats, which were used for trials and testing new generations of different drugs for treatments of mainly cancer.

John Belfield M.I.T.

Whilst on one of my many weekends down at the Hair & Scalp Hospital in Brixton, doing my hundred hours of training in practical treatments and diagnosis of a gamut of different hair and scalp conditions, one of the students on the course suggested we go up to Wembley. England was playing Scotland in a home international game. It was a Saturday evening kick off, which was great! I was up for that. We took a chance and got to Wembley about ten minutes after the start of the game. We didn't have tickets, and when we found the main entrance, there was a commissioner at the door, so we asked about getting two tickets, and to our surprise he gave us two.

Well the match had started, and there was one big drawback with those two tickets. You guessed it—they were on the Scottish End of the Stadium!

I learned a lot more that evening than the entire weekend down in Brixton. Number one; don't open your mouth and show an English accent. Two; don't cheer or have any resemblance to being an England fan, you would never leave the terrace alive. We were right at the top end of the away end, and everyone was hammered. There was a guy by me, and he had a long coat on with pockets on the inside full of bottles of booze and was passing them around to all his mates. Then I felt the back of my trousers go wet, as the drunk behind me was urinating where he stood, and I got most of it! Add the language and hate toward England, and we had no choice but to join in, My life was on the line here, but, mind you, I did draw the line at urinating. Once England had gone to four goals up with fifteen minutes to go, thankfully a good half of them started to leave. They'd seen enough, and I managed a trip to the loo. We waited until most had left, that was apart from those who were lying on the stairs too drunk to put one foot in front of the other. God knows what happened to them, but outside the Stadium, there were Scottish fans everywhere.

In the papers the next day, I read that the Scottish fans out numbered the England fans five to one.

The big embarrassment was still to come, as we walked around past the main entrance, the Duchess of Kent was just about to leave in her royal car, but the chauffeur couldn't drive because of all the drunken Scottish fans banging on the car shouting abuse, vocally and with a couple of fingers, and she sat there in the back, smiling, giving a true royal wave! That was a sight to see, but we both walked past with our heads down, desperately hoping we didn't get our collars felt! Which, now, some of the abusive fans were. Talk about being in the wrong place at the wrong time!

This was also the year I qualified with the Institute of Trichologist and finished my City & Guilds in Ladies Hairdressing. For my hairdressing practical exam, I had to go to a college in Oxford, which included a permanent wave and then finishing the hairstyle with finger waving. And to add to it for board work, i.e., wig making, this involved me completing a semi-transformation, including single/point and double knotting, plus two and three string fly weft. This transformation was a three-quarter wig, by the way.

Call me old fashioned, but the content of my courses were incredibly broad. Perhaps some would say nobody would want "that" sort of hairdressing today, but the difference in my basic training was learn or craft, and no matter how things may change, you will have the ability in your locker to change with it, whereas today, it's all about today, and these kids doing their NVQ's don't have enough meat on the bone in their craft to adapt to whatever and however fashion in hairdressing may change. As for this quick qualification of an NVQ, in my book, it means "not very qualified". Bring back my Arts and Crafts of Hairdressing, it's still all in there, but the only problem is—nobody is interested in reading it! Apart from me, that is.

I competed in my very first international hairdressing competition in the autumn of '68 in Brussels. I was hungry to have a go. The National Hairdressing Federation didn't show any interest in these events, and nobody from the men's side of hairdressing bothered with them.

The ladies' team was run by the Fellowship for British Hairdressing, and, sadly, both they and the federation never got on back then. There was a big divide between the two, as each organisation wanted to have control of both Ladies and the Men's International Hairdressing.

The competition I wanted to enter was in Brussels at the Atomium site. The building looked like the molecular structure of an atom and was the historic site for the 1958 World Trade Centre.

The event was on a Sunday, I couldn't afford to stay over for two nights, so I decided to take the overnight train on the Saturday night. It got me and my model Ron Spooner into Brussels at five a.m. on Sunday morning. We we're sitting outside the exhibition centre by six a.m., waiting for it to open at eight. My event was at nine.

I hadn't seen anything like it; the exhibition was massive. We enrolled for our event, then, like a child in a sweet shop, I went around the stands, buying combs and brushes I'd never imagined existed, thinking they might improve the standard of my work in my event.

I did okay in the competition. My model Ron was a great help the whole trip, but I didn't have a judge supporting me. A judge from your country helps to keep the marking even and balanced, but there was only myself from Britain in the men's event. We didn't stay for any results, as I'd achieved what I'd gone for, and we got the train back, crossing the channel from Ostend. This gave us both the chance of three-and-a-half-hours much needed sleep.

We ended up back in Stoke at four in the morning, and I was back at the shop at eight, ready for work like it was just the beginning of another week. But going up to Manchester to college was just a bit too far that Monday after my adventure going to Brussels. After this experience, Brussels became my first choice for International Hairdressing Competitions, as it was reasonably easy to get to over a weekend without having the cost of two people flying, and the exhibitions and shows gave me my inspiration I was looking for.

I followed up with entering the Irish Championships in Belfast. I'd been asked to do a day's teach-in there for a group of about fifty hairdressers, so I thought I might as well stay over and enter the competition on Sunday and do the teach-in, which was arranged for Monday. My fee for the teach-in helped cover entering the championships. Well, this trip didn't quite work out as planned, and I ended up with a ten-minute penalty in the competition for what they said was over preparation of my model, which in my view it wasn't. I felt an atmosphere toward me, to be honest. I was the only English competitor there, and this was at the end of 1968, a few months before all the trouble started in 69, but had I known how I was going to be received in that competition hall, I would never have entered.

When they announced me as the winner, all hell broke loose and a fight started. I never made it as far as going up on stage and receiving my award.

The guy who arranged the teach-in rushed over to me and said, "You need to leave, now!"

He got me out through a fire escape door and back to my hotel. As we were driving to the hotel, he explained that there was a £250 bet between two of the competitors, one who was from Dublin and the other from Belfast, both were favourites to win it.

£250 would have bought you a new mini car back then. It was a lot of money, and both thought they had it in the bag, and I messed it up for them both!

I did stay and to do my teach-in the next day, although the main talking point was the results the night before. I left as soon as I could, most of the hairdressers at my teach-in were okay with me, but it wasn't as good an atmosphere as I would have liked.

I never went back, and a few months later, the Northern Ireland trouble started. No, it wasn't down to me or hairdressing, but I could feel there was something not right. If I'd thought for a minute what it was building up to, I would never have gone. Having a warm connection to hairdressers was one thing, but the other was something else!

From there I went on to win The British Championships in Men's Hairdressing, and with that was also a place in the British Men's Hairdressing team to compete in the European Championships in Madrid later the same year, I was flying, on a real high, and it was unbelievable. My thoughts went back to Jimmy O'Neil and Albert

Harland, dreaming one day I could make the British Team just as they had. It may seem an easy road to take, but believe me; every hour of every day, I worked my socks off to make the British Team. However, as of yet, I'd won nothing. My journey was just beginning, and I wanted more!!

Robert James was our team manager and trainer for these European Championships.

This was my first opportunity to put on the blazer with the Union Jack on the breast pocket, and it was a very proud moment for me. I can understand the feeling it gave anyone who had the opportunity of representing their country, no matter what the reason was. Little did I know then that I would be putting that blazer on for the next sixteen years.

My confidence for the British Championships was high after Brussels, and I was using techniques I'd seen never seen or used before, which raised the attention of quite a few of the guys who were competing against me. It was highly competitive, and there were some big egos out there that day, all wanting to know about where I'd got this comb from and that brush. The curling tongs I used in one of the events definitely was the first time in a men's competition anywhere in the UK. Guess what, the next competition I entered, they all were having a go using curling irons. Copycats Galore!

I completed my Trichology Qualification in the summer, along with my City & Guilds in Ladies Hairdressing. I needed to stay focused on underpinning my education, which I hoped would stand up for me throughout my career when the hype of hairdressing competitions waned.

John Belfield M.I.T.

My British Championship win brought an unexpected surprise, I was awarded a Civic Plaque by the City of Stoke-on-Trent for my achievements in hairdressing. I was really made up about this because our local paper *The Evening Sentinel* hardly ever put anything in about my success. I got more editorial in *The Birmingham Post* than the *Sentinel*. I was pleasantly surprised at the award ceremony that goalkeeper Gordon Banks also received a Civic Plaque for his achievement in football. Maybe I was putting hairdressing on the map for my city. At least the local branch of The National Hairdressing Federation had now gone quiet!

The Euros in Madrid was a disjointed effort from us all. Robert didn't get us to gel as a team, and we were just competing against each other for who could be placed the highest instead of working together for a good team result. We bombed in every way individually and as a team. As much as I got on with the other guys, they were all from down south, and I can honestly say when asked –where are you from, if I said Stoke, I always had to add 'halfway between Birmingham and Manchester', and that is still the same today. In hairdressing, there is a big divide between north and south, and I can't see that changing. There was/is too much north in me to ever be totally accepted by southern hairdressers. I didn't hold it against them, because hairdressing-wise, I could hold my own, and that was okay with me.

With all that was going on, I still put in a shift at the salon, as most of what goes on in hairdressing usually happens over a weekend, mainly on Sundays, so if I wasn't away somewhere, the lights would be on at the salon, and I would be practicing. We had many an occasion when our local competitors would report us for being open on Sunday. It was illegal to open Sundays back then, but nothing to stop me either practicing on my own, or, at times, other hairdressers would travel and practice with me.

My days as a chorister and bell-ringer were over, I don't think I was missed that much at St Peters church in Stoke, as bell ringing wasn't my forte. Dad was disappointed, as he was still very active, and deeply committed as a chorister. Church and his Christian beliefs was a big part of his life, he would always call around the salon after church to say hello and meet my guests who had joined up with me for the day. Dad was never far away from what I was doing, and he was a great leveller. When he thought I was getting a bit too carried away with what was going on, he would quietly remind me. I did need it from time to time.

CHAPTER TEN

Japan Universal Championships

What a year 1970 turned out to be. I made it for the men's team to compete in the World Championships in Germany, but a new one-off event was offered to me by The National Hairdressing Federation, which was taking place in Japan to celebrate The World Trades Exhibition in Osaka, EXPO 70. I was to be the only men's team member to be asked, and I was going to be supported by the men's team manager Charles Clark from Brighton. He was also going to be judging for me.

Charles had a son, also named Charles, who was one of my main competitors. He wasn't the easiest of guys to get on with, so I was expecting more of the same of his dad.

The hairdressing event was to be called The Universal Hairdressing Championships, which was to take place in Tokyo, in June 1970, and the World Championships in Germany were set to take place in the autumn. I had no connection as to how the ladies' set-up was being arranged through The Fellowship for British Hairdressing, with the men's hairdressing competitor through The National Hairdressing Federation. And apart from Charles Clark, the federation wasn't sending any officials, just me and him and my model. Not exactly a united British team but I looked on it as a great opportunity.

We were Flying out from Paris via Alaska, crossing the international date line, with the return journey via Moscow, Russia.

It was one hell of a journey, flying to Paris, then changing airports, then a stop and re-fuel in Anchorage, and finally Tokyo. I had a very upset stomach after we left Anchorage, and by the time we'd crossed the international date line and Tuesday became Wednesday, I was all over the place. The event wasn't until Sunday, thank goodness, but my body clock was all over the place. This sort of travel was a million miles away from my travel experiences to places such as Rhyl in North Wales on a train.

We had a wonderfully nice hotel, that was an understatement considering my hotel experiences, or lack of it! This place was like a palace, just unbelievable. I planned to practice in my room and prepare for the two events I had to do. The first event was a ballot for models provided by the organisers, and it was to be a "Crew Cut" using only a comb/scissors and a razor. All other tools and products were forbidden. it was the same for the second event, the classic Sculpture Cut which was on my regular model Keith.

During the few days I had before the start of the event, I did join in for the different tourist attractions, which were organized during our stay in Tokyo. After the Championships, we travelled on the bullet train to Osaka for a visit to the World Trades Exhibition. This, I was really looking forward to, but before that, I needed to prepare for the Championship, and to my annoyance, Charles Clark was old enough to have been in the second world war, and all I got from him was war stories. Everyone he saw who looked old enough to have also been in the war he was having a right moan about, and by the time we were ready to go home, I felt like I'd been in the war with him!

You have to put your mind back to how different things were back then, this was 1970, and out on the streets of Tokyo, wives walked behind their husbands, not side by side. It was like a slight leaning forward shuffle.

We took in some temples and shrines, as Japan was mainly Shinto or Buddhist, no Christianity; that came much later. So there we were, standing outside this temple with the tourist guide explaining that it was unlucky to build something perfect, so one of the pillars at the front of the temple was upside down, and then she went on to say that this temple was 2000 years old, and it was re-build every four hundred years, work that one out!!.

I did well in the Championships, coming in 6th overall, which was higher than those in the ladies' team. I can't say I connected with any of them, to be honest, with the exception of a guy named Anthony Barnes Smith. He gave me some chat time, but really it was them and me, and there was a lot of them in this ladies' team group. Four hairdressers, judges, and half a dozen officials too. I was starting to realize how strong an organization the Fellowship was on the international scene compared with the federation, who, to be honest, I saw as a bunch of old-fashioned barbers who considered themselves important because they were on some committee or other.

I felt disconnected from the British group that was out there, and there I was with some out-of-date bloke who couldn't shut up about the war! And to make matters worse whilst there, I realised that the Fellowship's hierarchy was mainly Jewish and didn't want to listen to anything to do with the war, and neither did I.

The Man in the Mirror

One evening, something happened to me which changed my life, both as a hairdresser and as a person. There was a knock at my hotel room door, it was The Fellowship's President Xavier Wenger.

He was one of the most well-respected people in the international organisation, known to me as the OAI & CIC, which controlled all countries from around the world Hairdressing Organisations. Their headquarters were based in Paris.

So, Xavier introduced himself to me, he came into my room and asked me if I would cut his hair for him, he was a smart, elegant, well-spoken man, and I was in awe of him. He was an incredibly important man, so I gave him the best haircut I possibly could. He had a thick, wavy, greying head of hair, and I could understand why he wanted to keep it looking well groomed, it was also part of his image, and here he was trusting me with it.

So, during this haircut he talked to me. It was a bit like an interview, really, and by the time I'd finished his haircut, he knew enough about me to say, "Boy, are you here on your own, where are all your federation officials who should be here? There are important meetings taking place besides the competitions."

I said, "Apart from Charles, my judge, and Keith my model I'm on my own."

And he replied, "No, you're not. You must join us. We will never leave you on your own. The Fellowships ethos is a family of the best hairdressers Britain can offer and you. Boy, you are going to be one of us."

From that moment, my career took on another level. I joined The Fellowship, and he mentored me a lot wherever I was competing internationally. He got his haircut, too, and I've been in the

Fellowship for over fifty years now and am a "Fellow" of The Fellowship, the most elite group of top British Hairdressers. And I'm very proud to say I'm one of them.

CHAPTER ELEVEN

Almost an Astronaut

So, we packed our bags and left Tokyo for Osaka. When we got to the main station, we all had a ticket with a coach and seat number, the place was packed with people, and you panic a bit, standing there wondering if we would all fit on this bullet train, but we did. There were pushers literally pushing you on the train, but, to my surprise, we all sat at the seat on our tickets and in the right coach. I was very impressed. Then we travelled at a hundred miles per hour for three hours and had a view of three hours of rice fields!

But the purpose of the trip to the World Trades Exhibition was just amazing, forty-eight pavilions, with each country projecting their cultures and identities in the world.

Given it was 1970, the American Apollo space program was in full flow, having landed on the moon the year before, so the pavilion which stood out the most was the American Pavilion, where they had moon rock on display and APOLLO 8 on display. this was the one which circled the moon. I was completely blown away with it. There I was, all the way from Stoke, actually sitting in APOLLO 8, this cramped, almost bubble of a spaceship, which had been up in space and returned safely back to earth. The front of it had burnt lumps missing from its re-entry burn as it entered our atmosphere. If only PR and agents were around back then, I would have told everyone in my community at home!

I couldn't make it up if I'd tried, but this was by far the hi-light of my trip then and still is today.

We flew back over Siberia to Moscow on Areoflot. This was an uncomfortable experience, a no frills flight with a re-fuel in Siberia in the middle of the night, I had my first taste of caviar on that flight, which I mistook for marmalade, half of it ending up on the back of the seat in front of me. I was clueless as to what it was, maybe it was the slice of black cardboard bread that I spread it on, but one thing for sure, it didn't agree with my taste buds!

On arrival in Moscow, we spent five hours at the airport, filling in entry forms, declaring all our wealth, which was basically everything we had with us. This was then re checked when leaving, and the both had to match. In other words, we couldn't spend or buy anything, and the whole airport had huge pictures of Lenin everywhere you looked. Talk about hero worship/or brainwashing!

The whole German team and its party were quarantined for the entire weekend, there was no way they were being let in, don't ask me why, but, in hindsight, they drew the long straw, because we couldn't walk anywhere. There was no freedom to explore the city, total control was the order of the weekend. We were imprisoned without the prison! And if you gave or sold any of your belongings to the many people asking for stuff, I think I would still be in Moscow now.

The entire party got to see the Kremlin, which to be fair was a magnificent building. As for the rest of Moscow, it was a dump, except the underground, which we had to view, like it or not. This setup was quite impressive, to be honest. Although I was no expert on undergrounds, it had four classes of travel 1st, 2nd, 3rd, and 4th, not bad for a communist country, talk about equality!

Their tourist guide listed Moscow as seven times greater than London, three times greater than New York, and twice as big as Paris, with a population of seven million. Work that one out if you can.

Finally, the only shops we could buy anything from was Western shops, which had stuff you could have bought anywhere back home. I gave that a miss.

I was glad to get back to the airport for our flight to Paris. I'd seen enough of Moscow, so we had to re-declare everything we had taken in with us, and this had to match our arrival paperwork, or else! A

A few of us had some rubbles, which we couldn't take out of the country, so we put our money together and bought a plaque of Lenin with it. There was nothing else to buy, everything for sale had a picture of Lenin on it. Then drew lots for which one of us would keep it. Yeah, it was me, so I stood there in the middle of the airport with this plaque of Lenin, wondering what all my family would think if my mum and dad had it on top of the TV. I could imagine half our family saying Belfield's are commies! Problem solved, I binned it, what a relief.

We made it back eventually, via Paris Orly Airport, which was a basic airport on the south side of Paris. It never progressed and is now a commuter airport for France.

A middle school from Bentilee in Stoke sent over thirty letters to me from the children, asking for anything with Japanese writing on as souvenirs from my trip. I called the teacher who was responsible, informing her that the letters had arrived after I'd left. She went on to explain that they were staging the Mikado play, although it was Chinese, she thought my souvenirs with any sort Japanese/Chinese lettering would be near enough, as none of the children had ever been abroad nor ever on an aeroplane, so she invited me to go to the school and tell the children all about my trip. I agreed to this and said I would bring enough items with Japanese writing on them for all the children.

I turned up during the last lesson of the day and was warmly greeted by their teacher. But as for any preparation, I had no idea how to prepare for a talk to a classroom of ten- year-old children. This a whole new ballgame for me, a talk to hairdressers was one thing, but a class of thirty-odd ten-year-old children! I stood there after being introduced by the teacher, thinking, *What am I doing here, you're going to look a right whallie!* Well here goes.

I got the teacher dressed in a spare kimono I'd got, myself dressed in a male equivalent, and I gave them a full map of EXPO 70 with 48 cards of all the country's pavilions. Then I started my talk. I got the children's attention, standing there in my Japanese jacket on and the teacher looking like a geisha girl. My stage was set, so I started thinking the children would be interested in Japan, but no chance of that, my first question from a lad at the back—it's always the one at the back! Sir, what's it like on an aeroplane? Brilliant! I'd probably been on an aeroplane less than half a dozen times myself. I could connect with him! And, as it happened, most of the class, sorry—all of them, as none of them had been near a plane before. I was happy to give them insight on what they wanted to hear, and by the time I'd got to telling them all I'd sat in APOLLO 8 and seen an exhibit of moon rock, well that was it, to them I was almost the first man on the MOON!

The children really enjoyed my talk, and to be honest, standing there talking to those children, it was only then that I really took it all in; where and what I'd just experienced. It did make me feel special. None of the children wanted to go home, and the teacher was right made up about how it had gone.

When I was just thinking it was all over, out of the blue, the lad from the back of the class—yes, him again!—stood up and said, "Sir, can you play the harmonica?"

I couldn't make this up—he brought the harmonica down to me, and with all the children standing by their desks, I played "God Save The Queen". They all stood as straight as they could with their hands by their sides, unbelievable! I was Over the Moon! Well almost! It was and still is a very memorable occasion for me.

Stuff was going on all the time, I couldn't keep up with it all. getting back to my hairdressing roots wasn't easy, and I certainly wasn't prepared for any of it. My Boutique Salon was now becoming more unisex, though my dad was constantly being told at his federation meetings that my salon would fail, that women wouldn't have their hair done sitting next to a bloke. How wrong they were. In fact, from experience, if anything, it was the other way around. Men were a bit awkward talking about their vanity with women around. Wokery of 1970!

It sounds daft, but cast your minds back, those of you who can, it was a big change in hairdressing, a bloke having his hair washed or even permed next to a female, it was crazy. And for most, it was a bit too far! I'll re phrase that—a lot too far! The opposition my dad and I had from the local Hairdressing Federation was nuts. They wanted to cast us out of the federation. "You're ruining our businesses," they said, 'Get your hair cut short, you're encouraging young men to grow their hair, it's bad for business!"

"Wake up, for God's sake. This is a new ERA for men's hairdressing, and women's too. Embrace it," I said.

No chance of that.

I wasn't prepared to live in the past, so I went my own way, and dad supported me. Hairdressing both for men and women was more functional, not fashionable. Men had a short back and sides, and women had a weekly shampoo and set, so making changes in their outlook and routine was impossible. Salons were geared to that full stop. But as time went on, they got used to it. Well, it was my way if you wanted to have your hair cut upstairs in my Hair Boutique, or stay downstairs in the main salon. It got so busy, we couldn't cope with the demand. There was a queue of clients, men and women, trying to get in. And to be honest, the only way we could control it was by putting our prices up periodically just to help to ease the flow of people trying to get appointments.

The music got louder and so did the décor. We had a great atmosphere for that era, and we took the salon concept up to Stoke city centre opening in 1972, calling it John Belfield Progressive Unisex Haircutters! Yeah, that's a mouthful for a salon name, but it got the message across clear and simple.

To round of my competition history of 1970, after Japan, I competed in the World Championships in Stuttgart Germany. In those days, there was no Olympic style awards of Gold, Silver, and Bronze placing, just an outright winner and the title of World

Champion. It makes a massive statement: WORLD CHAMPION. The ultimate title. Be it hairdressing or any other sport.

Well, I came third overall, which I was really pleased with, and in the ladies' events, Colin Lewis from Britain won the outright World Champion. It was a good weekend's work all around for the British contingent. For me, just being there was amazing, with so many countries taking part and wearing the union jack on my blazer, it was a proud moment, a moment in time but a memory forever! If that moment never happened again, I would have been happy, but I felt I was at the beginning of more. In fact, I *wanted* more. Who wouldn't?

CHAPTER TWELVE

1971 - Hair Raising Luxembourg

Charles Clark, who I'd been to Japan with, was still our team manager. In fairness, he was at the top of the previous generation of successful men's competition workers in the UK, so was Tom Ahmed, Jimmy O'Neil, and Albert Hartland. All my heroes. But things were about to change. It had to change— our format was stale, and we now had the European Championships coming up in Luxembourg, and there was plenty of new competitors all knocking on the door for a place in the team or squad. New energy and ideas, not just about hairdressing competitions but about salon life how they saw it.

I was waking up to a new era, characters, and personalities, including how they ran their salons. These were big city guys from all over the UK; London, Cardiff, Southampton, Manchester, Birmingham, Glasgow.

We all practiced together in the months leading up to the European Championships in Luxembourg. We had new team members, Roy Chritchley from Manchester and Trevor Mitchell from Southampton, who travelled with us to Germany. I was pleased to have both of them around, as I connected with them both, a connection which lasted a lifetime.

The Man in the Mirror

When these events took place, there were always a lot of hairdressers travelling and supporting the teams. They were big occasions, with was a planeload of supporters, and both the federation and Fellowship connected to organize party evenings for these supporters. Some together and some separately. Which the teams had to attend and mix with everyone who travelled during the weekend. We even had autograph signings, too. It did make you feel honoured and proud to be part of it all.

On the back of such a successful year, you would expect it to continue in the same way, but how wrong it was to be.

For starters, we had to fly from Ashford in Kent, not exactly the best of airports to be flying from, but it was a charter flight and it suited all the southerners.

When we arrived at the airport and checked our bags in, we found out our plane was a Comet jet. At that time, jet flights were still in their infancy, as turbo prop planes were mostly used for short flights to Europe, and the Comet had a poor safety record. To make it worse, as we went to board the plane, each passenger had to stand on a set of scales and be weighed. Everyone was starting to feel a little bit concerned, and this was made worse as we got to the steps to get on the plane and were greeted by a stewardess and a mechanic with a spanner in his hand.

This set the tone for a disastrous weekend. I suppose I can say I flew on Comet and survived, but as for the rest of the weekend? Our Hotel was twenty miles away from the competition arena, we were in the middle of nowhere, and with some of our events starting at eight a.m., we needed to be leaving the hotel by six in the morning. Add the preparation time needed on your model, and it meant getting up around three-thirty a.m. None of us were happy.

We also had to share rooms, not just with team members but with supporters too, which was okay for me, as Keith and I shared, so getting up early wasn't a problem, but Roy Chritchley was having to share with one of the travelling supporters, and this guy turned out to be a big-mouthed know-it-all barber from Hull who was well past his sell-by date. He pissed us all off as the weekend unfolded. He was at us all, saying, "Ya shouldn't be doing that like that, son," and "Ya won't come anywhere if ya leave that like that," and, "If I was you_____." He went on and on all weekend. Well, our results were shocking. None of us placed, we bombed as they say, and after the parade of nations and the result ceremony, we got back to the hotel not in the best of moods. And Mr Hull was giving us, "I told you so," so it was time for revenge.

He eventually went to bed, thank God, and he wore a toupee, more like a RUG, as they say, which he took off before going to bed and put on his bedside table. Well, Roy, Critch as we called him, had a great idea. We'd give him time to nod off, then we'll nick his rug and stick it on the ceiling in the hotel's dining room—great idea!

So we did.

This was the best moment of the entire weekend by a mile! The next morning, we had to be leaving for the airport at eight a.m., and the dining room was packed with all our supporters, including the ladies' teams and models. So, in he walks, bald as a coot, "Okay what have you done with it?" he said to us.

"Done with what?" said Critch.

"Ya know what I mean, lad," he replied in his broad Yorkshire accent.

"We've no idea what you're on about," we all said, and then simultaneously, we all looked up at the ceiling. The whole dining room was in an uproar. Our revenge was sweet, and, amazingly, we never saw him again!

As fashion was changing, I was asked by the NHF to present their fashion forecast "New Look" hairstyle for 1970/71. This was to take place at the Winter Gardens Blackpool at the NHF Spring Hair exhibition and competitions. The Winter Gardens was a big event, and still is, not just for hairdressing but for many events; ballroom dancing was another.

I was also booked to work on one of the exhibition stands, where I styled a couple of star's from Coronation Street. Diedrie was one, the other was Elsie Tanner's son. My model for the Fashion Look of the Year presentation was Selwyn Johnson from Stone Staffs. He was a trendy client of mine, and our friendship has survived over fifty-seven years and was still counting until recently..

CHAPTER THIRTEEN

One of Britain's Super Salons

There something else that was to have an influence on my career in 1970/71, and that was during my training period with Robert James in Soho London, I was introduced to a guy named Graham Webb, he was a Wella product Rep for the West End of London. He called in all the big name London salons of that era.

Graham had a big effect on me, his connection to the squad that Robert was training was that Robert's "Magic Form" products were made by Wella. I got to know Graham well during my time at Robert's salon, and although Graham wasn't a hairdresser, his ambition was to open a progressive style salon based on his ideas from all the West End Salons he visited, with me as its art director. Well, it was all a bit of a fantasy, until he arranged for me to visit some of the salons he thought might swing me into getting on board.

So, our first port of call was to Harrods Salon. Wow! A staff of 164 and twelve receptionists sitting on God knows how many square feet of pink carpet—I'd never seen anything like it. My head was beginning to turn a bit.

The Man in the Mirror

We next went to Crimpers on Baker street, and all I could think about was, *Sherlock Holmes lived on this very street!* Despite him being a fictional character.

Lawrence Falk was one of two owners, a great guy with so much style and commercial fashion, I was really impressed. London was waking up to a new era of hair fashion, and the salon had a real buzz to it. We finally ended up on Beauchamp Place, a street just down the road from Harrods in Knightsbridge. This street was low-key, with shops that had style, none of them displaying any prices. I was getting the picture.

Half way down on the right was a basement salon called Sweeny's, nothing to look at from the outside, but down the stairs into a room/salon, there was one hairdresser cutting someone's hair without a gown wrapped around them. He was stop start, kept changing the music, then going back and trimming a bit more. Another was stoned, having a coffee with an extremely la-de-da woman with an Afgan dog. No pink carpet in this place! Just Cannabis and a stinking fog of smoke!

Graham introduced the owner Denny to me, he was arranging to travel to some place to attend to Mr Stewart's hair. Yeah—ROD. Then he sorted an appointment out for Bianca, with a give Mick my best.

I was now jaw dropped and turned to Graham. "Is he—"

Before I could get my words out, he said, "Yes, Jagger."

Well, this had my head spinning around and around, and if I wasn't sold on Graham's idea before, I was getting a bit more serious about it now. In fact, Denny was quite an okay guy once you put all that stuff on one side. He even travelled with me on a couple of occasions when I competed in Antwerp and Brussels.

My big problem with it all wasn't the hairdressing as much as my image just didn't fit with what was going on back then. I didn't do cannabis, and I wasn't camp enough to be interesting, which was how most of them in London expected a male hairdresser to be. I couldn't see me changing from saying, 'Hey, up duck," to saying, "Hello, Darling!" And in a Stokie accent, it was too false for me to adapt to. You just couldn't get the north out of me... and to be honest, I didn't want to be someone I wasn't.

Graham could understand this, but he wanted quality in his salon idea, and we settled for a loose relationship/connection, which for a couple of years worked well for us both. It gave our salon a London link, which kept our image interesting, and on the back of it, I opened my salon in the city centre of Stoke, which was to all the locals Hanley. We had in Hanley an exciting new discotheque called THE PLACE. It opened in 1968, and one of its owners, Kevin Donavan, who was originally from Manchester, brought a newness to the entertainment scene in the potteries I hadn't seen since my college days. Kevin was the most forward-thinking person I'd ever met, a great friend, and has influenced and guided my thinking throughout my career

From my college days in Manchester, we used to go to the Twisted Wheel, a quirky discotheque in the Manc's city centre. It was an outrageous place. Also the IN place to be. I'm not sure how IN I was being there, but it was something to impress your mates with, telling it like you were in with the IN crowd of Manchester. It was one-upmanship if nothing else.

The Man in the Mirror

The "Place" disco in Hanley (Stoke, that is) had a Twisted Wheel feel about it, and I wanted a salon in a similar style. Kevin Donavan's designer was a client of mine, John Victor Williams, and he was the man to go to in the pub and disco hospitality realm. Very much the man of the moment, and so we had him design the Hanley salon, which was well before its time. Stoke-on-Trent's first City Centre Unisex Salon, we called it John Belfield Progressive Unisex Haircutters. It was like entering a discotheque, and clients had never been in a salon like it. Graham had a big input into the name because his first salon in Lee Green London was the same, "Progressive Unisex Haircutters". He was so taken up by how the Salon looked that he had John Williams go down and re design his London salon in a similar style to my Hanley Salon. In fact, when we opened the salon, *The Hairdressers Journal,* our national hairdresser's trade magazine, did an article on our Hanley Salon, and in it the article referred to the salon as "One of Britain's Super Salons". I was well made up, one of Britain's Super Salons! It sounded amazing, I could keep saying it over and over again! We used this a lot in our promotion material on the salon. In fact, we used it on our Stoke salon too.

I was quite proud of that article, but back then, it really was what it said above the door, or on the tin, as they say.

CHAPTER FOURTEEN

Missed Opportunity

Graham's Salon in Lee Green wasn't the easiest for me to get to in those days, either by train or car. We continued our partnership for a while, but we both could see that it wasn't going to work. I was salon based, Graham was management based, and he wanted me to pull out of working on the shop floor and manage, the same way he was, but that wasn't me. So, we went our separate ways.

Graham expanded his salon group using John Williams as his designer, and it worked well for him in the medium term, or so he said, but I am pleased to say he did make it in the end. He opened a training school in Washington DC in the mid-80s, and through his connection with Wella, he brought out a range of products in the States, right at the time when Bill Clinton became president, and as a wild card, he sent Hilary Clinton a hamper of his products. She liked them so much, his product range sold in over thirty-eight countries worldwide, except the UK.

I got a phone call from him five or six years ago. The company sold for 250 million dollars, and although he only owned a half of one percent, he banked over a million and decided to retire. His salon group didn't hardly make anything. He was glad to get out of the industry, and I was left pondering what might have been.

I had a World Championship to prepare for, and opening a salon in the same year was probably a crazy idea, but somehow, the excitement gave me more confidence in my creative work, and this also brought the best out of me in my competition work.

There was plenty of long weekends practicing as a squad, the team hadn't been finalised, and at this stage, we decided to make it as fair as possible, so we moved the training around each of the squad members' salons; Roy Critch in Manchester, Mitch in Southampton, Wally Falkner in Northampton, Peter Pyne in Walsall, so that some weekends there was less travel for some than others. It evened out during the year, but being as central as I was, there was more times at Stoke than anywhere else, and I did have the best facilities.

As a group, we began to connect. We didn't know it at the time, but the format we created was quite successful. Well, much better than what went before. It stayed the same format over the next three World and European Championships, and all who joined the squad benefited in some way, even if they didn't make the team.

There were the user's, too, who connected with the squad just so they could go back to their salons and say, "Member of the British Hairdressing Squad". It wasn't a perfect format, as their hairdressing improved immensely also. We set a high standard, and those who used the system didn't stay around long. It wasn't my responsibility to say who stayed and who should go, I left it to the NHF (The Federation) to sort that out.

Barcelona was where the 1972 World Championships was held that autumn, and everything was working out well in training for me, plus the new salon was becoming a huge success, too. I was feeling good, really good.

There was another event added to these World Championships for the very first time, which was added hair, or toupees as its better known. You might ask why, but back then, toupees were becoming a major part of the men's hairdressing industry, so it was seen as a natural event to add to the championships. Finding a model for this event wasn't going to be easy, as I had my regular model Keith for the other two events. Keith was my Rock, he was always there for me, if only I could find a guy with a similar nature. Well, I found a guy, a very good-looking guy, who I first met playing football in the half holiday league on Thursday afternoons. His name was Bill Baddeley.

Everyone knew Bill, he was a real character, a good footballer and a charmer, too. He was good-looking, and he knew it,

In some ways, Bill was difficult. I put him in a world he never knew existed, and he wasn't that flexible in accepting it, but he liked the interest that people showed in him. However, believe me, the months leading up to the championships, Bill being Bill, was a pain. And he could wind me up something rotten! Especially after I'd paid him to model for me.

On one occasion, I had a show to do for a top hair piece company called Trendco. It was at The Tickled Trout Hotel in Preston and was also a fund raiser to help fund sending the team to the Barcelona Championships. Two hours before going, he changed his mind and said he wouldn't go. He dropped me right in it. I was a model short with only two hours to go before we opened the show. I was mad with him, but the show had to go on, and I learned how to compromise and always be prepared for the unexpected. Thanks to Bill, I learned to never rely on people; at some point, they will let you down just when it's least expected. How true that statement has turned out to be over the years—I could definitely write a book on that alone!

So, always be prepared for the unexpected. Not just with people but anything. My philosophy was to be prepared, and that included all my gear, too. I guarantee you, I'd always have anything and everything in my travelling work bag. This was especially beneficial doing shows, as you never knew what was expected of you and should always be prepared. If I was flying anywhere, I'd always be overweight.

CHAPTER FIFTEEN

Going for Gold

The Barcelona trip was better organized than the one before to Luxembourg. We flew out from Heathrow on a plane that at least looked like it could fly as far as Barcelona. We were all on this flight; the ladies' team and a plane load of supporters. There was a really good upbeat to this trip. At check in I was standing with Herbert from Liverpool, he always travelled with his mother and his aunty, one on each arm, and with his t-shirt on show with the logo I AM CAMP!, which also had the camp coffee symbol on it. But we all knew what message he was putting out, and when standing there at check-in with six large suitcases, the attendant asked, "Are these all yours?"

To which Herbert replied in an over-the-top way, "Yes, and the fourth one down has my shoes in it!"

We all laughed. He was a wonderfully warm guy and always supported the teams wherever we travelled to. If you sat anywhere near Herbert on the plane, it was entertainment all the way!

Our hotel was right on the Ramblers. We were warned about the locals who were up to no good, pickpocketing, but it was an interesting peoplewatching street, not that I had much time to experience it. In fact, you could say that wherever we went, it was a working trip every time, I never saw much of any of the places we competed at. All I got to show for it was a hairdressing demonstration or a teach-in to do, that was it—just get the job done and straight out.

The competitions went as well as I'd expected. The team worked well together, and I was captain for this championship, so it was my responsibility to get everyone working together.

As a bonus, we all had our own rooms, which, when doing what we were doing, you needed your own space. My room was set up like a salon, with everything I needed laid out just the same way and in place as when I practiced back home. Keith, Bill, and I worked together like clockwork; my room was now my salon, and it was to be the same on the day. I couldn't have asked any more of them.

In the competitions, I felt it was the best I'd done. If it wasn't good enough, well, I couldn't have done more. Looking around at all the other competitors' work was always a bit unnerving, trying to judge the standard of others against your own work. *If only I'd had a couple more minutes* was always in your thinking at that moment. But that was it, it was over—no going back.

It was time to be sociable with everyone, and we attended all the group receptions, mixing with all our supporters. I felt rather special, wearing my blazer with the union jack on my breast pocket. Before the evening of the Parade of Nations and the results, which was a bit like the Olympics, I did manage a stroll along the Ramblers, just reflecting on how the weekend had gone and the nervous anticipation of the Parade of Nations and results, which was in store for us all later that evening.

The competition area was now set up for the parade, with each Team walking around the arena, thirty-two countries in all, just the same as the Olympic Games. Each team with their flag bearer walking in front and the crowd cheering their support for their country. The atmosphere was amazing, there must have been five to ten thousand people sitting all around the arena ,waving their countries' flags!

Most of the results were announced in Spanish. It was the first time we'd had an Olympic style award, and each category was awarded Gold, Silver, and Bronze for first, second, and third placing. It was incredibly confusing, as most of us couldn't understand, with it was mostly all in Spanish.

All categories in all the ladies' events had been announced, and none of our ladies' team had been placed. Then came all the men's events, and one after the other was read out. We were all beginning to feel down, we thought as a team we had performed quite well. Then, out of the blue, all this Spanish was being announced, and there right at the end of it, I heard GOLD, JOHN BELFIELD, GREAT BRITAIN!

All the British contingent went wild. I stood up, flags went up in the air, and I excitedly made my way to the rostrum and stood on the pinnacle GOLD position. Someone gave me the union jack flag to wave, and then the National Anthem played. I could hear the crowd singing "God Save the Queen".

This was my moment!

It ended in a flash, but as I walked back to our team, the congratulations went on and on. It was and always will be a moment I will never forget.

With my Gold medal around my neck, people from other teams came over to congratulate me. I remember a French guy who was expected to win Gold, Julian Catchpole, came over and said I deserved it.

The celebrations went on most of the night, and a party was quickly laid out back at our hotel, with many of our supporters there. I must have spoken to them all. I was the first Brit to win a Gold Medal at The World Championships. It still feels good just writing it even now!

Back home, I had half a page in the Birmingham Post, but my local paper, *The Evening Sentinel*, disappointingly gave me just a small paragraph!

On the back of my success, the National Hairdressing Federation began to wake up to its commitment Internationally, with its membership to the OAI and the CIC. Until now, Britain had only been represented by the Fellowship, and this was at last a step in the right direction. The only problem was that the federation at that time had an insular national executive, most of them couldn't see beyond the barbershops that they ran. The whole setup was too political for my liking, and national and especially international hairdressing was just a bit beyond their comprehension. that was until they realized that there was a few free trips to Europe paid for by the federation and not out of their own pockets, plus an International credit, even if it was in meeting.

I stayed well away from it and focused on the direction I wanted my hairdressing to go, and fortunately the Fellowship held my hand when I was competing abroad. For that, I should mention Xavier Wenger, Tom Web, Leno D'Prano, and Jean Price, who helped my progress during this period.

I finished off that year in Brussels again, taking the international prize. Tom Webb judged for me because there was no federation officials there.

This was my most successful year to date, and I was getting requests for teach-ins all over the UK and beyond. I couldn't do them all, as it would have kept me away from the salon too much, so I compromised to Sunday only, or Monday evenings if it was within a two-hour car journey from Stoke.

Changes were taking place with the men's team for the European Championships in Lausanne Switzerland, I was an automatic choice off the back of my success in Barcelona, and the team was now under new management, with Vin Miller as team manager and Stan Gray as his number two. They were both from the northwest, Preston and Lancaster, and I got on okay with both of them, but their competition experience was at best regional. Both were much older than me, and to be honest, when it came down to it, both were dated in their outlook. Nice guys, but it was their way or no way, and my thought train wasn't connecting to theirs. However, they were in charge, and that was it.

I had, during my many teach-ins, developed a following, if you like. If I was doing a teach-in in one place, others from other towns nearby would also attend, and there was one guy who followed me all over the midlands, his name was Charlie Hussey, a very broad-spoken Irish guy who had a small barbershop in Albrighton just outside Wolverhampton. He was a good friend of Clive Basford from Tipton.

Clive was in the squad for the euros, so too was Peter Hipkin from Wolverhampton and Peter Pyne from Walsall. They all knew Charlie, and whenever they attended either my teach-ins or squad training, he got a ride with one of them. And so we became good friends.

The Man in the Mirror

When I was a long way away somewhere on a Sunday, I would get up early Sunday morning and pick him up and take him with me. We bonded, and on one of those occasions when I was working in Lincoln, a full day's teach-in for fifty hairdressers starting at ten a.m. until five p.m., I'd gotten up at three a.m. and drove and picked Charlie up. He did help with the driving, although I have to say—not the best driver, but during those lengthy drives in the car, I got to know his personal side. He originated from Connemara in southern Ireland, his only language was Gaelic until he was eleven. His main sport was boxing, and at his weight, he was an Irish schoolboy Boxing Champion. He'd moved to England, having been approached to join the IRA, something, according to him when asked, you couldn't say no to, so he moved to England, before he got asked to do something he might regret.

His business was a small barbershop, with just one other guy working for him. Charlie had other jobs, too. On top of working during the day in his salon, he was a part-time fireman three nights a week, had an early morning milk round five days a week, and was a bouncer at a nightclub in Wolverhampton on Saturday evenings. On top of that, his wife, who was working as a nurse in Wolverhampton General Hospital, between them, they had five children to support. By nature, his accent was deeply Irish, and so were his mannerisms—he always called me Luvva!

So, we got through the day in Lincoln, the teach-in went well, everyone at that time wanted to learn how to cut and blow-dry using barbering cutting methods on ladies' hairstyles. The shampoo and set was going out of fashion.

All the money I earned from these teach-ins went back into the business.

So, it was Sunday evening, and we started the five hour drive back. The road was all cross-country, winding its way west through Grantham, Nottingham. I had done all the driving back until we got as far as Derby, as four hours of those roads was enough, so we swopped over. He had been sleeping most of the way back, so Charlie continued the driving and I fell asleep almost instantly.

But before I did, Charlie said, "Where are we, Luvva?"

"We're on the Derby ring road, making our way to Wolverhampton," I said. So, he carried on with the driving, and I nodded off. The next minute, Charlie woke me up.

"Where to now, Luvva?"

"Where are we now?" I asked him.

Nottingham!

He'd only driven twenty miles back up the road I'd driven down an hour ago.

"Stop the car, Charlie, we're never going to get home at this rate."

So, back in the driver's seat I got, and back down the Derby road we went. I wasn't a happy bunny, but somehow I could never get mad at him. This experience wasn't the last one of this nature either, there were more to come!

CHAPTER SIXTEEN

The First Hairdresser to Have a Minder!

As I was most central to all those in the men's squad, it seemed sense to have the training days at our salon in Stoke. By now, we had the Liverpool rd. original salon, the Hanley salon, and we'd opened a first floor salon on the corner of Campbell Place in the town centre of Stoke.

I suppose because of my success, most of the squad were happy to travel to our salon, and it was central for everyone and convenient for the team manager Vin Miller and assistant Stan Gray, who used to travel together from their hometowns of Lancaster and Preston.

So, being the team captain, and because I was the most advantaged, I would arrange a sit down meal for everyone at our local pub, The Wheatsheaf in Stoke (not to be confused with the Wheatsheaf group of today). They had a nice middle of the road restaurant upstairs. I felt it was also team building after training, and we all had an opportunity to gel and do some brainstorming together as a group before going back home. We met about once a month, and as the Euro's got nearer, every other weekend.

Charlie was always present, and he'd get a lift up, usually with Clive Basford. Having said that all the squad members from the Birmingham area knew Charlie really well, he wasn't the best of barbers but a real character. He knew being around us all would be a big help to him, and we all liked him and his approach to everything. Basically, he'd do all the running around for us all.

The '73 Euros in Lausanne Switzerland was getting closer, and it was going to be another big event for me. expectations were high on the back of my Gold win in Barcelona. There was a lot of pressure on me to do well, and I was captain of this squad of hairdressers. I say squad because this wasn't a team as such—we had a max of six able to compete, i.e., six individuals. And unlike the World Championships, this was to be self-funding, apart from the entry money.

So, when the travel arrangements were put to everyone at our salon by the manager Vin Miller, it didn't go down well. Here we all were, trying to be a team, but with the financial expectation in the travel arrangements, I wasn't happy I was captain. I'd given my all to this group of six, and both Vin Miller and Stan Gray's travel was being paid by the federation, but my input meant nothing.

To top it all off, we were not flying out until the day before the championships—on a Saturday afternoon, with the competitions staring at nine a.m. on Sunday. This wasn't good planning. I'd been in this situation before two years before in Luxembourg. We should at least have travelled out on Friday, which gave us all at least one day to settle in and get a good run through on what we needed to do, settling in from the journey. Good preparation was a major part of getting it right.

On the back of this news, we finished the Sunday training day at our shop in Stoke. I'd booked the usual tables for everyone at the restaurant in the Wheatsheaf, but there was an atmosphere amongst us all. After dinner, the debate carried on in the bar downstairs. I was in a heated discussion with Vin Miller and Stan Gray, standing in a group of us at the bar. They were highly vocal and so was I, debating—nearly arguing—how these arrangements wouldn't work, when all of a sudden, over my shoulder came this fist that punched Stan Gray the assistant manager and knocked him to the floor, I turned around, and there was Charlie.

I said, "What the fuck are ya doing!"

To which he replied, "I didn't like the way he was talking to ya."

"WHAT!"

"I didn't like the way he was talking to ya!" he repeated.

Fortunately, Stan wasn't hurt. Well, not physically anyway, but his ego was. Then it got worse, as the landlord chucked us all out for brawling in the bar. This was my town and my local pub, and now I was banned! I was going to be the talk of the town, and my connection with the squad and the team management just when down the pan!

I decided that there was only one thing I could do, and that was stand my ground and make my own travel arrangements. After all, we had to pay our own way, though this was very much against the grain with me, as my captaincy didn't mean a thing. I didn't get much support from the squad either, they were all thinking of themselves, but there was a lot riding on this Euro Championship for me above everyone else. It was now looking like my last Championship, and I had a big point to make with Vin Miller and Stan Gray. Especially on how out of touch the pair of them were.

So, I decided to arrange my own travel and meet up with them all at the same hotel we were all booked into, but I'd arrive on Thursday, the rest of them on Saturday.

John Belfield M.I.T.

I was using a new male model, a local guy named John Hammond. He was a lorry driver for a local company, as my regular model Keith was getting a little tired of the commitment required. He'd been a great asset for me and a very good friend, but his life was moving on, and we both understood this. I wouldn't have achieved what I did without him—he was my rock.

John Hammond brought a new look to what I was wanting to create on the competition floor. His hair and head shape was more progressive, less traditional, he had a younger, youthful, fresher look to him for the events I was competing in.

I decided that we would travel by car over to Lausanne, arriving on Thursday two days before the rest of the squad. I was able to take extra gear with me travelling this way, as I always took too much stuff wherever I went—just in case was my motto!

That drive time helped me to bond with John. He was a great guy, but this was something a million miles away from being a lorry driver. He was up for whatever I asked of him, and he didn't let me down.

We got to our hotel by Thursday lunchtime, settled in, checked out the exhibition arena, which gave me an adrenaline rush for the weekend in front of us, then John and I practiced all day Friday. By Saturday, everything was as it should be. I felt the next time I was going to do John's hair would be the best I'd ever done. I felt organized, in control, and ready. Very ready.

The rest of our men's squad arrived that Friday evening. I'd had an extra day to prepare, but I kept my mouth shut and offered help to all those who needed it.

Some had never been to an event of this magnitude before, and everyone was nervous, bar me. Being nervous meant you hadn't practiced enough and you weren't quite sure how you would perform on the day. But for me, I knew exactly how I would perform on the day, all being well—the next time I did John's hair would be my best one, my build-up felt good. Whether that was enough to win anything, I wasn't sure; time would tell.

Both Vin and Stan were cool toward me. Mitch was his usual self, inviting us to his room for a cup of tea. Wherever we went, Mitch always had a pot of tea on the go, brewed for three minutes, and he had the second cup, it was his ritual. But there was more to Mitch. He knew how to be with you in times when there was a lot of pressure on. I could see him managing the team sometime in the future, and I liked having him around. He had a levelling look on things, and I knew he was happy with me because I always helped him with his work.

I kept to my preparation plan, the plan I wanted the managers to adopt for every person competing. But they had other ideas, and I became a loner, not with the other competitors so much but with both managers, I could feel them just hoping I fell flat on my face, then they could say 'you should have listened to what we told you, sunny boy'. They had that obvious attitude toward me, and they called themselves managers? Their attitude disgusted me, and on the eve of a big event, too. We weren't back in Stoke now, this was it! This only made me more determined.

The competitions went well all weekend, I thought. I was happy with my performance, and John my model worked really hard to keep everything in sync. I always had a game plan, leaving nothing to chance. I broke down each area of the head into so many minutes, even seconds, for each part. This way, you always finish. It was a method

I'd developed and wanted the squad to use the same method, but that wasn't going to happen under the current management team. But my method guaranteed you'd finish on time every time.

John kept me on time. He'd have a stopwatch clocking me, e.g., three minutes left side, three minutes right side, five minutes top, eight minutes on the back and nape, two minutes on each line out around the ears, ten minutes dressing and finish. This way, you always finished.

One major fault in competing is when one part of your style doesn't go right, you spend too much time on that part, which then is time lost on another part of your style. So, when finished, your hair style is not finished. My method, which I'd used for some time, worked. At least then everyone put up a finished job, and from a team performance, it kept a level standard with no weak links, and it was what I was wanting the two managers Vin and Stan to have everyone working the same way. But they disagreed, so we all did our own thing.

With the competitions now finished, there we went again with a Parade of Nations and results. I always felt deeply patriotic walking out wearing my union jack on my blazer. Twenty-five countries all doing the same, and the crowd all waving flags.

The ladies' results were the first to be announced. Chris Mann got a place in one of the ladies' events, and then came the men's results. I won a Bronze medal in one of the men's events, and none of the other men's squad came anywhere near to placing. I was happy with my result, although it was clear that judging in these sorts of championships can lead to some strange results. I'm not saying cheating, but groups of countries vote together, our team manager was our judge, and to be honest, he was out of his depth. but I was happy with Bronze, although a few competitors came to me asking why I didn't make Gold!

Back at the hotel, it was a great atmosphere. We had the usual celebrations and mixing with all our supporters. The hotel was Rocking! It was and is such a proud occasion, and with a medal around my neck, I was very popular. So too was Chris Mann with the ladies' team. Little did I know how much Chris and my paths would cross in the future.

As the evening unfolded, both Vin and Stan came over to me. We shook hands and called a truce on our differences. They asked me to train the team for the World Championships the following year in Vienna, and I accepted that. For a team performance, there couldn't be any weak links, otherwise we wouldn't come anywhere near winning.

They both accepted that my method of working would give a standard performance from the team in whole. I did add that for these Championships, Britain was allowed six places, and there was no team results in a European Championships. Had there been, our best four squad competitors at this event would not have made the top ten places. Thankfully, the team event was only in the World Champs. My biggest point was that we all had to pay our own expenses apart from the entry fee, and because of this, I felt we should have had flexibility on travel, so long as we all stayed in the same hotel once we got there. Plus, that extra couple of days before the championships made a massive difference for me and my performance, and it would have benefited everyone else too. So, we agreed not to disagree. Wonderful!

Back at home in Stoke, our original salon was at 58 Liverpool Rd Stoke. My father was born at this address, and eventually we relocated from no 58 to no 81 Liverpool Rd. This was a much bigger premises, and ultimately it detached hairdressing from no 58, where Aunty Doris and Uncle Eric still lived. The new city centre salon in Hanley, with the progressive unisex haircutters title, and the newest salon addition in Campbell place Stoke, which we called "Hair Mates", became our business model. All three salons offered something different, and so our profile increased throughout the Potteries Community. Although it must be said that demand more than anything created our salon group. I nor Dad had any idea on how to run three salons! So, it was decided we would introduce the salon manager from our Hanley salon, Dave Cook, as a partner. He was popular at that salon, although he had no management skills. Having said that, neither had I nor Dad. It just seemed the right thing to do.

So, the business just evolved, with no business plan. We did have Graham Webb's London input, and I still had a loose arrangement going on with Graham. He had now opened a second salon in Bromley, and John Victor Williams again did the design work, so the disco theme for a unisex was emerging, which did give Graham and I some belief that a national salon group could be achieved. Yeah, we both were still dreaming, Bromley by car back then was a good five-hour drive. We never had any practical planning on how we could ever bring the two businesses together. England's infrastructure meant we were just too far apart.

The main advantage for us was that we used to do an exchange week or two with Graham's apprentices. We shared the cost; he paid for his, and we paid the costs for ours. He would send one of his apprentices to us for training, and we would send one of ours the other way. It was a great opportunity for both, as it brought a London connection to our salon's in Stoke, which back then was unheard of. "London Hairdressers" in Belfield's salon, it did bring a new image to our shops, and when our apprentices returned, it gave then an "edge" that was impressive for our clients to see.

We were in a league of our own, Stoke-on-Trent. I was starting to realize that we did have something special. The clients were impressed by it, and our salon image went up a gear.

CHAPTER SEVENTEEN

It's Like a Rest Home for Retired Hairdressers

During this period, Graham's apprentices appeared to be getting better training that what ours were down at his salons, and one saying from our staff returning from London was, "It's like a rest home for tired hairdressers."

The point being made was that it wasn't as busy and demanding in Graham's salon as it was in ours. Graham's prices were three times the price of ours, and their appointment times were much more spaced out. With their prices, they could afford to be.

Graham wanted us to fall in line with what he was doing, but Dad and I thought it was too big a risk. Stoke wasn't quite ready for such a big jump in our prices. Maybe for an individual, but across three salons, it wouldn't have worked. I often wondered whether we should have gone with it, but we'll never know, because Graham and I decided that we should go our separate ways. It wasn't just the prices being an issue, there were other reasons as well.

Graham wanted me to be an art director, which involved training and stepping back from day-to-day behind the chair. Dad was very much against it, mainly because I was the one putting the most money in the tills in our three salons. Dad did have a point, it was a big risk business-wise. I did need to think it through, too, because back then, the image of an art director I certainly wasn't. I didn't look the part, nor did I have the right 'posh' in my locker. I was a Stokie through and through, very Northern.

Although we never made any official announcement, Graham and I went our separate ways. We stayed connected as friends and still shared our ideas, as it was good for us in Stoke to have this London connection. It's one thing I never quite understood with local people; "Oh, we get our hair done in London," or "Oh, we go to Manchester to get our hair done," as if because they are paying three times as much and have been to a BIG city to get their hair done it must be better than what Stoke can offer. And along with that comes a big snob value. Silly buggers. If only they knew what I knew. But, for those types of people or clients, you'll never change their mindset! Not back then, and not now either.

For the record, Graham never made any money through his salons. He had six in all, over a thirty-year period, but in the mid-80s, he opened the salon in Washington DC. The rest is history with the product line.

I too was very much products-aware, even back in the seventies. I had a hunger for newness, looking for products to match our developing hairdressing brand, anything new that I thought was better than what we were currently using, I would bring into our salons. Going abroad and competing so much was a big influencer, and the exhibitions were amazing. They had everything we didn't have back then, and I was determined to keep our international image strong. Not just because of my competition work abroad, nor all the teach-ins I was now being asked to do all over Europe, but because we had this international edge. It made us different from any other salon in the area.

CHAPTER EIGHTEEN

The Science of Hair on Our Doorstep

Something happened in 1973 which changed our philosophy in a way that was revolutionary and well before its time.

I was in London working, and I was introduced to a guy named James Blackburn. He was bringing a new product concept from America into the UK, and he was looking to create an exclusive group of specialized product salons in each town and city throughout the UK. These salons would have exclusivity in their area and would have special product knowledge like nothing the UK had seen before. And this American product was called "Redken".

Yes, our salons in Stoke were to be one of the very first Redken salons in Britain.

At last, there was a product range out there packed with science. Science of the hair, scalp, and skin. As a Trichologist, for the first time since qualifying in 1969, I could now have a product range which supported my qualification. Ph-balanced products might seem an everyday term on hair and skin preparations today, every manufacturer uses such terminology and technology, but back in 1973, believe me, it was unheard of. And we were about to re-educate not only our clientele but the entire area of North Staffs and beyond.

Redken laboratory in LA was the biggest research laboratory of hair and skin cosmetics in the entire world.

This was to be another big piece in our business model—Acid/PH-balanced shampoos and a load more products in the range too. Our salons became the only Redken salons in the area. Out went the local wholesalers bulk shampoo crap, and, sadly, I suspended making my Fixit blow dry product, and in its place was apple shampoo. Its PH value was 5.5 to 6. Yes, madam/sir, this backwash/retail shampoo has the same PH value as your hair and scalp. You can use it every day without causing any chemical damage to your hair, scalp, and skin. By the way, it doesn't lather very much either.

It took a lot of convincing clients that it actually cleaned their hair without much lather, in those days, we all thought the better the foam and bubbles the better the shampoo performed. What a load of rubbish. We'd convinced our clients that the nicer the smell, the thicker and creamier the product, the better its quality. Now we were saying just the opposite! We had an uphill battle for months, years even.

Also in the Redken range was a product called Volcanic Ash. it was for greasy hair, and you sprinkled it on after shampooing. Can you imagine the client? Blimey! This stuff has come out of a Volcano. We'd only just gotten clients to make an appointment, plus having a shampoo, or a perm for men, now they were chucking dust on their heads from Mount Edna!

We had a product called PPT. The nearest I'd ever been convinced that Keratin could possibly have a liquid state, because it doesn't—or should I now say didn't! With normal hair growth, apart from that very beginning at the base of the dermal papilla, the start of the growth stage, hair doesn't have a liquid state. When hair is heated, it goes from a solid to a gas. Think about it; if you heat your hair, it doesn't melt when you style it.

I see many products today that claim they contain Keratin, which is false, they definitely don't. But Redken's PPT was the nearest thing to Keratin I've ever come across. Back then, we used bucket loads of it, particularly on chemical treated hair as a repair treatment. We would also damp end papers in it when perming hair, it evened out the acidity/ porosity on the hair shaft. And to cap it all, Redken also had an acid wave perm lotion. It sounds weird saying acid, but hair is slightly acid, so it makes sense to work with products with the same PH value. Perm solution was always alkali, and it left the hair dry and brittle, but an acid wave perm left the hair feeling much the same as it was before it was permed. Less of a chemical feel, more of a natural curl to either blow dry or leave to dry naturally.

There was loads more philosophy behind this product range, and we needed to change the mindset of all our staff. And that, believe it or not, was harder than changing our clients' outlook toward their hair. The staff were set in their ways, and to a degree, some still are today. And I knew none of them would use these products at home because of the price, plus they were unconvinced about what it said on the tin, and what I had to say too. But time was on our side, and as the product performed as it should, our salons were as good as any one's out there anywhere!

Today, all manufactures have followed the Redken science and technology from all the research done back then, and I'm very fortunate to have been at the very beginning of this new era of hair science.

John Belfield M.I.T.

Our Salons reputation was the place to train as a hairdresser. We were getting two to three hundred apprenticeship letters a year, asking for job applications. We would get them between Christmas and Easter every year. My employment skills were poor, and I had never expected the demand we were getting. I was still progressing my own skills and career; it was crazy, and in some ways all a bit foggy sitting here writing about it now.

CHAPTER NINETEEN

Going Hungry in Paris

The year of 1973 wasn't over, and I had one more practice event to do in Paris. There was an international event on the agenda alongside the French Championships. It was a good opportunity to watch the French Championships and check out any new equipment that might improve my competition and Salon work.

I was always hungry for anything and everything at these events. It was so motivational and at the same time exiting.

Charlie was going to come along and model for me. His hair I knew well, and I used him as a practice model many times, as with many types of competitions, you needed practice. It's the same as in any sporting event, and I did treat it with a sporting attitude. Yes, I'm very competitive!

This was my last event of the year for match practice, and I did believe in keeping match fit. I didn't have a budget for this weekend in Paris. To be honest, I was pretty much skint. I knew Charlie would go along with however it played out, so we flew out from Gatwick to Le Touquet on the northern coast of France and then by train into Paris. This was a new cheap travel method from Gatwick; the whole

John Belfield M.I.T.

journey was mainly by train, i.e., Stoke to London, then London again by train right into Gatwick airport.

It was a mammoth journey, but travel back then was trains and boats and planes. Fortunately, the exhibition centre where it was all taking place was near Place de la Bastille, so we settled in Saturday evening. We'd gotten the cheapest flea pit we could find.

It was going to be a long weekend, as this event was not due to end until Tuesday lunchtime. There was a result evening on the Monday evening at the exhibition centre, then an award ceremony at the CIC Building at the BOURG in Paris and then the same journey in reverse back on train and plane and train back home.

It was about eight-fifty a.m. on Sunday morning, and I'd prepped up Charlie's hair and what clothes I was going to present his look in earlier, so we were about ten minutes from starting the competition. All of a sudden, I heard a voice calling my name from the audience. It was one of my clients. I recall talking to him about my competition in Paris when he was in having his hair cut. He did say he was travelling back from the south of France that weekend, and here he was at the side of the competition stage. It was Dr Eric Trowler from Nantwich.

He was travelling alone, and he could see we were about to start, so he said, "John, I'm staying at such and such hotel, let's get together for diner later." I took the details off him and agreed to catch up with him later.

Charlie and I got through the day's competitions, and it went really well I thought. We went over to Eric's posh hotel and met up for drinks.

Charlie had no money with him, apart from what Clive Basford, one of our squad/team members from Birmingham had given him to buy some brushes and combs with, so what ever came next financially was down to me.

So, we joined up with Eric, had a few drinks, and then he said, wait for it, "I've booked us into a fantastic Michelin starred restaurant for diner."

Wonderful, no half measures with Eric. I wasn't expecting such a high-end restaurant, and I was going to be picking up the bill for Charlie too. Credit Cards didn't exist back then.

Well, the meal was a blast, and I sat next to a Canadian government minister, who was eating alone and decided to join in with us. The conversation was well over the top, and Eric coped with it. Charlie's knowledge of the world beyond either Wolverhampton or Conamara was limited, and mine wasn't much better, but in hairdressing, you got used to going with the flow conversation-wise.

We had an exquisite meal, and our day was the talk of the table. I can confirm, you know when you've had a Michelin starred gastronomic experience—one is you're skint, and two, you leave your table still hungry! On top of that, I paid for Charlie too. Clive B was going to go nuts when he found out all his money was gone on one bloody meal and he wasn't even going to get a comb to show for it.

It was Sunday evening, and Charlie and I were in Paris until Tuesday afternoon. We said our farewells to Eric, and when out of sight, we went and shared a bag of French fries with the last few Francs I had left. We were starving. And starving we stayed, well, nearly, apart from breakfast rolls from the flea bag hotel's continental breakfast, for the rest of our time in Paris. We bagged up as much as we could to see us through the day until our next breakfast on Tuesday morning.

John Belfield M.I.T.

We attended the results announcement at the awards ceremony on Monday evening. All the usual Fellowship crowd were there, and Charlie and I joined up with them. They were very warm toward me, and I appreciated it.

My name was announced for an award, and I was over the moon. All the Fellowship crowd were really excited for me. Chris Mann explained that the awards were given at the CIC building at lunchtime the next day, and you had to attend to see what you'd won.

Well, we had a much as we could eat of bread and jam for breakfast on the Tuesday morning, which was going to have to last us both until we got back home on Wednesday. We packed our bags and killed a bit of time until two p.m., then set off for the awards at the CIC headquarters.

All the weekend's competitors were there, plus all the officials from the different countries. The Fellowship from the UK was there but no federation officials as usual.

The event was quite posh but casual too. There were tables and tables of trays of posh nosh plus bottles of Champagne a plenty. We were starving, and there were loads of speeches going on, so Charlie and I grabbed a large tray of food and a bottle of Champagne each and found a quiet place where we could sit and stuff our faces with what the trays had to offer, washing it down with the champagne.

A good hour or two must have passed, and we managed another tray each and a bottle too, whilst staff were watching the speeches.

Eventually, Chris Mann from the Fellowship found us, saying, "John, I've accepted your prize for you, nobody knew where you were."

At that point, I wasn't sure where I was either.

"Thanks, Chris have we won any money? We haven't been here long," I said, lying. Only a couple of hours, two trays of nosh, and a couple of bottles of bubbly.

I thanked him as best I could, not even asking which event I'd won, I was still sitting unmoved. Charlie and I left, staggering, and made our way back to Gare du Nord station for the beginning of our journey back home.

What a weekend. You might not believe this, but back then, a shandy was about as much as I ever drank. At least we had a long trip home to sleep it off. And 'never again' was starting to creep into my mind as the journey unfolded.

We got back at the crack of dawn, but it was straight into work. I'd two days to catch up on, and Charlie went back to his salon.

CHAPTER TWENTY

Dodgy Hairdryers and Drunken Staff

We had a good balance of staff across the three salons. I was mainly working at the Campbell place salon in Stoke. It was a first floor salon, again designed by John Williams. My boutique salon upstairs at Liverpool Rd was too small to expand any more than it was, and at some point in the future, there was a possibility of the ground floor at Campbell place coming available. The shop was on a corner, so it was a good position for the town.

Our main stylist at Stoke was a guy named Neil, and at Hanley on Stafford St. Dave Cook was our main stylist, backed up by a more mature fella named Len. Len had a big personality. What he lacked in ability, he certainly made up for it in other ways. He was very popular with clients and a genuine nice guy.

At the old Liverpool Rd salon, we had Tony and Alan, and I tried to be everywhere, spending one day a week at Liverpool Rd, all day Thursday at Hanley, and the rest of the week I was at the Campbell place salon. Dad was Liverpool Rd through and through, but as a trading street, it was in decline, a lot of the one-man businesses were closing. It used to be the main road from Stoke Town through to Hanley, but people were moving out of the town, not just the town of Stoke, all the Potteries town centres were slowly in decline. They relied on the Pot Banks workers, and these industries were all on the edge of each town, hence the name The Potteries.

Also, new council housing developments were being built, people were encouraged to move out of all the towns to live. For example, we lived on one of these sort of council estate in Trent Vale on the south side of the town of Stoke, so I wasn't struck on developing the Stoke/Liverpool Road salon. It was now less than a secondary trading area of Stoke. My dad was still dead against us leaving Liverpool rd. If the ground floor space at Campbell place ever became available, this would be an obvious move with a better location in the town than Liverpool road, and the space would accommodate all the staff from the old Liverpool road shop too.

At that time, I was also contracted to do some shows for a French hand dryer company called Paramount. These shows were in different towns around England, the show format would start off with a visual presentation about me, my achievements, my philosophy about hairdressing, and how cutting and blow drying was the new era for all hairdressers, both barbers and ladies' hairdressers. And yes, the Paramount hair dryer was a must for all, too. Then I'd do a couple of haircuts, taking the show to an interval. In the second half, I was to bring on Neil from the Stoke salon and Dave from the Hanley salon, thus adding a bigger demonstration of different haircuts and hairstyles on male and female models. This also gave the salons they both worked in an extra factor. By doing demonstrations in other towns in England, their clients would be impressed that their hairdresser was doing such things—most impressive!

John Belfield M.I.T.

We would do one a week, normally on a Monday evening, Monday being the day most salons were closed. We kept to the same format at all the venues, and most of the time we would drive back later that night after the show. But there were two occasions when we needed to stay over. The first was in Taunton Somerset. The show was in a hotel, so we were staying at the same hotel, still using the same format, which meant Dave and Neil joined me on stage for the second part through to the finish. Little did I know that whist I was on stage, Neil and Dave decided as a prank to swap the hotel room numbers around, so apart from our room, which we always shared because of the cost, all the room numbers to the others' rooms on our floor were changed. It caused chaos, and the next morning I got it in the neck from the management when they realized the only room that wasn't affected was the room we were in! Oh, the pair of then thought it was hilarious, laughing all the way back.

The next week, we were in Scunthorpe. It was another Monday evening with a stopover, only this time we weren't staying where the show was, so no monkey business, you two. I laid the law down with the pair of them.

So, I got the first half of my bit of the show done, and then in the second half introduced Dave and Neil. Well, when they both got on stage, I thought, *What's up with the pair of them?* They were a bit different looking, and after about half an hour, I realized they had been drinking. Particularly Neil; he was hammered. When we finished, I gave them both a right telling off. We got back to our room, which was a three-bed room with a freestanding wardrobe, and Neil tried to open the wardrobe door.

The Man in the Mirror

He was so drunk, he pulled the wardrobe down onto himself, and there he was, in a drunken stupor, laying flat on his back with a wardrobe on top of himself! I must admit it was funny. He was legless and couldn't move the wardrobe off himself.

I was tempted to say, "Well, ya made your bed, now you can lay in it!"

Dave and I got him into bed, as we had an early start back the next morning. We had a long journey back, with clients in starting from noon, and Neil was in a stat and a half!

We set off, but after an hour in the car, Neil was, "Stop the car quick, I'm going to be sick!"

I pulled over, not realizing I'd stopped by a queue of people at a bus stop. The car door swung open, Neil threw up right in front of the people standing there, then shut the door, and I drove off quickly, leaving a bus stop full of people with a pile of sick to look at! And me saying for the rest of the journey back, "Don't you dare chuck up in my car, Neil."

We made it back bang on twelve noon. I pulled up right outside the Stoke salon door to unpack all the gear we'd taken with us.

Neil's first client, Miss Weight, who owned the town's travel agency (a real nice, posh lady who came to Neil every week) was waiting outside.

Neil opened his car door and threw up right in front of Miss Weight.

"Oh dear," she said.

And I quickly responded by saying, "I'm so sorry, Miss Weight. We've done a Show in Scunthorpe last night, and Neil suffers from travel sickness." He was supposed to be doing her hair! I talked her into having someone else do her hair, and Neil spent the rest of the afternoon asleep on the staffroom floor with his coat over him.

That was the end of me using Neil or Dave again. I was better off doing everything in my shows myself.

During 73/74, there was a major inconvenience we all had to deal with, and that was two-hour power cuts.

The Heath government was at war with the unions, so everyone had to endure two hours on and two hours off with their electricity. We had a flat roof at the Campbell place salon, so we fixed up a generator for when to power was off. Some staff from the other two salons used the Stoke Salon. It went on for ages, we kept all our staff on throughout that crisis, but as soon as it was over, we had staff leave. Little did I know back then how many times as a business we would experience this in the future. Loyalty was not a two-way street.

CHAPTER TWENTY-ONE

A Sad Loss – A time to Remember

In 1974, my main focus was to achieve a good result in the World Championships in Vienna Austria in the late summer. I'd had seven months to put my head down and practice. This meant practicing after work or on weekends. I never took time out of the salon to practice, I always put my share of money in the till. It was full on for me.

John Hammond was going to be my model for these Championships, as after Lausanne, I felt John brought a newness to my work, and as a team, we gelled really well.

We had training in different Salons with the British squad to even up the fairness for travelling, the farthest being Trevor Mitchell's salon in Southampton, Adrian Fuller's salon in Leeds, and occasionally Gordon Stuart's salon in Glasgow. In between was Sundays at mine, but there was no after meals at the Wheatsheaf anymore because of my ban there.

I felt I needed to give my all to this year. I may not get such a good chance of winning something again; it was my time, particularly after my previous success, and I wanted to make the most of it.

I had pencilled in a trip to the German Championships in Stuttgart around early May. The German Championships were a good insight to how the German teams were performing, and the exhibition was amazing. I was by now quite interested in trying for the ladies' team at some point in the future, and the hairdressing standard not only in the competitions but also in the exhibitions too.

With Wella, Schwarzkopf, Goldwell, and Indola being German companies, they always had large stands, with some of the biggest names in Europe demonstrating. It gave me ideas for the shows I was doing back home, plus salon design ideas.

With the style of furniture from Wella and Olymp, this would give our salons an international ambiance with the European trends in salon design. At some point, it was my intension, money permitting, to pursue this this new European style and format the salons to them instead of the disco theme we'd had so much success with.

So, off I went, driving overnight, down to Stuttgart.

Driving was the norm for me, I'd be crossing the channel three or four times a year, usually over a Saturday night to save money, and on this trip, there was the Dutch Championships the following weekend in Amsterdam, so I decided to go and watch them both. there was no international event at the German Championships, so I went on my own, agreeing to meet up with some of the squad in Holland the following weekend. The Dutch, too, were knocking out some great work, and I couldn't get enough of it all.

I'd driven up to Amsterdam from Stuttgart, and there I was, meeting up with most of the squad members who were trying for the team. I suppose my trip down to Stuttgart was a bit extravagant, but I couldn't get enough of it all, and I treated this time as my holidays, so It didn't mean me taking anymore time away from the salon than was necessary. In Stuttgart, I paid particular attention to the members of the German team I'd competed against many times before. I photographed every member of their team's work, plus others I thought may improve my inspiration for new ideas.

I drove back up to Amsterdam, having pre-arranged where we were staying and when we would all arrive. Remember, there was no such thing as mobile phones, and calls from hotels were mega expensive. This whole trip was cleaning me out, but it was going to be my ultimate year, and everything was feeling right, all my preparation, both at home in training plus these two observation/motivational trips; all was good, very good.

When I arrived at the hotel in Amsterdam where we'd all arranged to stay, Adrian Fuller from Leeds was the first one of the group I met up with. Adrian was an up-and-coming name in the Leeds area in a big salon group called Carlo & Geoffrey. He was well known as Comedian Freddie Star's hairdresser. Adrian travelled with Freddie and did his show wigs, particularly Freddie's Elvis character.

Adrian approached me and said, "Your dad has asked me to tell you to get home as quickly as you can. You have some very important overseas visitors arriving back at your salon!" Adrian expressed this in such a way that was obvious how serious he was in getting me to change my plans and get back to the salon as quickly as I could.

And that's what I did. *What could it be? I wondered. Am I going to be approached by a big manufacturer, was this the beginning of fame for me?* I had plenty of time to dream of all the different scenarios as I headed for Ostend and then drove back as quickly as I could to Stoke.

Would they wait for me? Would I not make it back in time? All these thoughts throughout my journey kept going over in my mind.

When I finally arrived back at the Stoke salon it was Monday lunchtime, so I approached my dad.

"So, what's going on, then? Who's coming that's made it so important that I needed to get back as quickly as I could?"

Dad turned to me. "I'm sorry to say this, but your Model John Hammond has been killed. He was delivering a lorry load of goods, to a yard in Buckinghamshire. His lorry had a tarpaulin cover over the goods he was unloading, and across the yard was a single cable. John didn't know or realize that the cable was "live". He was electrocuted. He lay there on the top of his lorry for two hours before he was found. His funeral is at two today, you need to get going."

I was shattered by this news. My mind was racing with so many thoughts.

I just made it in time to his funeral, and I just couldn't believe it. After my long journey expecting one thing and finding out this, it was like a nightmare. I went through the motions, his wife and her sister were in a right state, we all were. John was a careful guy, he was a responsible kind of person, how could this happen? So many questions, we were all saying the same thing.

I was in a daze. I'd spent my entire journey dreaming of fame and fortune, I just hit a brick wall.

John wasn't just a hair model to me, he was my friend. A very good friend. Our time together driving down to Lausanne, we bonded, and now he was gone.

I went back to work after the funeral.

The Man in the Mirror

I can't explain how it felt. John—we bonded not just about modelling for me, we really got on in so many ways. Our friendship was growing, really growing, and now there was just a deep, empty feeling.

Back at work, I filled my days trying to come to terms with his death. I was also deep down angry with Dad and Adrian in the way they decided to get me to return home.

Word also got round the squad. Adrian knew when I met him in Amsterdam, so they all knew before I'd even got back home.

Inevitably, the questions started. What are you going to do? It's seven weeks to the World Championships, and your main model is gone, what are you going to do?

This isn't easy to explain to a non-competition hairdresser, so someone who isn't even a hairdresser won't understand what I'm about to try and explain. Preparing a haircut on a classic sculpture model for a World Championship would take several haircuts to achieve a precise growing pattern needed to produce what you felt would be the exact correct one on the day you were going to do it, and you would need at least 1.5 cm of hair to be removed on the day, but underneath that 1.5 cm lays the ultimate haircut you've been preparing each time you've practiced on your model, and bearing in mind everyone's hair growth is different. But here we are talking very, very fine detail. My preparation on John's hair started back in Lausanne a year prior, and of my spare stand-in models, including Keith, I'd been cutting for practice, none would have 1.5cm of hair growth to remove on the competition day. Without the correct growth to be cut, I would be penalized, and it wouldn't be worth even going. Plus, I was one of the favourites to take a medal place, so any opportunity I presented my other country competitors with, they would take it. I had to be perfectly prepared to avoid anyone penalizing me, and that with a model. Now I didn't have a suitable model, so it was a no win situation for me. Having said that, my work was consistent, I never turned in a poor job, so as a team member, I was still a good choice to have even if I didn't take a top prize. A top fifteen would keep the team in with a chance of a top three placing.

The manager Vin Miller was going to have to make the final decision. It was going to be his last championship.

Well, he didn't like me, that was for sure after the fuss I made the previous year on his management methods, but I was his most experience team member. Would he play it safe with me should I be able to find a model from somewhere on such short notice, or would he pick a less experienced person and take a chance?

The decision was going to be made within the following two weeks, leaving just four weeks to the championships.

I was in a quandary. John was my model for these championships. We'd put in a lot of time together since our success in Lausanne. He'd just died, and here I was moving on to another model. It didn't feel right, me just carrying on, not showing any respect for John, but I also felt he would want me to carry on. I was at a loss as what to do. Missing these championships, I'd put four years of my life into, ending it like this wasn't what John would have wanted.

Charles Clark from Brighton called me. He'd heard the news. His son Charles Junior had packed in hairdressing and gone working on the fishing boats, and his old model was still around and was up for standing in. His hair was long, so I could use him.

The Man in the Mirror

There was the problem of travel, on top of getting his hair in some sort of prepared shape. He was a good model, not quite in the same league as John, but Vin Miller called and said I should stay with it and use Charles' model. He was a good standard, and he felt the team would be best if it was kept the same.

And so I decided to see it through.

CHAPTER TWENTY-TWO

Cheating Germans!

The next four weeks flew by. I put a shift and a half in preparing Vic's hair. He was a great guy, and he made himself available whenever I asked. And he didn't mind what I did with his hair. In fairness, he knew the ropes from his time with Charles Clark junior.

I'd never fully cut his hair, so my first haircut on him would be on the day in the World Championships. I had to leave the 1.5 cm of growth needing to be cut on the day, and also back then it was customary for all the models' hair color to be black, but I'd used a very warm, slightly dark burgundy tone on John's hair, and it went down really well, it looked more modern. This way, my thinking was to give something extra to my work to make up for the lack of cutting preparation which I couldn't build into Vic's hair because of the timescale.

The trip started well. We had a good hotel on the outskirts of Vienna. The rooms were a good size, and the light was good to prepare my model's hair in. We never had our rooms cleaned, as there was always a risk of being chucked out of the hotel because there would be stuff everywhere; tint stains in the bathroom sink, hair on the carpets, towels with colour stains on them, that's how it was.

The Man in the Mirror

Apart from our events using our own models, there was also a ballot for models' competition. This was the first event of the weekend. There would be a member of the public sitting in front of a mirror, and each mirror had a number on it, so the stage area would have around 130 people sitting at a mirror and each team would line up in alphabetical order and draw a mirror number out of a bag, and that would be your model to produce a commercial hairstyle on someone you'd never seen before. For want of a better word, it was a lottery as to the standard of the model and the quality of their hair, too. You had forty-five minutes to perform something wonderful.

We always carried extra clothes and bits of make-up so that you could at least present your model better. Right or wrong, we always had a good walk around the stage area, looking at the different models and which ones would be the best, and also the worst ones, too, because there was always a pool of spare models should you draw a model which you felt was not up to an average standard. So we would always check the pool models just in case the model you'd drawn was not up to standard.

So, there I was, walking around, observing the models and looking at the numbers of the best ones, hoping I got a good one. I noticed that there were four models that I'd seen earlier in the year when I went to watch the German Championships in Stuttgart. I was surprised that there would be four outstanding models sitting there in this ballot for models event.

I talked to our manager Vin Miller and the rest of the team. We discussed it between each other, as I thinking something was going on here, but to be honest, the others weren't that bothered, thinking about their own performance, and my mind should have been too.

John Belfield M.I.T.

Maybe I was overthinking, perhaps I would draw one of those four models. I wouldn't be complaining then, would I...

It was time for us to get in line for the ballot draw. We were represented as Great Britain, so we were letter G in the queue standing just behind the German team. We each picked out of the ballot bag our model mirror number and went to the model with the corresponding number. My model was okay, middle of the road, but okay. I checked on our other three team members to see if they were happy with their respective models, and all were okay, with them.

As I walked back to my model, I noticed that the four German Team members had drawn the four outstanding models I'd seen at the German Championships! Well, that didn't take much working out, did it? I quickly informed our team manager what I'd seen. This was a big distraction for me right before the start of the first event, but Vin wasn't that willing to say anything. He was well out of his depth. I had to do or say something, by which time I was now getting angry. I complained to one of the stewards and said there was cheating going on, that this wasn't fair. Other competitors started to notice me complaining, but nothing was being done about it.

I was angry, the competition was about to start, and I hadn't got myself organised properly with the balloted model I'd drawn. I complained to the stewards, who were supposed to be checking all competitors were abiding by the rules, but nobody was going to stop the German team. They were getting away with it.

My head was all over the place. The event finished, and I made sure I'd presented my model as best I could, then left the competition floor to see the finished hairstyles of the four German team members, they stood out, their hair was pre-coloured, their clothes were high fashion, well over the top for a person off the street event. I was disgusted.

I knew two members of the German team and made it quite clear I knew what had gone on, but they were non-committal.

We finished the championships off over the next two days, and we all felt we'd done well, the best we could have done on the day, but my gut feeling was not quite well enough.

The Parade of Nations and results was on Tuesday evening. We had a free day, and this was the first time I felt the need for a bit of space from it all. We were stuck in our hotel just outside of Vienna, and I decided to take a train and go up to the Semmering Ski slopes.

Three of us went, and we got up early and took the train. It was out of season, but the scenery was amazing. I'd never been anywhere near a ski slope, skiing was for the well-off, and that definitely wasn't me. When we got up there, I couldn't believe anyone would attempt to ski down what was a really steep slope, I'd never been skiing, but I soon realized the first lesson was learning how to stop!

It was a pleasant change, even just taking the train, something new for all three of us. We felt the benefit of it after weeks of stressful training, as it put life into an equalising perspective.

We got back mid-afternoon and got ready for the Parade of Nations and the results. I was still annoyed about the ballot situation. A few other teams were talking, and it was mentioned in the ladies' events too. We did the usual parade, walking behind our Union Jack. All our models were well presented, and it was a special/proud moment. A moment in one's life that stays with you forever. I'm getting goosebumps just writing this now, that's what it does to you, and I'm sure it's the same for all the other thirty-odd countries and competitors who took part too.

Well, as expected, the results went to the German teams. Both men's and ladies'. There was a fair few thousand people in the arena, it was quite a spectacle, because after the parade and before the results, there were shows and entertainment, usually themed to the history of the host nation.

The German national anthem was playing, both teams with their models stood on the stage, flags flying high, it was a spectacle sitting there watching. But what happened next shocked everyone, because as soon as the German team stood on that stage receiving their awards, the ENTIRE American team, both men's and ladies', staged a protest and just stood up en-masse and walked out!

Well, I wasn't expecting that!

Other teams, including ours, stood up and applauded them for doing it, and parts of the audience joined in too. I'd never seen anything like it. It was jaw-dropping just standing there watching, taking in this scene. Everyone knew the Germans had cheated, and there they all stood on the stage, expecting a standing ovation, but all they got was humiliation, and well deserved, too.

That night will go down in the folklore of hairdressing history.

We came 5th overall, which, out of thirty-two countries, wasn't bad, we usually made it in the top six.

When we arrived back in the UK, we heard that the OAI and the CIC (the two governing bodies who control the World/European Championships) had disqualified the German Teams. It should have never got as far as it did, but there ya go, what goes around comes around, so we again placed 4th.

Given the circumstances, I couldn't complain. I performed well and didn't let the team down. We all felt 4th was about right.

Going back home to reality wasn't easy. Whenever I did a World/European Championship, the months prior in the build-up was really intense, it takes over your life, and then it was like dropping off a cliff, just an emptiness. I was always down for quite a few weeks afterward. Getting back in the salon just didn't give me the buzz that the competitions did. Taking a holiday didn't work either.

I settled back in, getting on with the day-to-day things as best I could, working off the empty feeling I was experiencing.

I got a phone call one day from a guy who was working for Charlie at his Albrighton Salon. He hadn't seen or heard from Charlie for a few days, and he wasn't answering his phone at home, either. I was concerned, as this wasn't like him at all. In fact, just the opposite.

I decided to go to his house and see if he was there. I was concerned, as this was completely out of character.

Well, I found him in the street where he was living, but I didn't get as far as his house. He was laying in the gutter. What made it worse was it was chucking down with rain.

He was in a state, he didn't know where he was, nor who I was. I thought he was drunk at first, but I couldn't smell alcohol, though it was raining heavy. I got him up and took him to a local A&E and stayed with him until they admitted him. I left him there and called the next day to see how he was. They told me over the phone that they needed a next of kin.

John Belfield M.I.T.

I decided to go that evening and visit him. He was sitting up in bed, not quite himself, but he recognized me, and we talked. I knew he'd found times hard; after all, he had four different jobs. I could see he'd gone over the edge—he certainly wasn't himself.

The staff asked me if he had any next of kin, as Charlie was reluctant to say anything to any of the staff that were looking after him. What on earth had happened that got him in the state he was in?

I knew his wife was a nurse at a hospital in Wolverhampton, but whether it was this one, I wasn't sure. As I sat there, he started to tell me his wife had left him. They had five children, and she had just packed her bags, up and gone, taking their five children with her. Unfortunately, she hadn't just gone down the road where I could go and see her and hopefully get to the bottom of it all to see if they both could resolve whatever it was between them.

But, as Charlie said she'd left him for good, taking all their children with her to live with her sister, who lived in America. Overnight, she'd decided she wasn't going to live with him anymore and the life they had together, and so off she'd gone, permanently.

It didn't surprise me to learn that he was up to his eyeballs in debt, and had just worked himself into the ground trying to make ends meet. I knew from what he'd told me that she was a dominant type of person. Her family had originated from Jamaica. She didn't give him any warning—she just up and went.

I did feel some responsibility. I knew he thought a lot of me, as friends and professionally, and I left the hospital feeling really sorry for him. His family meant a lot to him, although with all the jobs he had going, I doubt how much time he could have put into his family.

He was, in his own way, trying to improve his ability and standards as a hairdresser/barber, but that wasn't a quick fix financially.

I came back to stoke and had a chat with my mum and dad. Mum was still active in the business as a bookkeeper, and she also did the wages. I was thinking could we make a go of his business for him in some way. I felt I had to do something.

I went back down to his shop in Albrighton to see his only employee, Michael Evans, and put him in the picture as to Charlie's situation. I asked if he would stay on working in the salon, as it was my intention to run the business and pay off all Charlie's debts, or as much as we could within reason.

I put our business plan to Michael, explaining he could either stay on and have the business once Charles was free of any liability, assuming we could return the business into profit, that is, or he could move on. The only way this was going to work was Michael staying on. I did also say we would give him a job if he wanted to after we sorted Charlie's finances out.

Michael decided he would do the right thing and stay.

Mum and Dad were going to help me, too, and I did promise Michael that he would get paid one way or another..

So, that was that. We started sorting Charlie's shop out. He wasn't fit for work even after he left hospital, so, since I had a spare bedroom, I brought him up to Stoke to live with me. Between us, we sorted out his rented accommodation, set up the business plan with Michael Evans, and with Mum and Dad helping me, we started to pay off his debts.

It was going to take some time to do. We covered some days at his salon with one or two staff from our Stoke salon to cover when Michael was on holiday. Charlie rested at my house for weeks until he was well enough to think about starting back to doing hairdressing again.

Charlie's first language was Gaelic, he spoke nothing else until the age of eleven. He knew I'd done some self-taught German, because of my interest in the German Championships and the exhibitions in Germany, and he realized he could pick German up quite easily. I knew a guy from the German team who had a salon in Cologne, so before Charlie started back working, we both had a few days with Wolfgang Steinbach at his salon.

He took to Charlie. His salon was huge, with fifteen hairdressers and bar area for clients to sit and enjoy the experience. It was the norm for German salons to serve alcohol in those days.

I knew Wolfgang from him being with the German team, and I hasten to add that he wasn't in the German team that cheated.

We had a few days in Cologne, camping to save money right on the river Rhine.

On the way back, we talked about Charlie's future. He could stay in Stoke and work for us, but he felt working in Germany would give him a new start. I couldn't disagree; he needed a whole new start, that was for sure.

He stayed living with me for a while and started working in our Liverpool road salon, his salon. His work was okay, but it needed a lot more to his game if he was going to work with Wolfgang. He appreciated that we were sorting his finances out, and that wasn't going to happen overnight, and he also needed to try and find his wife and five children. You never know, they might have wanted him to go and join them, and I didn't fancy picking up the pieces for him again if he threw a wobbly in Germany!

CHAPTER TWENTY-THREE

Alcohol in the Workplace

Working in the salon in those days, there wasn't the workplace structure that we all know exists these days. There was always something to deal with, whether it was staff or clients or both. Conversation and freedom of expression was still in its infancy. Yes, we had staff rules, of course, but there was always something.

I was still working all day on a Thursday at our Hanley salon. It was very bang up to date, and our staff projected a trendy image. The salon design was something clients had never experienced, and most of the music we played matched the tone we set.

Well, we had one young guy working for us who was an up and coming hairdresser. I'd taken him on one of my overseas trips to Paris to give him a taste of international hairdressing, and it was motivational, too. Having staff with those extra experiences was client building.

His name was Paul, and we used his photo on some of our promotional stuff. I knew he liked a drink, and we did have occasions when we'd find him on the doorstep of the salon after a heavy nights bender, fast asleep. My thoughts were, *Well, at least he's turning up for work.*

The Man in the Mirror

It was one of those Thursdays, and we were really busy. The salon styling units were triangular, standing off each wall. It was about four o'clock in the afternoon, and Paul had two children in, a brother and sister aged around ten and twelve, just a normal afternoon.

About five o'clock, I got a phone call from the children's mother.

"My children have just been to your salon and are now in my office drunk. Do you realize I work in the council's education department at the town hall just up from your salon and they are under the influence?"

"What? I don't understand what you're talking about."

And then I looked a Paul.

Full of apologies to the lady, I hung up. He was drunk too, very drunk.

"What the hell are you playing at giving alcohol to two very young children, and in my salon, too!"

It turned out he kept a bottle of sherry hidden behind the units he was working at, and unknown to any of us, he'd been drinking most of the day, apparently, and took it on himself to give the two children a tipple, too.

I sent him home. I didn't need to fire him, he never came back.

That just about finished off one hell of a year!

When I think of this time in my life, I wasn't prepared for any of it. As the song goes, "Life is a Rollercoaster." Well, it certainly was for me. Everyone expected so much from me—my input into the salons, staff training, development of our brand, and also for me to improve on my competition success, which at the level I was at needed time, a lot of time, not just to practice but also network a crowd of like-minded people who I'd connected to all over Europe and beyond, where I could improve my all-around ability as a hairdresser.

This was my future, and it doesn't come round twice. Everyone's expectations of me, I felt, were higher than I could achieve. The pressure was enormous.

The Man in the Mirror

CHAPTER TWENTY-FOUR

An Unexpected Japanese Visitor

1975 started off in the craziest of ways.

I was working at our first floor salon in Campbell place in Stoke. It was a Friday morning, the salon was rammed as usual, it was the start of our weekends trade, and I got a phone call from Stoke Station. "There is a man here with a card with your name on it, he's looking for you."

"Eh! What for?"

"We don't know, he can't speak English. He's from Japan and is looking for you!"

So, they sent him round to me. There was a lot of bowing and nodding going on, but I couldn't for the life of me understand what on earth he was doing looking for me in Stoke!

I needed some quick thinking; where on earth was I going to find someone who could speak Japanese? It was bad enough trying to understand clients from "neck end" (Longton that is, southeast end of the potteries), let alone Japan.

Well, I had some good fortune, as I called Keele University, which at that time was our only University in North Staffs. I explained my circumstances, and, luckily, they had a far east student. Not Japanese, but she could understand Japanese. This was a life saver.

She came down to the salon and spoke to this guy, discovering that his name was Masataka Tanaka. Come on, how many letter As can you possibly have in your name?

So, it was Friday afternoon in our Salon in Stoke. And folks around Stoke were quite insular, if we had a client in from Tunstall, north end of the potteries, that is, it was quite something. And here we were with a guy from Japan—at my shop in Stoke!

Crazy as it was, it turned out he'd won a prize funded by Gillette to tour Europe. He'd read about me in some of the Japanese hair magazines. At that time, I was doing stuff for Japanese hair mags, particularly cutting, styling, and perming men's hair, also coloring, too. I'd been doing this since my trip to Osaka in 1970.

I'd no idea he was visiting me, nor Europe, he just turned up and stayed for the rest of the afternoon, as did the student interpreter.

He didn't have any pre-booked accommodation, and I think he just thought he'd wing it and play it by ear. I found out he needed to be in London Monday morning, so I booked him in the North Staffs Hotel, which in those days was a good hotel, and it was right opposite the railway station. Our interpreter could only help on Friday afternoon, as she had plans for Saturday, so I needed to make the most of his visit for him.

We had dinner together back at the hotel, which was a bit difficult, as Stoke wasn't exactly Tokyo. But I made the best of it for him, and decided to take him up to the PLACE in Hanley. It was the "in place" in the area. I'd no idea about discos in Tokyo, but his eyes lit up. I suppose he did stand out because of his looks, and while it wouldn't mean much now, back then, he was the center of attention.

I had to drag him out at two a.m., he was buzzing. But I'd had a busy day, and the added problem of having him all day in the salon, too. He was at my salon by nine-thirty a.m. the next morning, and I made sure he had a good day. He was a barber by trade, but we were now full on unisex, and he enjoyed the mix it offered him. I'd got him another night, before agreeing to travel with him down to London on Sunday, ready for his four days with Gillette.

We had diner again back at the North Staffs, and all he really wanted to do was to go back to the Place for more of the same as the night before. He couldn't wait to go there again.

By two a.m., I organized a taxi back to the hotel, only this time there was three of us in the cab, not two! He had got a grin from ear to ear. I left him to it, and we met up at Stoke Station the next day and travelled down to London by train. With no interpreter, it wasn't easy trying to communicate, just plenty of nodding and hand signs.

I booked a room at his hotel, we managed a few sights later in the afternoon, and he booked dinner at a Japanese Restaurant, a very authentic restaurant, I might add. We had a private dining room, with a table about nine inches off the floor. we sat on the floor cross legged throughout our meal, my joints were never the same after that meal. We had a geisha waiting on us, and she did everything, all very traditional. Most of our food was raw, and not well presented, either, not a bit westernized like todays Japanese food. I got it down, with plenty of Sake, but it's not the best sitting position for your digestion. However, after my time back in Tokyo, the food was what I expected, and it was his evening, I suppose, as a thank you for his time in Stoke.

John Belfield M.I.T.

He was still talking about his nights at the Place, and I hope his time at my Salon, too.

After dinner, we said our farewells. I could tell he'd really appreciated his time with me, and considering it wasn't planned, I was happy he'd go home with fond memories of his time in Stoke. I know he did, because he sent me his feature in the Japanese hair magazines that Gillette had organized, and I was well mentioned in his article.

CHAPTER TWENTY-FIVE

Pickled Herring and Gun Boats

Three weekends later, I was judging and demonstrating in Reykjavik in Iceland. I was flying out from Glasgow, and I never had time to unpack my travel bags, It was straight back into work from London, then a full-on weekend in Iceland from Saturday to Monday, plus a train journey to and from Glasgow.

At that time, Britain was in the middle of the "Cod War". Not the best time to be in Iceland as a Brit, as fishing was the only industry back then that Iceland had, and we were fighting them over it.

The worldwide hairdressing community stays pretty neutral when it comes to these sorts if issues, although I doubt whether this would have applied in 1939.

I had my first taste of pickled herrings on this trip. The President of the Scandinavia Hairdressing Federation held an welcome evening for all invited guests. They were very warm toward me, and I knew some of the Norweigian contingent because I had done a couple of teachings over in Norway, both in Oslo and Trondhiem around that time, and twice a year I had organized groups over from Norway to London for three days of styling and cutting classes. I used to use a lecture room at the London College of Fashion, The head was good to me from my days at Hollings College when he was head there. I suppose it was also a feather in his cap having overseas hairdressers at the college, and as I was on their advisory committee, setting their City & Guilds standards, it all fit quite well.

I had a very busy but friendly weekend in Iceland, and it was my first time there, but as it turned out, not my last.

I did get a couple of hours doing a reckie in Reykjavik!

Almost a poet.

The place itself was quite small, but the two things about the place which stay in my mind was the gun boats in the harbor, with the war on, and as I was walking down the main street, there was a river which ran through the town, and standing on a bridge, looking into the river, the amount of salmon I could see was unbelievable, it was packed with them, a bit like the herrings the night before!

If I had to add a third memory, it would be the natural hot water they had. The thing that puts you off is taking a bath in hot, brown, smelly water. It is amazing that a cold place such as Iceland has its own natural hot water supply; that's cooool!

The judging was quite boring, really, sitting in a room somewhere in an exhibition center, and just being let out at the end of each event, then back in the room again. It was like that all day, apart from my thirty minutes on stage doing my thing!

I flew back Monday morning to Glasgow, then a train back to Stoke, and by Tuesday morning, I was back in the Salon.

Things were beginning to get on top of me, and I was hoping to make the Euro's in the Autumn, which were back in Austria again, but I didn't have a model, and with the amount of commitments I had, it was looking unlikely I'd make the team. I would need to practice, plus coming up with a new hair look, too.

It was a crazy time. If I wasn't away judging or demonstrating, then Sunday was a training day, which usually was in Stoke or down in Southampton at Mitch's salon. Something was going to break, I was going a hundred miles an hour, and that time came on Easter.

I'd been booked to do a Sunday afternoon show in Edinburgh and an evening Show in Southampton, which I was doing with Mitch. I worked all day on Saturday, then drove up to Edinburgh in the evening after work. I had models to audition and prep on Sunday morning.

I used to have my music taped, and I'd always carry a suitcase of clothes and a bag of make-up and just about anything and everything in a big box with all my hair stuff.

My models were really good, and I sorted out the ones I wanted, got their hair looks prepped up, and we even had an hour to run through the music to practice how I wanted it to pan out.

One of my very dear friends Gordon Alcock back then was active with our local amateur operatic society. He could act, sing, dance, choreograph, and do just about anything I would need to present an interesting hair show. So I would walk the models to music, focusing on a good intro and a good finish.

The afternoon went well. There was a couple of local hairdressers presenting, and we gelled well, with an audience of around 250, which wasn't a bad turnout. At least the majority were sober, which was better than my last trip to Glasgow. I was expecting a similar reaction from the audience, but the Edinburgh hairdressers were a lot more civilized than over in Glasgow.

It ended by five p.m., and I packed everything away, ready for another show the next night in Southampton. I drove back as far as Stoke, went straight to bed, ready for my drive down to Southampton. I had arranged with Mitch to audition the models and also prepare them, too, so, basically, I just needed to turn up, which I did, just in time to run through everything.

Mitch was on stage with me, so we were familiar with how we wanted it to go. He did all the male models, and I did the females. There was another couple hundred in the audience, who were very appreciative of my work. I knew most of them, too, which does help.

I got back to Stoke at five in the morning, with my first client due at eleven. I'd arranged with one of our staff to call me to make sure I didn't oversleep.

Well, one thing was for sure—that weekend put me off fancying being a rally driver!

But things had come to a head at work. My personal life was at a crossroads. It wasn't anything to do with either my dad nor Dave Cooke, the business was going well, it was all me. I was trying to do everything; put my five days in behind the chair for the business, and also pursue my ambitions as a hairdresser and put down my mark as a name within my industry.

When I got back from Southampton, Dave Cooke crossed the line with me, stepping into my private life, and my mum and dad were doing the same, too.

It was too much for me, I just needed some space so things would settle. I certainly wasn't neglecting my commitment to the business, and in my eyes, I started to wonder where the business would be without me. We were all being paid the same, the only difference was

The Man in the Mirror

Dave Cooke went home on time every night and he had his two days off every week, and here I was working all over the place, I didn't even know who my next-door neighbor was.

Mum and Dad had a car on the business and four free tickets to Stoke City football club every home game, two of them were for my brother and his wife, and for that I had to do someone's hair for free every Saturday morning so they had a nice freebee at Stoke. And in between, Dad went to Port Vale home games, too.

I just snapped, and I walked away, I told them they could get on with it on their own.

My personal life was not in any way affecting my work, I was just putting more into the business than any of them, maybe too much, and I needed some time away. I was burning out. I hadn't taken any holidays for a long time.

I called Mitch and asked if I could spend sometime with him. I also called Charlie. He was still living at my house, and he could see it coming. He understood. I knew he would eventually move on, we had paid off his debts and closed his business down, and the guy who was working for him came up to Stoke and worked at our Hanley Salon, settling in Stoke.

I did a few days at Mitch's Salon and basically sat back and waited to see how the business would get on without me.

CHAPTER TWENTY-SIX

Retirement for Dad and the Door to Dave Cooke

After a month or so, I decided to chill out down on the beach in Newquay Cornwall. Summer was coming up, and I wasn't in any mood to return. In fact, I'd looked at a small salon in Truro, sort of plan B. If the business back in Stoke was surviving without me, I considered staying where I was.

Charlie came down one weekend, and I caught up with how things were back at the salons. Sure enough, it wasn't good. Although neither Dave Cooke or my Dad was going to admit it.

I think during those weeks, I got the best suntan I'd ever had. My flat was just a bedsit a couple of miles out of Newquay, so I wasn't in the holiday trap of rentals.

I'd kept in contact with all the guys in the squad, and I kept my commitment to training over at Mitch's salon in Southampton, too.

A couple things happened which changed my circumstances, more or less at the same time. Dad called me and said he wanted to meet up with me. In fact, he drove down to Cornwall, and we sat down and talked things through.

At the same time, Mitch called me, as he'd dropped on a really good model if I wanted to use him for the Euros, and that was a game changer for me.

Dad said the business was suffering badly, and it needed me back on board, and pretty quickly, too. I said I would return on two conditions, one was that Dave Cooke left, and the other was that Dad retired. Those were my terms, and it was not negotiable.

So, I packed up my things, said goodbye to the beaches of Newquay, and returned to the salons. I met up with Dave Cooke for the last time, and we gave him the Hanley Business, which to me was more than generous. He should have paid something for it, but to be honest I was glad to see the back of him.

And Dad took retirement.

My mother wasn't too warm toward me, but time was a big healer. Dad kept his car, his football tickets, and I paid him his normal wage, too. Neither mum nor dad had any pension pot apart from their state pensions, so it was down to me to provide. We did it quietly, not even my brother knew of how I'd committed to basically keeping my parents. But when it came down to it, it was a family business, and to the outside world, nobody knew any different.

I got back into the swing of things. The Hanley shop was gone, and our original salon in Liverpool Road where Charlie was working was looking dated. Liverpool Road wasn't the main road to Hanley it used to be; in fact, it was becoming a dump of a place, and it wasn't worth investing in a refurb at those premises.

The ground floor at the Campbell place salon had come available, so too was the freehold on the premises, so Dad and I decided to sell the Liverpool Road property and move the remaining staff to the Campbell place salon. It gave me a new beginning and a fresh start, which was something I really needed.

Our business model worked extremely well, with salon designs looking like discos, and unisex hairdressing being our main theme, but though we were the forerunners of unisex hairdressing, having started it back in 1968, other salons were copying. In fact, the whole hairdressing industry was going in that direction

And from my many trips abroad competing and doing teach-ins I felt it was time to bring the salon up to date, having the ground floor salon as a ladies' salon, and the first floor as a men's salon. I felt unisex was over, and we needed to provide a more professional approach to our business. This was going to be a work in progress, as it was too big a project to do in one go, and I still had one more crack at a European championship in the Autumn.

The salon was doing well, and we were getting good publicity with having Alan and Maureen Hudson as clients. I did have a rule as far as footballers were concerned because we did have a time at our Liverpool Road salon when some of the Stoke footballers came in, but none of them wanted to pay, which went down like a lead balloon with me.

But Alan was different. When we first met, he laid down his rules. "If I send any of the Stoke lot around to you and you don't charge them, you won't see me again. They expect everything for nothing."

That was music to my ears.

During the time Alan was at Stoke, we became good friends and have periodically still kept in touch. He was a warm, friendly guy and would do anything to help me if he could. Unfortunately, he attracted too many hangers on, and I didn't connect with them.

I did meet a very special couple at that time when dining out with Alan and Maureen. Michael and Jackie Hamnett. We became and still are very good friends. I always had a view that you take people the way you find them, and Alan Hudson was a very giving not a taking sort of person, I focused for the rest of the year preparing for the Euros. Mitch came up with my new model, Gerry. He had a young look to him and was adventurous.

I felt it was time I stepped outside my comfort zone and really had a go for something more fashionable rather than staying in the mold that we all conformed to in the past. I'd decided this would be my last Euro with the men's team. I wanted to have a crack at making the ladies' team, as nobody world-wide had ever been in both and actually won medals in both teams. This was to be my goal, but the time wasn't right yet. I had more to give the men's team, and a new salon to get off the ground too.

Gerry was a good, enthusiastic model. The euro's was my main goal, but we all knew the big one was next year; The World Championships in New York. This was to coincide with the Bicentenary of the United States, and everyone wanted to be involved for that. But first we had to get through the Euros, which was back at the same exhibition Center in Vienna. The '74 World Championship fiasco was still very clear in my mind, and, quietly, I did have some reservations about going back there so soon. After all, I had been one of the competitors who had kicked off about how the Germans had fixed the ballot event. Trust me to open my big mouth!

Vin Millar was still team manager, though I didn't see much of Stan Gray after my run-in with him in Lausanne in '73. Upon reflection, I was a new kid on the block, and the federation was full of past generation barbers who were hanging on to what political glory they could still use in the promotion of their businesses, which most had pictures of men's hairstyles in their windows that had been there for years. And then I come along with a different mindset, and I did ruffle a few feathers. But I was the first of a new generation of men's hairdressers, and I really wanted to make a difference for this new squad of hairdressers who were of the same mindset as me but were not quite up there.

My legacy for that was to leave it in a better place than when I started.

I wasn't interested in the political side of the federation. Hairdressing was my real interest, and I never saw myself fitting in with what the federation was all about, even though my grandfather was one if its oldest members, which likely made our family business of 113 years their oldest business member. For that, we'd had one paragraph in the federation's focus magazine, and that was that. Nothing! It meant nothing.

I was, in my eyes, doing a good job training a squad of about a dozen hairdressers. Some would come into the squad just to learn more and then leave, having the title of British Team Squad Member. It didn't bother me that much, as I felt this got the message out to a wider audience nationally, and any publicity at that time was good for British Hairdressing, in my view.

We did have a publicity officer, a friend of Vin Millar and Stan Gray. He was a nice guy, to be honest, but he had no connections with the media, as such, and that was my first insight to what the media could do for our industry. He also didn't have a the personality I see in today's hair industry. There were publicity agents, yet almost all of the squad came from areas where there was no media, i.e., no national newspapers or television. In today's hair and beauty industries, these agents can create publicity out of almost nothing. However, back then, we created plenty of interesting things to use for publicity, yet we made nothing off it.

The year was good. I had a solid core of exceptional hairdressers in the squad, and I knew my team for the World event even before the euro's, but I also had an open mind. I never closed the door. We were building a future for British men's hairdressing, and I felt success would come, just keep it flowing.

Trevor Mitchell was a great asset for me. He had a very outlook and vision, plus a modern maturity, which I lacked. He knew it, and he mentored me with his vision, while I sorted out some of his hairdressing failing.

We also inherited some big egos. Mitch handled these guys really well, matching like with like. they were big in their areas and sadly always displayed a single mindedness which annoyed all the squad members, including me.

There was one who was in line to be my star man, his name was Adrian Fuller from Leeds, and he pissed everyone on the squad off for one reason or another, mainly by trying to upstage everyone. I managed to get it to work for the squad. They all wanted to be better than him, and he became my benchmark. If they could out-do him, the team was going to go all the way.

I had one international in with Gerry in Paris, and I didn't expect a top three, but I was happy with how it went. A few of the squad came along for the experience. Charlie, of course, was with me, so too was Adrian Fuller.

I got to know and understand Adrian from that weekend in Paris. He was a big city guy, fronting one of the biggest hair salon groups in the Leeds area, called Carlo & Jeffery, and Adrian was Freddie Star's hairdresser. He did Freddie's wigs for his shows. I think his "Elvis" character was his most outstanding.

Freddie was making a big name for himself in TV, and Adrian entertained us on that Paris trip with some amazing stories of him working with Freddie on his shows. I remember him telling us about the time he'd done a show with Freddie in London and they were travelling back up to Leeds in Freddies XJS speeding! There was a police chase, so Freddie drove onto the first service station they came to and Adrian swapped places with Freddie, pretending that he was the driver. When the police arrived, they both had to get out of their car. The police then accused Freddie of actually being the driver. At that point, Freddie stripped down to his underpants and climbed onto the roof of his car whilst the police began giving him a speeding ticket in the middle of a service station car park. They asked him to climb down, but Freddie was insistent, saying there was no law in stopping him getting a speeding ticket whilst standing on the roof of his car in his underpants!

Adrian had loads of similar stories, some best left unread. But this helped those of the squad who were with me to gel, just being together. For me, it was a successful weekend as a team building exercise, but it didn't end there, Ray Bridger from Birmingham was also with us.

We had been to the results evening, which was rather glitzy, and after, we made our way to a wine bar close to the flea pit of a hotel we were staying in. We'd settled in, and everyone was relaxed and happy-ish. There was a guy playing the piano, and Ray was in good spirits, as usual. I remembered his stint in Gravesend after a show when we ended up in a pub and he talked the band into performing, with Ray singing a "Johnny Be Good" number together. They turned out to be the backing band for Jimmy Hendrix! So, here we went again, up he got.

"Okay," he said, "who's betting me I can't sing "Jonny be Good" with the piano player?"

Well, the piano player was playing some gentle, relaxing, background music, not exactly in Ray's kind of music, and he must have been at least sixty years old if he was a day, but, we all chucked in a few bob toward a bottle of wine, and off Ray went to approach the piano player. The guy didn't look like he had any sort of entertainment style in him—in fact, he looked like he was ready for bed.

And then it started!

The pair of them kicked off with "Johnny Be Good," and another hour load of full on entertainment. The whole place came alive, and we had a great night—not just us but everyone in the place. The owner covered Ray's wine for the night, and the atmosphere was just magic. It finished off a brilliant weekend for all of us, and for me, team building and bonding, it couldn't have worked out better. I had an ace card in my squad. There was more to come from Ray Bridger!

I'd always kept in reasonably close contact with the ladies' squad members because of my membership with the fellowship, and also those from up north. At that time, I became quite close to a guy from St Helens named David Appleton. We shared ideas on occasions when we were travelling together, and he proposed that we should get together and start a training school. Our salons were close enough, just an hour apart on the M6 for it to work, and it seemed a natural expansion from a business point of view, as well as a new challenge to add to my re-branding the Stoke salon.

I'd gone in with a German salon furniture company called Wellonda, which was an offshoot of the German hair coloring manufacturer Wella. David had an excellent pedigree as a ladies' hairdresser, and the ground floor salon was looking like nothing anyone had seen in my area before. Salons were changing to unisex and cut and blow-drying, and I'd gone full circle back to a traditional ladies' and men's salon set-up. We were planning on opening the new ground floor salon with a bang, so we'd planned an opening in the spring of 1976.

David was very keen to get going with our training school, and it was all coming together nicely. We'd started off just doing teach-ins around the country, which was mainly in the midlands and the north where we were well known for our British Team success.

And so, this was how the year of '76 started.

Most Monday evenings, David and I were on stage somewhere, promoting our training school, which was now looking like it was going to be in my new salon in Stoke.

We'd connected as amateur photographers, too, though he was more advanced than me at that time. He was an Olympus camera fan and I was Nikon. He enjoyed this part of us working together, and all the photography was at my Stoke salon, as were all the models and largely most of my hairdressing.

I picked up a lot as a photographer, and David's fashion work improved. His ladies work was more traditionally based, whereas mine was hair dryer and brush.

After doing a number of shows, we had then created a demand for all-day training, which we did on a Monday at our salon in Stoke. I'd actually never been to Davids salon, and I don't know why, but it never occurred to me to go. In hindsight, perhaps I should have, because David decided to come and work in Stoke and close down his salon. This way, he could develop the training school on Mondays and work three days on the Stoke salon. Well, the salon was about to open on the ground floor, and we needed an experienced hairdresser on board, so I agreed to it. Although he would actually work for himself but on the school payroll.

At the same time, I was still training the squad on Sunday and Tuesday evenings for those near enough to travel. Adrian Fuller always attended both sessions, so too did Clive Basford from Birmingham, John Julien from Bolton, and Peter Hipkin from Wolverhampton; basically my team, with Mitch coming up on Sundays from Southampton. A few others attended on Sundays, including the manager Vin Millar. It suited me not seeing Vin, and I think he thought the same. These guy's I had were highly motivated, and apart from Vin bringing his photographer mate, taking pictures for the federation, he wasn't really needed.

So, there was a lot going on, and I had a new salon to open, too. Never a dull moment! But that was how my working life was... and still is.

CHAPTER TWENTY-SEVEN

Alan Hudson Opening the New Salon

I'd asked Alan and Maureen Hudson to do the opening of the salon for me. Alan was back then a celebrity in the area, having moved from Chelsea football club to Stoke City, and a cockney through and through. So, the invites when out. We chose businesspeople, mostly retailers who had boutiques, and I suppose in "In Crowd" for a want of a better description, plus our regular clients, and of course the press.

I'd booked a full page in our local *Evening Sentinel*, with businesspeople having supporting adverts to go along with it. The spread in the paper ended up being over two pages, and there wasn't a salon around who could pull that sort of publicity.

For entertainment, we had Dave (Arry) Roberts singing, so the stage was set for a Monday, early evening bash. We were expecting around eighty guests, as all had accepted their invitations, and then a disaster happened.

Four days before, Stoke City transferred Alan Hudson to Arsenal on the Thursday before my opening on the following Monday. Alan Hudson left, and I wasn't sure who would still turn up, because Alan was a big draw. I hadn't a clue what to do.

The Man in the Mirror

Peter Shilton was now playing for Stoke City, and I was doing his hair for him, but at that time, I didn't know him well enough, and Alan Hudson's name was on all the invites. I couldn't ask him, because he would see he wasn't my first choice.

Well, a couple of days went by, it was getting toward the weekend, and I'd had no success in finding a stand-in for Alan. All the catering was in place, as well as the entertainment, but no star man to open the salon. Then, out of the blue on the day before, I got a phone call from Alan asking me what time the opening was and what time did I want him to get there.

I said, "Alan, how is that going to work? You're in London with Arsenal, how on earth are you going to be here" We hope to have everyone in place by four p.m. to make the official opening about forty-five minutes after everyone has arrived and had a drink."

He said, "That's fine, I'll be finished training by noon, and I'll drive straight up to you."

I needed to sit down.

I said, "Alan, I can't ask you to do that."

He replied, "I said I would open the salon for you, and that's what I'm going to do."

And he did. He arrived on time, with everyone else. He had photos taken with guests, mixed and spoke to everyone, and did a brilliant job. So did Maureen.

Dave Roberts sang his usual stuff, and my mum un dad were amazed at how the whole evening had come together, especially my mother, as she loved a party. The evening was a huge success, and Alan wouldn't take a penny off me. Not even his petrol money. He left about nine p.m., sober, and drove back down to London. That's the Alan Hudson I knew and loved.

If I had to single out one thing above everything else that evening was it brought me back closer to my folks, especially my mother. She wanted more of it, and on the back of that, I asked her if she would like to go to New York with me to watch the World Championships. She jumped at it!

What a year this was turning into.

The salon design looked amazing. We had a circular waiting area right in the middle of the salon, and a traditional bank of hood driers with a coffee bar behind it. Newness brings something else out in you, and I needed that excitement from time to time. I think we all did.

But right then, there was too much going on. Excitement is one thing, but commitment is another, and I was committed.

David settled in, doing the training school and his time in the salon. All our staff seem happy with it all, and so they should, we had the best salon in the area, and great working conditions, too.

The salon on the first floor for was men's hairstyling. I say this because there is a difference between that and barbering, which is the same today; a short back and sides, and that makes the difference between the two. Upstairs was increasing in turnover and footfall. Even a few footballers from Stoke City were paying for a haircut! That was something.

My time was full on, and we were fully preparing for New York and the World Championships. It wasn't my final decision who would make the team, that would be Vin Millar's, the team manager's decision.

The Man in the Mirror

Around that time, there was a fashion for football/sports teams to have a team song. Ray Bridger called me and said he'd talked Vin Millar into doing a team song. I wasn't sure how much Vin put into this song, but Ray knew Roy Wood from Wizard pop group, and had arranged a studio in Birmingham to record a song called "Were on our Way to USA."

So, half a dozen of us went down to Birmingham and recorded this team song, I also played harmonica on it, plus singing. It was a completely new experience for all of us. Ray was comfortable with it all, but tracking a song in a studio was strange, far different from playing my harmonica on the back of a bus coming home after an away game of water polo. The drum section was the first part to be tracked, and then it was me, all I had to follow was the drumming, ya know—whack a do, whack a do in my earphones.

Roy Wood started calling me Larry, after the famous harmonica player Larry Adler, so there I was, standing in a sound-proof cubicle with my headphones on and Ray Wood standing outside, timing me when to come in on my harmonica.

Well, the beginning was easy enough, because I started the song off. I didn't re-join in until the middle 8, and then continued through to the end. The problem I had, having never done anything like this and not knowing the music until we got to the studio, when it came to joining in at the middle 8 part, by the time I'd taken a breath, I was half a beat out. So, I had Roy Wood counting my timing, standing in front of my sound-proof booth, calling me Larry. it took me ages to get it right.

Roy was a real likeable character, and he basically put all of the music together, including him playing most of the instruments except drums and my harmonica. Then we all sang together, and it was quadrupled over a 16-track tape to make it sound like there was a lot of us as a large team. So, we had a 45 single record with music just on one side of the disc. This was all down to Ray Bridger, we were now at the final preparation stage with the team/squad. I'll just give you a taster of the lyric's:

> "Snip and cutting with the razor,
> looking smart in dark blue blazer.
> Oh, how our styling will amaze ya
> as we cut and blow,
> we'll steal the show!"

We all had smart, dark-blue blazers with our British team union jack badges on the breast pocket and grey trousers to match.

Because this Championship was to coincide with the United States Bi-Centenary celebrations, on the back of that, we decided to present a very British theme for our models' clothing. particularly for the added hair event. We had the models fitted out as Grenadier Guards with Busby hats to match, just on their lap as window dressing, really.

We all had to finance this, so we organized hair shows and fund raising events around the country over the previous two years to help. The federation did add to it all. I can't think of a time previously where we put so much effort and detail into our preparations. Whoever took this over following this event was going to have a benchmark standard to follow, assuming we were successful in the championships, but we hadn't got there yet, and there was so much more to do before we left.

The Man in the Mirror

Our added hair event was what we hoped would swing it for the team. The ballot for models was a lottery, really, and the classic trend was everyone brought evening wear and trendy cloths, which we all felt was okay, left to each team member.

Wed had a dress rehearsal to check everything, from the finished hairstyles to all the matching clothes. We covered absolutely everything, including one little extra which would give us the edge if it worked but could also get us disqualified; this was to add very fine, small lace hair pieces to thicken up the temple area of each model in the grenadier guard event and also fine lace pieces added to the back of each ear area down to the nape. These added pieces would give each model a much stronger profile than without them, the risk was these little extra's weren't allowed. Having said that, nobody had tried it before, so there was no reason for the "wise men," these are stewards who checked each model before the start of each event to make shore that each model had the right length of hair growth to be cut. So, as long as we had the right amount of hair length to cut off each model, there was no need for these wise men to actually inspect each model's hair. We collectively decided we would chance it, and believe me these hairpieces were almost invisible. In theatrical terms, they were perfect. I wouldn't go as far as to say we were cheating, as there wasn't anything in the rules to say we couldn't, but there was also nothing in the rules to say we could. So, we chanced it!

John Belfield M.I.T.

CHAPTER TWENTY-EIGHT

New York, New York

The final team selection had to be announced because of the expense of making up these grenadier guard outfits. The team was Adrian Fuller, Clive Basford, Peter Hipkin, and John Julien, with Trevor Mitchell as reserve. I was already trainer and captain, plus the added responsibility of being our judge. Vin Millar was team manager, as before.

The record we made became news in the media, and most of us sang it live on TV. I was in Pebble Mill studio in Birmingham with three of the squad, a couple more in London, and Gordon Stupart up in a studio in Glasgow, and we sang it live as if we were all in one studio and not spread out all over the country. It gave us that added recognition we were hoping for, and as a massive bonus, when we flew out to New York from Heathrow, our team song was played on BBC national radio as a well-wishing gesture. British Airways did us proud, too, flying us out on a 747 jumbo jet, which at that time was its flagship plane.

We met up with all our supporters at Heathrow, including the Ladies' British Team. We filled the plane with hairdressers, and it was a special feeing. My Mother was over the moon that she was going with me. by the time we'd been in the air a couple of hours, she'd made friends with some of the show dancers who were working in the exhibition and some of the federation officials who she'd met before at the federation's annual conferences. this was good news for me, because I could see that she would have someone around once we got there, particularly because, in reality, I wasn't going to be able to be with her most of the time whilst there.

There was a lot riding on this World Championships. Six years of preparation, and for me experience on the big stage, I didn't want anyone in my team to bottle it. The big prize was the team event. If anyone picked up medals individually, all the better.

I don't think any of us had been to New York before, and we were all incredibly excited and also nervous. It had been a long journey of competing for me. Now, I'd coached this team, and I had the responsibility of judging for them.

We had a great hotel location on Central Park South called the Barbizon Plaza, with the Coliseum exhibition Center at the top of the road, which by NY distance was about three blocks. I'm not sure why, but we were still having to share a room, this hotel must have been about seventy floors, but we still had to share. I suppose costs had to come into it, but each team member shared with another team member, with their models doing the same. It kept everyone reasonably close together. The reserve shared with me, which was Trevor Mitchell, and when we got to our room, the number was 1418.

Mitch looked at me, and I said, looking back, "If you say anything about the bloody first world war, I am going to go nuts."

He replied, "It's an omen, I can feel it." Mitch always had something to say about the War, any bloody war, un off he went—"We're in for a bloody war!"

My mum shared a room with one of the dancers working in one of the shows for L'Oreal. Not only was she a stunner but a really nice person, and she stayed with my mum most of the week, when she wasn't working in the exhibition. They went sightseeing all over Manhattan together.

I did have a good feeling about everything; the hotel, the location, and we had a couple of days to get over the time difference. With the team and models together, we were able to practice in each room, and I could easily get around them all. Mitch was using one of the models for the reserve events the day after the main event, so he was a big help to me. And Vin Millar let me get on with it, apart from us all eating dinner together and keeping a curfew of ten p.m.

We were room only, with no fare, which was the case with most New York Hotels, but there was always a deli or a coffee shop close by, and most were open until the early hours. From six a.m., you could see the bag ladies hanging around them. This was a common site in Manhattan.

But right from day one, Mitch and I had room service, courtesy of my mum. She made us breakfast every day. "Just let me know what time," she said, "and I'll bring your breakfast to your room for you."

Good old Mum! It saved us both a good half hour going out for something, and in the evening, I would take her for something to eat, usually around the corner at Wolf's Restaurant. It was the place everyone seemed to eat at, so we all used it.

I had a good feeling about our chances. The team was ready, and I was ready too. I had Mitch coordinating the team from the team changing room to the competition floor, whilst I was locked up in the jury room for the day. Not the best of places to spend a day, to be honest. Thirty-two countries taking part meant thirty-two judges, and that was my battle to win, because some countries joined with others to improve their teams' chances. How was I going to connect with some of those judges of countries I thought would be British friendly? And at the same time, could I trust some of them to do us an odd favor? What was my plan, how did I do my team justice in this room? Well, there was a rectification points system, so if your marks were more than two points above or below the average mark for each contestant, your points wouldn't count and the average mark would replace it. I was confident my team would be consistent throughout each event, so I asked myself, do I need to get into bed with any of them? And so I didn't.

I was approached by all the major European Judges, and I pretended to go along with their plan, which was, when walking around all the models, assessing the overall standard, each judge would pause just a little so that I would know which country that particular contestant was from. I didn't do the same for our entries because I didn't trust any of them, and knowing the standard, we had a risk of a judge or judges marking one of ours down by one or two points. It wasn't worth taking the risk. I felt we were in with a good chance without it. The best way forward for me was to make sure the marks I gave to our team was as high as I could without my marks going to rectification, and that's how I always judged. If one of our team didn't perform as we expected on the day, I needed to make sure whatever my mark for that team member was, it was one or two marks up on what the average was so my marks counted. If we had a top three placing, all the better. I then could give a top first place without any possibility of rectification, and each judge knew that. If it was a top three mark, then mark it, because when it was all over and the championships were finished, every country would get to see all the judges' scores, and if you were a rogue judge, you'd never get accepted to judge internationally anywhere again.

I was well respected by most countries, and my reputation was most important to me. So, we did very well on the first day. It couldn't have gone better. I regrouped with the team, giving positive feedback to all of them. Now wasn't the time to dissect each performance, that was for when we got back to the UK. But right now, we had one more event to get through, and I knew it was going to either make or break our chances of winning something, because this was the event for added hair, the one where we were risking have fine hair piece fillers to improve the profile and neck line hair density of each model. On top of that, we were presenting the models as grenadier guards, each wearing the full uniform plus sitting holding their busby hats to complete the visual presentation of each model. In doing this, we were telling everyone that these models were the contestants of the British Team.

Had I won over enough of the jury to think I was in their pocket, or had I made enemies of enough of them to scupper any chance of us winning the event? I had no idea until the event was over and I got back into the jury room to find out.

So, we had one more run through the evening before, just to give our final touches if it was needed and also to give each team member a fresh image in their minds now that their other two events were over. I needed them now to just focus on this last event for tomorrow. It had been a tough few months keeping a team spirit of together- ness, as we all knew, given a chance, that Adrian Fuller would try and go one better just to have that image in his head that he was better than everyone else.

The Man in the Mirror

So, there I was, overviewing the dress rehearsal of each competitor's model. Fortunately, each competitor was with his model in their own rooms, and I went around each room, so none of them would actually see each model until on the competition floor the next day. Then, what I feared most happened. This might sound trivial, but try and see it through the eyes of the team. I got to Adrian Fuller's room and checked over his model's final dress presentation, only to find that he'd put tree stripes on the upper arm of his model's uniform, so that as a team together, his model was a Sergeant! He just had to go one better. We all knew in our minds that, as trivial as that was, to the other team members, he had to get one-upmanship with them, and though it may seem like nothing now, when you've prepared for as long as these guys had, something as stupid as this could throw them out of focus. Tomorrow was their biggest day in their professional lives. They had given up most of their family lives for this moment, and tomorrow was for all of us—our families, friends, supporters, the National Hairdressers Federation, our models, who'd given so much of their time, and above all, we were representing our country; that union jack on our blazers! That ultimate reason why, above everything else, we'd all put everything we had into this one moment. And my mum was watching, too!

I went to speak with all the rest of the team and prepared them for this stupid on upmanship Adrian had created, and unbeknownst to me, this stupid act brought the best out of the rest of the team. They all got motivated by this and had something to prove that he wasn't any better than any of them.

CHAPTER TWENTY-NINE

Sharing a Room with Trevor Mitchell

That next morning, I had one big added problem before we all went to the competition area. I was sharing my room with Trevor Mitchell.

Mitch didn't sleep, he was one of those people who would savor every moment of that time and say, "Ya can sleep when ya get home."

"Ah come on, Mitch, get off to sleep. It's a big day tomorrow!"

He said, "I can't sleep laying here looking at you!"

We we're in single beds, and he got up and moved the TV between our beds so he couldn't look at me. Great, so now can we get off to sleep!

Well, that worked for an hour or two, and then *CRASH*!

What the bloody ell was that?

He'd kicked the TV over. Oh my god! How the hell are we going to explain that? Then I remembered, our room number was 1418.

"Mitch, the bloody room looks like a war zone!"

We bantered about it, and joked on how we were going to explain the TV, then my mum showed up with our breakfasts. Good old, Mum, just when she was needed most.

The three of us had breakfast together having a laugh about the bloody TV, and then Mitch and I looked at each other.

"Mum, we've got to get going, it's our final day." D-Day as Mitch put it. "Can we leave you to sort out the TV for us? Just tell them you knocked it over, you'll be fine." With a bit of bribery, I said I'd take her to Wolf's later for dinner.

She looked at me and didn't need to say anything. I knew she knew. Mitch and I started the teams' final day, and we left her to sort our mess out.

I'll say it again, D-Day was about to begin.

Everyone was ready, I'd told the guys in advance about Adrian trying to go one better. They knew he would do something, and now they knew, there was to be no shock from any of them once they got on the competition floor.

Once organized, I left Mitch to stay with them and help, and I went to the jury room.

The next couple of hours was the longest I'd had in years.

When the event was over, I walked out with the rest of the jury. We all spread out, walking around the competition floor, and our four model's just stood out. It felt amazing. It took all the jury by surprise. I caught Mitch's eye, because I was concerned that the small infill hair pieces might get noticed, but he gave me the thumbs up discreetly, and I relaxed and got on with judging.

Back in the jury room, quite a number of them came and congratulated me. We might not win this thing, but the whole coliseum knew who the British team was. I felt so proud, everyone on the team did their very best work. A few words were said to Adrian, but that was to be expected. All the guys knew his work was right up there.

We had another day to go with the reserve event, but when you get to the finished bit, it's like dropping off a cliff. There's this emptiness, all those months, weeks, and days leading up to this, and then nothing. Everyone deals with it in different ways, usually back at the hotel bar!

I had a quick blitz around the exhibition, Mitch went back to the hotel to get sorted for what he needed to do, and we all just regrouped later at the hotel, just so I could get all their views and feeling on how it had been for them.

My mum came by our room, she'd sorted the TV and said she'd knocked the tele over by accident, and we got away with not having to pay for it. Good old Mum. I left Mitch to it, and as promised I took my mum around the corner to Wolf's, which was on 58th street, for dinner. Wolf's was a "in" place back then, with good food and a great atmosphere. Mum and I talked about how her day had been, and I about mine. There was one little incident when we'd finished our meal and we were paying to leave. *All sorted*, I thought, but no, our waiter came by, and asked for her tip. Mum more or less told her where to go, but I cottoned on, the waiters worked on their tips , so a few dollars shut this very rude waitress up and it gave us both something to laugh about walking back to our hotel. This is New York, Mum, not Stoke!

It was now the day we'd been waiting for. The RESULTS!

We had a free morning, so Mitch, John J , Peter H, and my mum and I took a trip over to Liberty Island. We had to see something of NY, NY before we went home.

Then we spent the afternoon getting all our models prepared, we only had a relatively short distance from our hotel up to the colosseum, but with everyone all dressed up, it was a few pre-booked stretched limos for the short trip. I'd not had much time to find out how the ladies' team had done, but their reserve was a guy from Wigan, Phillip Hodgkinson. Phillip, David Appleton, and I were considered Northerners, and we supported each other. Also, Phillip's boyfriend/partner had an antique business, and they both were down in Stoke regularly, buying stuff for his shop. Little did I know back them how much Phillip was to feature in my ambition in making the ladies' team.

Everyone from the federation had been on a high about what our results might be, and there was back then a rivalry between them and the fellowship. The federation was responsible for the men's team, and the fellowship the ladies' team. I wasn't interested in the political side of hairdressing. In fact, in some ways , because I was also a fellowship member, the federation hierarchy didn't like me for that, and I felt at some point I would need to make a more decisive decision who I should be supporting, when really my only support was to British hairdressing, and in my opinion, so should theirs be.

The Parade of Nations was what we expected from the Americans—plenty of razmataz! As for the results, we were in America, so it was always going to be them or Italy, you can work that out for yourselves, but, we got Silver, the highest place a British men's team had ever been. For our ladies' team, it wasn't to be. For the federation, it was a huge one-up on the fellowship, but for me, I was sad the as a country we couldn't be more united.

John Belfield M.I.T.

But this evening was for my team, these guys had been brilliant. Mitch was a good leveler for me, he had good vision, and I had a lot of respect for him that night. He gave me guidance, as I was young and headstrong in my goal for British hairdressing and how far we had come.

Back at our hotel, we celebrated with all of the federation, supporters, and our team. At last, we'd arrived. British hairdressing was on the map as a team and not as individual winners as I'd been.

Michael Fanthorpe The federation's national president came to me during our evening and said, "John, the federation will be awarding you a Gold medal from the federation for this fantastic achievement."

I was over the moon. My mum was there, and she said, "Your Dad will be so pleased and proud. The NHF are finally recognizing what you've done for British hairdressing, and the City of Stoke-on-Trent."

I felt so proud of that moment. My mind went back to when I left school, I'd not achieved anything worth a dime. Yes, my swimming was something, but in the eyes of my schoolmates who'd got apprenticeships on the Michelin, my brother and cousin, who'd gone to high school and dropped me from their circle, I was to them a non-achiever! Just a lather boy in a barber's shop.

My mum came to me that evening, and something was different. I felt it, she felt it. Nothing was said, but we both were taking back something our family had never dreamed of nor experienced before. We came together that evening, my past was behind both of us. Yes, it took something like this.

Both Mum and Dad could now go to the NHF conferences and enjoy this family achievement, and it stayed with us as a family forever.

For me, there was only one big disappointment from that evening. The NHF Gold medal for achievement to British hairdressing as promised by the President of the NHF, Michael Fanthorpe, never arrived, and I'm still waiting!

This unkept promise changed me toward the NHF. This outstanding success should have been given to each member of that team and squad, not just me. We all did it together. Instead, those NHF representatives who were there took this success for themselves, and my team didn't mean anything to any of them. They went back to their salons and NHF committees and took the credit. Shame on them, then and now!

CHAPTER THIRTY

Policing the Salon Front Door on Match Days

My time with the Men's team was coming to an end, as I wasn't getting a buzz from it anymore. I continued to judge and help toward training the team, but those who were replacing me had other ideas about the direction the team should go.

I remember judging at the winter gardens in Blackpool; this was a big event, always well supported, with entries for the competitions, but my opinion with the federation deteriorated even more, because when I arrived to take part in the judging, there was only three people on the men's jury instead of the normal five. The other two were old fashioned barbers with very little judging experience. With these two judging similarly, it might make my judging look "wild." I wasn't prepared to take part unless two more people joined the jury to make a more balanced five. I got my way, but it just made me look bad in the federation's eyes. They just didn't get it. I was never asked back after that, but I stood my ground for the benefit of the competitors.

It was time for me to move on from this dated setup.

Sometime things make decisions for you, and this was the case here. My good friend Trevor Mitchell took over as manager of the team, and he brought a new way of selecting. This was a master stroke on his part because it kept the prima donnas in check. There was one in particular who thought he was better than anyone else, good on ya, Mitch!

Things were progressing at our salons, and we were now moving away from unisex. The Campbell Place salon was a separate ground floor ladies salon, with a barbers/men's hair styling salon on the first floor. We closed the Liverpool Road shop completely, Hanley was gone too, and we had the most up-to-date hairdressing business in North Staffs. In fact, we were probably the biggest business apart from Bourne Sports shop in the Town of Stoke.

Every salon has its character clients, and Stoke was no exception. I remember one afternoon, we were really busy, and there was a row of clients sitting under each dryer, having a roller set, when the salon went quiet, no hair dryers were on and a very recognizable "phist!!" noise came from the dryer bank. There was an old lady sitting under the dryer with a can of lager in her hand, she must have been seventy years old if she was a day! She was certainly enjoying her moment! Good on her! We had no rules for that, and why should we? So long as she could walk out of the salon without help and wasn't driving. Those were the days!

Stoke City was still playing football at the Victoria ground, which wasn't far from where our Stoke salon was, and being on a corner, it was one of the walking routes to the stadium. We used to have major problems with football fan's leaving the pubs around two p.m., heading for the stadium, opening the front door and shouting all sorts of stuff at our clients and staff. It wasn't just football banter, either. Not only was it annoying, but it was affecting our business, too!

We were always being asked to support different local community fundraising projects, and our local constabulary was no exception. The old police station in Stoke had been closed and replaced with a more modern, up-to-date building, which also included a social room facility. We were asked by them to put on a Hair and Fashion Show to help them raise funds to support its usage by the staff who worked at the station, and so we did. Our shows were always well supported, as we had a lot of entertainment incorporated in the content of these shows. It was a great night and well supported too.

One of the organizers, on thanking us for putting the show on, made a friendly comment, saying, if ever we can do anything to help you, just ask. Well this didn't register with me at the time, but after a few more Saturday afternoon experiences with the Stoke fans making their presence known at our salon front door, I decided to see if we could cash in the offer that was mentioned at the show.

So, we had a police officer outside our salon front door on a Saturday afternoon, controlling the football crowds that walked past our front door before and after each Saturday afternoon football game at Stoke City Victoria Ground. I'm sure our neighboring shops benefitted too, not that they had any idea how it came about.

Stoke Traders in those days were no different than a small shop trader today. they'd attend trader's meeting complaining about their businesses, expecting the council to somehow improve the town, which would then improve their businesses too. Most traders back then couldn't see beyond their own business, and so these trader's meetings in Stoke were just moaning, negative, monthly meetings, blaming everything and everyone but themselves.

Every time I turned up with a constructive idea of collective things we could do, which could have given the town solidarity to show the council and the local community at that time that it was worth another look, it was ignored. I also suggested the local press i.e., *The Evening Sentinel* feature the town more often when a free space in its pages came available with local news.

I left them to it in the end. if I spent any more time in those meetings, I'd end up doing what they were doing. No chance! You have to look beyond your own front door, in my view.

My Dad was born in the town of Stoke, 58 Liverpool Rd. As a family, we had a loyalty to the town beyond the front door of our business. He and my granddad Ralph both engaged with all aspects of the local community. I felt a commitment to do the same.

I lived in Penkhull back then. It was and still is a great place to live, but in Stoke, there was an initiative from the council to move people out of the towns. Not just Stoke but all the towns of Stoke-on-Trent. It was the beginning of the end. The locals moved out, and slowly, the town center died. Would my small contribution made any difference? I am afraid it wouldn't, but at least the town traders could have given the council some conscience on their decisions, because a town without its community is a death nell to its heart!

With this in mind, for our business to grow, we needed to seek a wider audience back in Hanley, which was then considered the city center of the Potteries.

However, we stayed another couple years in Stoke Town. We couldn't afford to just up and go. We had an investment where we were, both in business and the property we were using, and 1977 was a year which I still had industry commitments.

But my personal life was about to change, too.

CHAPTER THIRTY-ONE

The Start of Photography

I'd been playing around with photography for quite some time, and I decided to do an "O" level in the subject at what was then at Cauldon College in Shelton, just off the city center.

Well, no disrespect to most of the dozen or so on the course, but there were a number of blokes with Polaroid cameras who seemed to have a single direction in their photography ambitions. I kept my head down and learned a lot about the history of photography, but as for taking none polaroid photos, it was sort yourself out, which I did, and scraped in with a C grade. It was a pass, but I did learn the art of problem based learning, which basically is teach yourself. So much for college-based learning. As for hairdressing, it's still my opinion today.

My very dear friend Mike Hamnett introduced me to an accountant named Neil Bradley, he was supposed to be a real wiz of an accountant, and I got taken in by him, so much so that I couldn't make a decision without his help. He had total control somehow over everything about us and our business, and he never wrote anything down. Our business plan was all in his head, and as far as being a wiz of an accountant, over time, I came to realize there was more Fizz than Wiz. Yeah, he always liked his meetings late in the afternoons so that when he was completely legless, I would drive him all the way home to Crewe, where his suffering wife Francis would look at me, and all the blame for Neil's state of intoxication was down to me. Bradley's appearance at my back door increased, so no matter where and who he'd been doing his intoxicating with, I ended up as a taxi driver back to his home in Crewe! This wasn't an overnight situation, it went on for a number of years, well into the 80s before I said enough was enough.

But '77 and '78 was a time to re-engage in developing our business. We had recruited Karl as a Stylist, and there were another two addition's. One was a young lady who had just finished her apprenticeship with a locally known salon. Her name was Liz, and she had a basic background in hairdressing but had an open and eager mind to get up to where we as a salon were in all the latest cutting, coloring, and blow drying skills. Plus perming, too. Sassoon had just introduced his short-cropped, curly, Greek Goddess look, and the Coupe Sauvage on long hair was becoming fashionable, too, most with the help of perming, I'd already had a few years by then perming men's hair, so we were well into the most up-to-date perming products. However, I do remember Liz's first perm with us. She started her perm wind using very small, pink, perm rollers, the sort you would use on an older, traditional shampoo and set lady who wanted her set to last at least a week, and her very frizzy perm to last about five month's!

As for trying to blow dry on a perm done on pink rollers, it would have just looked like wool! Liz soon got the hang of it and became central to our team for the next thirty-four years. There's more to come about Liz as this book unfolds.

The other was an apprentice named Christine. She left school in the summer of 78 and stayed for another forty years plus! She too was central to our salon team. One of the main reason's I'm able sit here and tell my story is because of the loyalty and commitment both Christine and Liz gave me, not only as employee's but as dear friends too. And that is still true today.

As with many salons, you develop a regular clientele, and Phil Maskery and Selwyn Johnson both have been clients and close friends for well over fifty years, and thankfully still are. But I can't exclude two other clients , both who became clients in the late 70s, and with the exception of holidays, they came to the Salon every week. One is Gwenda Jones, who sadly passed away on St Davids Day, 1st March, 2020, just before the country went into lockdown on 23rd March, 2020. Her funeral was on 24th March, 2020, one day into the pandemic lockdown. What was to be a large celebration of Gwen's life became just a few of us at a simple graveside service. I was very proud and honored to be asked to do a reading, Corinthians 1-13.

The other lady is Mrs Briscoe. Christine was still attending her hair until she passed recently, although in her later years, she was still able to come to the salon. Where would we be as a business without such loyal clients?

I could fill this book with so many names, all are so special to me and my family. As a business, it's because of this that we are still hairdressing today. Thank you! Before this book is finished their names will come up again and again.

Having a business in Stoke town, one of the six towns back then in the 70s, it wasn't the most vibrant of towns or even places to be trading in, but Stoke-on-Trent is my home. I was born here, my dad was, and my grandfather started his business here in 1908.

John Belfield M.I.T.

I was constantly being advised to go to London, make a name for myself, but by that time, I'd seen enough of London hairdressing. Yes there were some I could name who I looked up to and respected, but as a Northerner, having been looked down on and when asked where are you from, having replied Stoke-on-Trent, I always had to add halfway between Manchester and Birmingham, because them lot from down south had no idea where Stoke-on-Trent was, and I still get that same response even today! Talk about the government bringing the north and south together as one, which all the governments then and now keep saying, but from my experience, it's not just the government of the time, it's about the people, because if you look at hairdressing as an example, anything north of Watford not only have they not heard of, they have no interest in, either, and probably likewise, too.

But Stoke is where my roots are, and later Newcastle, which is where we are today and have been since 1985. And I'm very proud to say I wouldn't want to live anywhere else, nor work anywhere else, either! There's and old saying in hairdressing: "You get the clients you deserve." The people from North Staffs and beyond have been amazing people to have as clients, their loyalty is why we're still here today. Just the other day, a guy came in to pick his daughter up, and when I saw who he was, I recalled giving him his first haircut at five years old. He's now sixty-four. So many stories about so many clients, and staff too.

I should add too that after starting with my dad in a traditional barbershop, I wanted to dissociate with the name barber. To me, it represented cheap, fast, haircutting on dry, dirty hair with no job satisfaction whatsoever. And it's still the same today. Six haircuts an hour, forty a day just to make your money. Whereas men's hairstyling signified quality, producing a hair styling service with an individual cut and style, with products to go, too. A massive difference—job satisfaction. If ya want a short back and sides, not a problem, but you'll have a hairstyle to match it as well, and that is the main difference between the two!

CHAPTER THIRTY-TWO

Candles, Wine, Sue

The stoke salon was buzzing, we had a great team of staff and a good apprenticeship system for training, too. I believed in apprenticeships back then, and I still do today. It's where your tomorrow hairdressers are. Throughout my career, I've always had this ethos—build your team of tomorrow from within, make your standards stand out, it where your businesses future is. A loyalty as a team grows from it and brings everyone together, then work becomes something else; a team, and with it is job satisfaction on a large scale, and the clients notice it, too. It's what makes our salons different, then and now!

I would be remiss if I didn't mention meeting my beautiful wife during this time. I stumbled upon the love of my life at Candles Wine Bar in Newcastle-under-Lyme, near Stoke and between Birmingham and Manchester. We married on St Georges Day, 23rd April 1979. Forty-four years on and three wonderful children Jonathan, Hannah, and Harrison.

It was around this time that I was introduced to an accountant named Neil Bradley. He came across as a more progressive and connected accountant than our current once a year traditional accountant who basically just produced a set of accounts, full stop. I got drawn into his ambitious nature and decided to accept his style of accountancy, which was over a semi-formal dinner at Rookery Hall near Nantwich. This was the most up market restaurant in the area at that time.

Dinner was arranged by Neil, who also wanted to introduce me to a solicitor friend of his named Oliver Bull, so the six of us, Neil with his wife, Oliver Bull with his wife, plus Sue and myself, were just making small talk, getting to know each other. It was very formal at this stage, the dining room was full apart from a large table at the far end, whose diners had yet to arrive, but it was very quiet, and everyone eating seemed posh, if you get the picture.

Then it all changed. The party of people dining at the large table entered the room, and amongst them was a friend of mine, Jimmy Westwood!

Wherever Jim was, you would know he was there, and on this occasion, he excelled himself. Picture an extremely up-market restaurant with a quiet ambient atmosphere, when all of a sudden, front the far end of the restaurant, Jim Westwood stands up and in a loud voice right across the room, shouts, "Hey, Belly, do you remember to night we got chucked out of Phil Baily's party for having a swimming race in the nude?" Well, if you needed an ice breaker, we certainly got one! Everyone in the restaurant looked our way, Sue gave me a kick from under the table, and with a few sniggers from our dinner guests, our formal dinner ended.

Jim sat down, thank God, and I wished the floor would swallow me up. I did have some explaining to do, including when Sue and I got back home.

Jim and I are still good friends, don't ask me why, because that incident wasn't a one off from him, there were many more!

But he's a very loyal friend too.

My relationship with Neil Bradley developed, and not just on a professional level, that was just the beginning.

Sue and I were living on Trent Valley Road in Penkhull, an area close to Stoke where the salon was. Penkhull is a nice, mixed community of people, and we both enjoyed our time living there.

I was drawn in to working with Neil, his attitude on finance and money was a new world to my humble business background, and I went along with his way, starting with opening a salon in the city center of Stoke-on-Trent in the town of Hanley. Anyone not from Stoke reading this is going to say what? Surely the city center of Stoke-on-Trent is Stoke. Anywhere else, it would be, but not here. Stoke-on-Trent is made up of six towns, and Hanley Town is the city centre. No wonder Stoke never got off the ground as a city.

After my dealing with Wellonda and the German style of salon furniture, I was aware of an independent German salon furniture company called Olymp based in Stuttgart, I was very much taken by the German salon interior designs. It gave us an edge over everyone else's salons in the area, and with this in mind, and Neil's enthusiasm for business, the idea came up about approaching Olymp about us opening a new salon with their furniture as an import agency into the UKT through my friendship with Kevin Donavan, who was well known in the area for his disco and entertainment businesses, and having already in the past used Kevin's interior designer John Victor Williams, I connected with a guy who worked for John named Rod Travers (Rod the Mod).

The Man in the Mirror

Now that John had moved down south, Rod was drifting, doing different stuff. So I put the idea to him about importing this high-end salon furniture, incorporating a salon design service alongside it. Sounds great, doesn't it? Read on...

Neil thought it a great idea, so did Rod. So, Rod and I decided to put our new venture idea to Olymp. Rod didn't fancy flying down, so we decided to drive to Stuttgart in my new 260Z Datsun pose mobile, which Jim Westwood had sold me a few weeks earlier (he owned the Datsun dealership in the potteries). I'd put the basic proposition to Olymp and their export director Heinz Pasha. So, off Rod and I went, all the way down to Stuttgart in my pose mobile sports car.

During our journey down, we joked about not mentioning the war, defo don't mention the war.

We met most of the board of directors, including the owner of the company, Karl Hertzog, had a tour of their factory and design facility, followed by a structured lunch. By that I mean we were sat in an organized way—you sit here, you there. So much for a friendly lunch, in my book, this wasn't friendly, it was business.

So we started off with small talk, but not the usual chit chat, this was more like an interview, I sat next to their export director Heinz Pasha, and he spoke very good English. I later found out why, but for now, small talk!

Out of the blue, he turned to me and said, "It was a terrible thing, the war."

To which I stupidly replied, "Yeah."

And it happened twice! Oh shit, that did it. Rod had a right smirk on his face, get out of that one, Belly!

Heinz Pasha had a certain style to him; he wore his big coat thrown over his shoulders and a white scarf around his neck. I couldn't make my mind up whether (in my imagination) he was in the Gestapo or standing up in a tank on the Russia front, shouting out his orders! He was old enough, and had "the look," so I thought, *Sod* it, and turned to him and said, "Where did ya learn such good English, Heinz?"

That changed everything, as he said, "I was a prisoner of war in a camp in Blackpool."

Bugger me. He offloaded the lot, caught in the Russian front, and ended up in an English prisoner of war camp in Blackpool, where he learnt his English. He did a lot of sales, wheelin' and dealin' in the camp.

I looked at Rod, and with a nod to each other, thought, *Here we go we're off with a deal.*

We got everything we asked for. My new city center salon in Hanley (Stoke on Trent, that is) would be an Olymp flagship salon in the UK. Their very first. It would be a ladies and separate men's salon with a combined main reception area servicing both salons, all designed in Olymp Studios in Stuttgart. Rod would learn their design methods and have a drawing/studio above the salon so that clients could see an Olymp working salon and then go upstairs to Rod's studio to discuss their needs and for Rod to show all the Olymp salon furniture, i.e., styling chairs, wash units, salon styling units, plus reception, seating, and displays, which there were many. Every custom built could be done. What on earth could go wrong? The whole concept was perfect, so I thought.

So, with everything agreed, the next morning, Rod and I said our farewells to all the directors of Olymp at their headquarters. My 260

Z Datsun pose mobile was parked overnight in the director's parking area, alongside ten or so Mercedes cars belonging to the management. It seemed logical; we were in Germany, Mercedes' main factory was just up the road.

So, in my Datsun we both got, and it wouldn't start! Unbelievable, right in the middle of all these Merc's, and my bloody 260Z Datsun wouldn't start. I could see their smirking faces all nodding. Oh God, I just wished the earth would open up.

They called a tow truck, and Rod and I stayed for lunch, but the joke was on us. It had rained heavily overnight, and water had gotten in the distributor.

We got the car back after lunch, and their parting shot was, "Buy a Mercedes." I don't know about now, but back then, you could turn up at the Mercedes factory gates and buy a Merc.

We got back home without any more car issues, but I never trusted that bloody Datsun after that.

This new city center salon was the most up-to-date European style salon in England, and to match our new image, I dropped The progressive unisex salon name to John Belfield International. This matched all aspects of my true image.

Along with my success with the British hairdressing team, we now had a truly European style salon to complete an international image.

CHAPTER THIRTY-THREE
The Beginning & End of Travers Belfield Design Ltd.

Peter Shilton (England's goalkeeper) opened the salon for me. It was the usual affair, with Arry (Dave) Roberts providing the entertainment, Pete Swindells organized most of the guests, i.e., anyone I didn't know, Peter certainly did, he was well known in the business community, and of course Heinz Pasha from Olymp, too.

So, we were up and running. It didn't take long for the salon to take off. We kept the Stoke salon going, and Liz stayed there and did a great job in the short term, but it was in the short term because I'd borrowed the money for the Hanley salon against the shop property at Stoke, and one cancelled out the other. Except for me selling the business to Jim Cullen's sister, the deal was a monthly payment, but you guessed it, she did a runner to Tenerife after six months. That's friends for you.

I knew Jim when he was a furniture salesman at a shop where my mum worked, opposite the original shop in Liverpool Road, Stoke. Jim modeled for me back in the early 60s. His wife to be, Judy, had a hair salon over her dad's fish and chip shop on College Rd Shelton. When they got married, Dad and I through a mutual friend got

The Man in the Mirror

them their first home in a new Council Built block of flats on the Honeywall in the town of Stoke.

There's a lot more to say about my friendship with Jim, but not at this stage of the book, for now, he was supportive, modeling for me during the 60s. We even had a guest slot on local tea time TV on the BBC. We were in a program with other experts of their different professions, including a Men's tailor from Saville Row in London (the most famous street in London for bespoke Tailoring). He explained the quality of the material he used in his suits, and Jim piped up, "I've seen better cloth on Cheese." That was the end of my bit in the program. This was live TV!

More about my friendship with Jim Cullen later, but for now, his sister had taken out a bank loan against the fixtures and fittings in the salon. This bank had loaned with no knowledge of her debt to me, which was a monthly payment. What she did with the money, I've no idea, it certainly never landed in my pocket, but when she up and left, I got a call from a trader nearby the salon to say that all the fixtures and fitting were being removed from the premises. I went straight down to the salon only to be told that the bank had a charge on the fixtures and fittings against her loan and they were removing them. The interesting thing here is the same bank turned me down for a loan for the fitting out the Hanley salon project, and I was offering the freehold of the Stoke premises as collateral, and the manager was the same person. So, you get the picture, a female with no collateral apart from the fixtures and fitting in my salon, which she was paying me monthly for, managed to get a substantial loan, and a male with substantial collateral got turned down. Say no more. Well, actually, I did, which was quite out of character for me, considering a bank manager in those days had a big standing within the business community and beyond. Pillars of our society, only I told him otherwise!

It didn't finish there, either, because in the sale agreement of the salon, the fixtures and fittings belonged to me until fully paid for. And I took great pleasure in informing him that he could put all the fixtures and fitting back in the salon premises exactly where they were when he had them removed, as they were my property. His face was a picture.

To be honest, the fixtures and fittings were worthless by the time I got them back. They were a mess. And yes, I should have pursued the bank for the damages, but it was time to draw a line under the Stoke salon. I tried chasing Jim's sister, who by now was in Tenerife enjoying the sun. But there was no chance of resolving that without chucking more money after bad. I am sure the bank would have been chasing her too.

The Hanley Salon got off to a flying start. Liz joined us from the Stoke salon to complete our styling team. Sue, my wife, ran the reception on Saturdays. I mention this now because, in those days, Hanley was a Saturday trading town, and many of the local community shopped in Hanley town center on Saturdays, so over half our business was done on Saturdays, and the reception area was hammered, it needed a cool head controlling what basically was two salons; one side ladies' hairdressing, the other side men's hairdressing, with a central, semi-circular reception desk and retail displays all the way along between the two.

Rod had his design studio on the upper floor, and in my mind, we were in business. Well, at least the salon was. Rod had a different perspective about work, or more accurately; the meaning of the word "work." We had agreed that I would travel to those salon enquiries, which sounded to most positive. Rod didn't fancy the driving, and we didn't have a sales policy, we just went for every enquiry that sounded worth visiting, this meant me giving up either a Sunday or, more than likely, a Monday. So, off I went. Penrith one Monday, Kings Lynn another, I would present the overall design and supply product, and we offered a free design service for the first couple of months. The design was a necessity in order to price the equipment we were selling, so during my sales pitch, if I thought we were in with a possible chance of selling something, I would measure out the salon floor space so that Rod could draw it out to scale, usually 1-20 or 1-50, and we could price it accordingly, there was no computer software back then, it was down to the drawing board and Rod.

A month went by, and I'd gotten four salons interested. All it needed was for Rod to design a floorplan so I could rearrange a site meeting to show the salon owner what we could achieve with Olymp salon fittings, plus the cost, too.

There were two problems to overcome to get the design business off the ground. First problem, we opened the salon at eight-thirty a.m. six days a week, but Rod would stroll in around ten-ish, and then at twelve-ish, he'd put his Cuban heeled shoes back on (Rod was a small guy) and go out to lunch with his girlfriend Fiona, who he called Bones (she was ultra slim), his terminology not mine. Anyway, he'd come back about two-ish and leave at four. If you're thinking this was a one off, you're wrong, very wrong. In fact, some days, he'd turn up as late as ten forty-five and still go out at noon for lunch. This was the norm, and after a month, not one completed salon floorplan. All my leads had gone quiet. Time I had a chat with Rod. So in I went, into his design studio. Once the air had cleared enough to see, Rod was a heavy smoker, and coffee drinker too, one went with the other. So, there I was, standing in front of his drawing board, a fag burning in the ashtray, and coffee on the side.

He was standing beside me, looking down at this half-drawn salon floorplan, smiling, feeling quite proud of his achievement, and turned to me and said, "What do you think so far? It's starting to come together. "He'd have a fag and a slurp of coffee, and I'm not sure I can print what I was really thinking, but here goes.

"Rod, we've got to move things on a bit quicker. For example, your time keeping. Even the staff are raising their eyebrows. You need to have a structured working day. You know, starting at nine not ten some days later, having a two-hour lunch and gone at four."

Now, Rod is quite an intelligent sort of guy, you know, good company in the pub after nine p.m., but what came next was a shock I hadn't expected.

"John, I'm a director. Directors don't start work at nine a.m.! Really, I suppose that's left to the workers, isn't it"

"Well, when the smoke clears, have a look around, because there ain't nobody here, only you, get it? And I'm paying your salary. The company is joint, but with no money input from you, I would expect you're here before anyone else and the last to go, and lunch is a sarney whilst your working, get it?

"Now, I'm no superstar designer, I left school at fifteen with no qualifications, but I know how to draw. My tech drawing was good, good enough to get me into college to study architecture, too late for that now, but if I may show you something: Take a 1-20 floor plan, you have two stencils from Olymp, one scaled to 1-20, the other 1-50, so make paper shapes of say the 1-20, i.e., chair shapes, styling units, etc., and place them over the blank 1-20 floor plan and shuffle them around until the layout works, then draw it in and price it. Your time schedule per plan is four hours. Get it? Two plans a day. My four salon owners should have had something to look at and me to present to them after the first week in business. Are you okay, Rod? Do ya need to sit down? I'll get ya a coffee, have another fag, the dizziness will go in a minute. I won't use the word *work* again, I can see it upsets ya!"

I did try with him for as long as I could, but it wasn't working for either of us. After six months and not one order, it was time to say goodbye. It wasn't him, we both agreed, that was the end of our working partnership. It was mutual. We stayed good friends for a long time after. Rod was happier working from home doing his thing, and I needed to move on.

I needed to try and stay focused on getting the salon established rather than driving around the country flogging German salon furniture.

How I wished I'd never gotten myself into to this. My ego needed a good kick up the arse, and nobody better to tell me so than my dad.

Yeah, Dad was still around, just pottering about, and Mum still did the wages for the staff, in a fashion. We kept a family image as far as anyone else was concerned. It suited Mum un Dad and me too. We'd come back together as a family.

Before I told Olymp anything about rod I needed to sell some salon furniture. Luckily, Graham Webb was doing a new salon with Rod's old boss John Williams, I sold him a complete salon, including chairs, styling units, wash basins, and reception units at cost. At the same time, the Constantinou Brothers in Cardiff were refurbishing. They got the same deal as Graham, two big orders. I was nearly up and running, time to be honest with Olymp. They too had gone too far to pull out. We met back in Stuttgart, and I took Graham Webb over with me. He had more expansion plans using the Olymp style of furniture, so I treated it as a sales meeting as well.

Olymp knew of a guy in London named Tony Lunch. He'd worked as a freelance advisor to a British salon furniture company named Henry Serventi. They had done salons in Harrods and Selfridges, two of the biggest salons in the UK back then. Tony introduced me to a guy who seemed to fit the bill named Peter Blythe, he lived in Nottingham, so location-wise it could work. So, he started where Rod had left off, picking up on all the leads we had. As to doing floorplans and salon design, we backed off until we got a feeling of commitment. Sometimes, we'd use Olymp's design facility in Stuttgart.

So, the upper floor design studio became Peter's domain. He too was a heavy smoker, just like Rod, and I still did some chasing up salon enquires or deliveries over the weekends and Mondays.

CHAPTER THIRTY-FOUR

Fire Down Below

We'd been running now for about nine months in all, so the salon was still like new. One Tuesday evening after the salon had closed, Sue and I were working over upstairs in the smoky design studio with Peter. It was about seven p.m. and I suddenly thought I could hear someone down stairs in the salon, then there was another noise, and suddenly the office door burst open like someone had almost smashed it open, and there in the doorway was a fully kitted out fireman with an axe in his hand.

He ordered us to immediately follow him and exit the building. What the hell was going on?

As we left the office/studio into the landing corridor, the place was full of thick smoke. I couldn't see my hands in front of me as we followed the fireman through the thick smoke, down into the main salon area, which was full of dense, black smoke.

The firemen had smashed open the salon doors to get into the salon, the arcade area too was full of smoke.

We continued to be instructed by this fireman down a stairway onto the main street outside, where a large crowd of people had gathered in an area higher up the street. They started to applaud us, clapping loudly, then we saw why. The shop in the main street right below our salon was fully on FIRE! We had no idea at all, the main building fire alarm system didn't go off, and there we were, up on the top floor of the building, totally oblivious that the shop right below us was on fire,

It made us realize how lucky we were. Our salon didn't have smoke alarms in those days. The main building and shopping walkways should have had proper fire alarm facilities, but nothing, no alarm was sounding in the shop that was on fire, and no smoke detectors were fitted in the entire building.

The caretaker of the building had no idea either. We were lucky that it was early evening, and Lewis's department store right opposite had customers exiting who could see the shop that was on fire. How lucky we all were.

But our newly fitted Salon now smelt of smoke, and it affected everything, from salon towels/gowns, the fitted, cushioned, waiting seats, packaging, everything we touched left a smell on your fingers, it took months to get rid of the smell of a fire and the thought of what might have been.

Peter settled in, becoming familiar with the Olymp product and design concept, I still had to travel to see new leads over the weekends, and Peter wasn't a "no fingers on the clock" type of person, he valued his own time, which was fair enough. Olymp liked him, so I accepted his terms of employment. I didn't have much choice anyway.

I got back working in the salon, and after about a year, we separated the two businesses and moved the salon furniture business just out of the town center to a larger space, more of a showroom with shop windows. we never really had people come and visit the salon, so this seemed a natural progression. If I'm honest, I thought I had something of a business model with the salon furniture. My accountant Neil Bradley was masterminding it all. I did everything he advised me to do, and the bottom line to it was Olymp was going to buy into the business. Their company also designed optical businesses, so, over time, we did supply a couple of high-end opticians in the London and Bristol areas.

I did begin to rely on Neil Bradley more and more. This business model was all in Neal's head, not mine, but I went along with everything he advised. The Germans liked him, and so did I at that point, why wouldn't I? he'd gotten Olymp saying they would buy into the business, so, financially, I was going to make some money, maybe a lot of money, and that carrot started to grow in my head. Just keep it going a little longer, and it'll all be worth it in the long run.

Sue was a big help back at the salon. She covered the reception every Saturday, and believe me, Saturdays were manic. We turned over more than half our weekly trade on a Saturday.

Sue and I had settled on living in Penkhull, a mixed community close to the local hospitals, and I loved living there. An ideal place to start a family, and we did. Sue was expecting our first child, and we were really happy. It was a boy! Jonathan!

There was a lot going on, the story of my life, as they say.

If only I could make some money. Neil was very convincing, just go with it a little longer and we'll have the Germans buying into the design business. Well, what more incentive did I need? Peter Blythe had almost all control of the design business, and it was expanding.

Not only were we designing and selling salon furniture, we started shop fitting too. It seemed a natural progression. In fact, it was the only way we could get our money in. Salon owners only needed half of an excuse not to pay, and these half excuses were eating into our profit. We had supplied to a salon in southeast London in Bexleyheath, and we just couldn't get them to pay. The reason was we'd supplied faulty washbasins and mixer valves. We were standing at about 5K, so after about three months I went all the way down to Bexleyheath. Peter was too busy, and Olymp had been paid, so with cashflow, we were strung out.

Well, back then, travel wasn't what it is nowadays. It was a five hour drive, and when I got there, the owner had gone to the wholesalers, so I had to wait. While I was waiting and observing, our salon equipment was in full use, so what was up with it, I wondered. I couldn't see any problems, no leaks or chips, everything seemed fine. Then the owner returned.

"So, what seems to be the problem?" I kept it as pleasant as I could, be she had an angry face on her.

"I'll show you," she said sternly, "they are faulty, we've got hot water coming out of the cold taps and cold water coming out of the hot taps on all these expensive wash units."

Now, I'm no plumber, but I looked at the units, and sure enough, turn on the single lever tap toward the hot, and cold water came out, and turn the mixer valve the other way, and hot water came out of the cold side. Now, back then, we were the first supplier to have these new, single lever mixer valves. Each unit had a red emblem for hot and a blue one for cold, her plumber had connected the hot water supply to the cold side and the cold water pipe to the hot side, so he'd fitted them the wrong way round, and for his mistake, she wasn't going to pay us.

Any excuse, you can imagine what was going through my mind. 5K, almost a five hour drive, and I had to get home that night too. I wasn't an happy bunny. She knew it, alright.

So I said to her, "Our terms are the equipment belongs to us until its paid for, so either you pay right now, or I'll have a local company I know round here in the morning and take it all out, or instruct a local bailiff to do the same (in those days, you could remove what belonged to you), so what's it going to be?"

I got my cheque off her reluctantly and said, "I'll be going to the nearest Barclays Bank and cashing this cheque before they close."

It cleared, but I had honestly thought all hairdressers were like me. how wrong I was.

I carried on with the business plan that Neil had in his head. I kept thinking, *If I just keep it going a little longer, Olymp will buy my out, and Peter Blythe can have his job running the UK design business for Olymp and I can get back to the salon.* At least there, I felt I had control of my own destiny. I'd never worked for anyone before, and I had no idea how to set up a company nor how to run one, just Neil saying to me, "Leave it to me, Duckie," (Pottery talk) and I did.

CHAPTER THIRTY-FIVE

New York Once More

We carried on. The salon furniture showroom was a base to work from. At least we had styling units and chairs to show people, and products, i.e., bits and pieces to steal from when we were short on the shopfitting side.

By today's standards you wouldn't need a showroom using modern technology, but this was 1980, no computers/mobile phones, emails, etc., we're talking over forty years ago!

I trusted Peter Blythe to run the furniture side whilst I got on running our salon. It wasn't perfect, but my gut feeling was always short term. With Olymp baiting me, saying they'd buy into the business, and my investment and effort would be all worthwhile, in the back of my mind I was always wondering when and if it would ever happen!

Well, something did happen. Neil Bradley our accountant came to see me one day. "Duckie," he said, "you know some hairdressers in the States, don't you?"

"Yeah why?"

The Man in the Mirror

"Olymp has some enquiries from the States, they would be interested in using a British Company to enter the American market. The pound is 2-45 against the dollar, and five Deutsche Marks to the pound. It's ideal currency wise. Apparently, the British hair magazines are popular in the states, and that's where the interest has come from."

My ego got the better of me.

"Pull this off, Duckie, and they will buy into the business, and you've made your money, more than you could wish for."

Before I knew it, I was on an exporting course with International Accountants and a good to go handshake from Olymp.

I contacted my hairdressing friends in New York, and off Neil Bradley and I went. Neil had it all planned out. As for me, I wasn't so sure, but Neil had done okay for me so far, and I was hooked on the main objective—get this sorted, and Olymp would take over, job done! Well, I found a salon that was up for sale, or should I say going cheap. It was a first floor salon on 62nd and Lex, two blocks up from Bloomingdales with a studio apartment on the 5th floor. It was a low rise building, the owner was an eighty-year-old Jewish guy who had a pharmacy business on the ground floor, the salon was over his store, then the rest of the building was six apartments.

My plan was to use the salon as a working showroom as we did back home. I moved into the apartment but hesitated over the salon. It didn't feel right. Did I need to be running a salon as well as flogging salon furniture?

I was glad I waited a while. I connected with my hairdressing friends, particularly a guy named Sal Fodera, the president of the whole of the American Hairdressing Federation. He was a big help to me in settling in, and we got on well during my competition time in Europe. It wasn't long before I was helping out with the American Men's Team training sessions. It helped me to network most of the East Coast Team members, and before long, I was over in Anaheim, i.e., Disney on the West Coast, judging the American Hairdressing Championships.

Yes, Sal was a big help and a good friend, too. I soon learned how different their culture was to mine. Sal was Italian, and Manhattan had a large community of Italians. They all traded together, whether you were a hairdresser, tailor, or owner of a restaurant, they spent money with each other.

One of Sal's clients, who he called "Poppa" had his hair done at seven every morning, that also included a shoeshine and manicure. When it came to mortgages for the Italian communities on Long Island where Sal lived, Poppa arranged the money. Enough said.

I soon started to realize I didn't need a salon, American hairdresser's weren't going to travel to New York to view hairdressing furniture, I needed someone who worked with distributors. Not only that, I had someone try and break into my flat one night, at three in the morning. They were really having a right go at the door. It should have clicked why there was a metal plate on the door and so many locks and bolts too! Fortunately, they gave up and left, and only a few days later, so did I. But not before I told my landlord. So, there I was, standing with him on the doorstep of his drug store, and he said to me, "Ya know, John, in five years' time, they are going to build a subway entrance and exit right outside my front door. Can you imagine the footfall that's going to bring to my store?

So, I'm standing there thinking, here's an eighty-year-old guy talking about how good his business will be after they've put the

The Man in the Mirror

subway access in in five years. He's going to be well on his way to ninety by that time. That's a New Yorker for ya!

Back then, twenty-five percent of the population of Manhattan was Jewish. I have always had a lot of respect for the Jewish community in hairdressing, my membership in the fellowship gave me a platform to be successful not only in my hairdressing competitions but for me as a person. They were always there for me when I needed someone. That respect has never left me in all the years I've been hairdressing and a fellowship member.

New York proved to be no different. My accountant and Larry, my attorney, were both Jewish, and in that moment in time Belfield became Belfieldt. Why not!

I abandoned the salon idea, and the flat, and moved down to 31st and Lex in a slightly better apartment and rented a first-floor space for an office and a small showroom, which was over an artist's materials kind of shop, just a couple of blocks down from the flat. I was glad of the insight Sal Fodera was able to give me about the hairdressing industry back then. It made me realize the products I was trying to sell was far above the average salon owner. Europe was miles in front of the average American salon in style and design.

I recruited a guy who worked within the Distributor system, as it was the only way to go. His name was Bob Apatow, and he knew the hairdressing industry well, which was lucky for me because apart from the hairdressers I knew, this was going the be an uphill challenge.

I was there and committed, so, no going back. I had to give it a go. The exchange rate was on my side, but the profit margin of 40% was going to prove difficult using distributors, I had a few leads on the books, direct leads with salon owners, which kept Olymp happy.

Heinz Pasha, the sales director, soon visited to see how I was doing. Fortunately I had enough going on to send him back to Germany happy. Bob focused on the east coast distributors, and I followed up direct enquiries with the salon owners.

I picked up a positive lead in Atlanta, a big salon needing a complete refit, and if I could seal this deal, we would be up and running. So, I was down in Atlanta, sorting out the design, the style of furniture, while Olymp in Stuttgart would be doing the design work. The idea of this was to provide the owner and his new salon a truly European style, boosting his image.

All was good so far, and then he invited me to have Sunday lunch with him. He wanted to take me to an authentic Southern restaurant. It sounded great, an opportunity to experience Southern cuisine. Well, we sat at our table, drinks were ordered, but no menus, then I was shocked when the menu arrived, it was an "A" hanging around the neck of a young negro boy who couldn't have been more than twelve or thirteen. He went from table to table with the menu hanging around his neck and shoulders. It was 1980 in Georgia, and the salon owner expected me to be impressed! Far from it. I left Atlanta with a very poor opinion of what I'd experienced. It certainly put racism in a clearer light. What I'd witnessed I ever thought existed.

He got his Salon, I never went back. Not even for the opening. I was beginning to see America in a completely different light.

CHAPTER THIRTY-SIX

Flying Concorde

I was following the guidance of my accountant Neil Bradley. In fact, I was more of a puppet, just doing what business plan he had in his head. He came to New York a couple of times, so did Heinz Pasha from Olymp. They all had their little moments of the big Apple. I suppose in some ways, I was getting a little homesick, I was missing Sue, and now we had Jonathan, who was just a year old. New York certainly was no place to bring up a family, and though I was flying back about once a month, and the salon was doing okay, Peter Blythe was slow in converting leads into orders, and I began to get suspicious that he was using his expenses account for his girlfriend's wholesale beauty business. Wherever he went, she tagged along. I started thinking was that trip he made for the benefit of our business or hers? She was on a nice little earner if that was the case. Running her around the North of England at our expense!

In those days, there used to be a standby deal at Kennedy Airport with British Airways on their morning flights to Heathrow. Basically, you just stood in line. There were never many people waiting, I would say not many people knew it was on offer, so , if there were seats available, they would sell them off. The morning flights weren't popular, most flights back to the UK were in the evening. Well, on this rare occasion, there were no seats available on standby. The flight was full.

Well, I did the craziest thing. Over the loud speak came an announcement, "Would all passengers flying Concorde please proceed to the gate?"

Like a fool, I went to the BA desk. "Are there any standby seats available on the Concorde fight?" I asked.

The attendant looked up at me like I was nuts. "It's first class only, sir."

Well, I wasn't going to back down, my pride was at stake. "No problem, just thought I'd ask."

"We do have seats available, but you'll have to hurry, the flight is about to leave."

Out came my diners card, and I bought a ticket, checked my bags, and ran to the gate. I was surprised how small it was. Anyway, here goes three and a half hours super-sonic to London, and silver service all the way.

During the flight, the guilt began to wash over me. £850. Sue was going to give me a grilling when I got back. And she did, for days after! I was brasic, and I'd just blown a fortune flying Concorde! Looking back now, I think, oh yeah, I've flown Concorde, like it was my usual flight choice.

I had a good relationship with my attorney Larry. He liked the English connection. He lived on Long Island and commuted into Manhattan by train. He had a thing about wanting a European Manufactured Mercedes. Through my Olymp connection, he got his European Mercedes. It was his pride and joy, so each day he'd drive

The Man in the Mirror

and park at his local station, and everyone admired his pose mobile, which suited me, because he used to let me have his old Buick if I needed a car, which was better than the Rent a Wreck car hire I used to use. Believe me, the cheaper the car, the bigger a wreck it was.

One day, somebody keyed the Merc whilst it was parked. After that, he went back to using his Buick, that is until one of his major clients saw him parking up the Buick.

He turned to him and said, "Larry, what's gone wrong, it doesn't look good you getting out of an old Buick. Is Business That Bad?"

That's the way people perceive you, so his client assumed he was doing badly based on him parking up an old car. Larry was back the next day in the Mercedes.

Larry invited me over one evening, he lived in a lovely location on Long Island with a water view of Long Island Sound. Larry's wife was an interior decorator, to me it meant interior designer. Their house was as expected, a very modern almost state of the art, or a bit over the top! So, Larry is showing me around, and upstairs we go to the master bedroom. It had a 180 degree view of long Island sound, which was really nice, but then Larry had to demonstrate that the bed turned around facing the east in the morning so that you got a lovely view of the sunrise, then in the evening, the bed swung round 180 degrees so that you got a lovely view of the sunset. Fancy stuff, and all down to his wife's skills as an interior decorator, but it didn't end there. So, back downstairs we went in to the entryway, where Larry turned to me and said, would you like to freshen up before dinner? He gestured toward the bathroom, so in I went to freshen up. Well, it was floor to ceiling mirrors, I got a couple hundred images of myself standing using the toilet. Then I got it, the lower down the mirrors went, the more they magnified. Yes, that's right, my private bits looked like something belonging to a donkey!

Back in the entryway, Larry was standing there smirking and waiting for me to say something complementary.

"Well, Larry that's a first in anyone's book." All the while, I was thinking how tacky that was. I could write a book on the number of tacky salons I walked into. Only in America.

I was beginning to realize the only thing we shared with Americans was the language. Their culture was so different, it was like chucking together fifty different countries and pretending they were all the same. No chance!!.

I was waking up to the thoughts that Olymp wasn't going to buy into either the UK nor the bit that I was doing in New York. I had a long chat with Neil about things, and concluded there was no way I was going to make my fortune flogging Salon Furniture in the States, nor back home. As things happened, circumstances made the decision for me. The pound crashed against the dollar, from 2.45 down to 1.76, and the deutsche mark dropped from 5 to 2.8, it was either get involved, Olymp, or I'm getting out. I sold what business I'd garnered to Bob Apatow for ten thousand dollars. His son was going to join him in the business. Olymp agreed to trade with him, and I got a few dollars out of it, or so I thought.

I was saying my farewells over dinner with Sal Fodera, including my frustration of not being able to get my money from Bob Apatow, and what came next in the conversation shocked me. Popa would pay me the 10k less twenty percent. It was guaranteed payment, to which

I commented, "And what happens to Bob to make this a guaranteed payment?"

"Don't ask."

"Well, reading between the lines, there was no way I was getting involved in that sort of activity. I'd try myself when I got back home. As I said, same language, different culture, call it what you will.

I packed my bags and left New York to Bob Apatow and his son. I never got paid by them, and it was about time I made my own decisions instead of relying on Neil Bradley to make them for me.

The same was the case for the Olymp business back home. I'd had enough sucking up to the Germans. Either back me financially, or its time for me to walk. I was going to get my own back in some way, so, the last order which went to the States, and the same at home, I deliberately didn't pay. And in fairness to Olymp, they didn't try very hard to get their money off me.

Peter Blythe took over the UK business and moved it to Nottingham where he lived, and I returned to doing what I do best—Cutting Hair.

CHAPTER THIRTY-SEVEN

Judging in Paris

I'd turned my back on my international career with the British men's team in favor of flogging Salon furniture. Trevor Mitchell was now their manager and jury person. Mitch was a good friend, and there was no way I was going to rock the boat with him. He had a good vision of what was needed, and after New York, it was time for someone else to re-build a new group of hairdressers.

Clive Basford was still around from the New York Team, and he was an asset for Mitch. Clive was very reliable and loyal, too, just the sort of person Mitch needed. I continued having team members up to my salon for tuition, and Mitch would authorize this. I was happy just being on the edge of it all.

Mitch was successful in the World Championships in Amsterdam, taking Gold in the Men's category. The Constantinou brothers were outstanding but a law to themselves. Mitch's people skills in were outstanding the way he handled them.

I was happy just leaving it all behind—salon furniture, the men's team, even the National Hairdressers Federation.

I was now back to one salon, in Market square Arcade Hanley (the city center of Stoke-on-Trent). And I was settling into salon life again. Dad was happy with somewhere to go to when he felt like it, Mum was still doing the bookkeeping and wages, with the odd stint on the reception desk for half an hour at lunchtime. It was hilarious, she never turned anyone away. As soon as she was on the desk, the staff was on edge, in a nice way, that is. Our most loyal employee Christine and I even today laugh at the memories of my mother on the reception and the chaos it caused. Saturdays, it was standing room only at times. My wife Susan ran the salon on Saturdays, and we could have more the half a dozen people waiting in each area for men's and women's. Clients turning for appointments, clients paying and leaving, the phone would be ringing all the time, and then there were the walk-ins too! It took someone very special running the reception on Saturdays, and believe me, Sue ran it like clockwork!

As stressful as Saturdays were back then, it was the most enjoyable and rewarding day. At the end when we finished, the feeling of getting through it was amazing. Managing stress is very rewarding, a job without any managed stress in it is boring, that's what a busy hairdressing salon does to you. We always went home on a Saturday feeling a huge amount of achievement and job satisfaction.

After the men's team winning in Amsterdam in 1980, Trevor Mitchell was to be applauded for the success he brought to the team. However, for the World Championships in Paris in 1982, he asked me to judge the men's events for Great Britain. Having stayed away from it for a couple of years, I was happy to accept his offer of judging. After all, I was the most experienced British judge in men's hairdressing, how hard could it be!

When I turned up at the jury room on the weekend of the championships, our men's team was expecting to do extremely well again, as they were more or less the same team that won in Amsterdam, but this time there was one big difference. Great Britain was at war with Argentina.

There were around thirty-two countries taking part in these championships, and so there was thirty-two judges in the jury room. So, there I was, sitting at the table across from a block of judges from South America, and sitting in the middle of them was the judge from Argentina. They were all looking at me, or so it felt.

"Well, gentlemen," I said, "I hope we can leave our differences at the door of this jury room and focus as hairdressers on the job at hand in judging these championships." That was it, no gesture of friendliness from any of them. What could I do? It was obvious they would judge on block and against me.

I never trusted anyone when it came down to it. You just never knew.

I expressed my concerns to Trevor Mitchell, our team manager, but what could he or I do?

As a team, we came third. A Bronze medal position, and nothing exiting individually. That didn't surprise me, because there was marginally better work in each event than ours, but someone had to be blamed, and I felt the finger was being pointed at me. Not by Mitch but certainly by the Constantinous. It was in their nature to find some sort of an excuse.

That weekend, as I was out on the competition floor judging the men's events, and glancing across at the ladies' competitions, I had a strong feeling that, if that was the standard of the ladies' championships, I could do that. Certainly looking at the work of our ladies' team, I wouldn't be far off that standard, with a bit of practicing, that was it.

The Man in the Mirror

The beginning of my ambition to make the ladies' team!

Well, if they can, so can I.

Sue and I talked about it, and she had been modelling for me on photo shoots. It seemed the obvious for her to become my competition model, and it became our/my ambition to make the ladies' team, even win a medal. It had never been done before anywhere in the world. Could I really achieve such an ambitious thing?

Sue had already done quite a bit of make-up work for us on different projects.

In 1980, we had one of our senior staff Karl enter the Wella Vogue awards. He won the regional heats and came runner-up in the grand finale, with a lot of help from me and Sue. But all credit to Karl, he still had to go out on the competition floor and do it! A Bo-Dereck look won it, but maybe a person at the end of the results felt that Karl's look should have won it; a great haircut with futuristic color work to match, what a night we had, not to mention a feature in *Vogue* magazine, too. The only salon in the area to achieve it.

Sue and I started practicing and entering some regional competitions in different types of categories, i.e., day wear, evening wear, cut & blow dry, etc. All this we practiced after work. We used to have Jonathan with us in the salon running around, and later even riding his little bike around the salon. It was the only way we could practice after everyone had gone home.

We got lucky in a few competitions, and started to get noticed. It was leading up to the British Championships, and we got a phone call from Central TV to appear in their *Midlands Today* program, which in those days went out live. They wanted me to do one of the hairstyles

John Belfield M.I.T.

I was going to do in the British Championships. This was a great opportunity for us, being on TV.

We arrived at the studio early afternoon. There was a rehearsal prior to the program going out live, and I'd decided to do an evening hairstyle, which I thought would be more impressive. Chris Tarrant was fronting the show, with Jimmy Greaves doing his thing, too, which included a pre-recorded interview with John McEnroe the tennis player.

The program was a new format from what the previous show was, and it ran for an hour. During the rehearsal, it started to appear not what I expected. The producer was getting frustrated with Chris Tarrant, who wasn't paying too much attention to what the producer was asking him to do. The show was to start and finish with a new competition for viewers to enter. We noticed that Chris was drinking alcohol; in fact, he'd come over to where Sue and I were positioned in the studio and made a crude remark about the evening dress Sue was wearing. It upset us both, and at the end of the rehearsal, the producer asked Chris if he was going to change for the show because he had a tear in his trousers. In the end, Chris had to borrow a jacket off one of the studio crew to hide the worn trousers.

The program was chaotic, nothing went according to plan, and Chris forgot to remind viewers at the end of the program to enter the competition.

As we were about to leave, Jimmy Greaves came over to us both and commented, "The only people who knew what they were doing in there was you two. Do you fancy a cup of tea with me down the canteen?" So, off we went down to the canteen with Jimmy and left the studio producer giving Chris Tarrant a piece of his mind.

There we were, having a cup of tea with one of the greatest goal scoring footballer of the 60s era. I was really made up, he was very genuine toward us both and wanted to know more about us and what we were doing. At the same time, he was telling us what a nice guy John McEnroe was, saying after his interview with him, which was done on a tennis court, and was starting to pack things up, McEnroe turned to Jimmy and said, "What are you doing?"

Jimmy said, "We've finished the interview."

To which McEnroe replied, "Get back on court, we're having a game before you go."

What a story, I was amazed, both by Jimmy and McEnroe. As for our experience in that TV studio, I came away with a different opinion of live television.

CHAPTER THIRTY-EIGHT
All Roads Lead to Vegas

We didn't come anywhere in the nationals, but I felt we were moving in the right direction. Places were up for grabs for the European Championships in Gothenburg in '83, and I had time for me to be seen by the fellowships team manager Christopher Mann and trainer Phillip Hodgkinson. So, wherever they were competing, I'd go there too. We did the nationals, then in the Autumn of '82, Sue and I did a bridal event at the French open Championships in Paris, and it was there that Xavier Wenger saw us competing. He had been my mentor way back in Japan in 1970.

"John, what are you doing here?" he asked.

"I'm trying to make the ladies' team for Las Vegas in '84." That was all that was said, but for me, I was so pleased to see him.

In the spring of '83 I got Sue's sister Pat modelling for me too. I needed more than one model, but also having more experience working on different hair types, too.

Christopher Mann was insisting his team selection would be on international results. It was starting to get crazy, and expensive. I competed with Pat as my model in Saarbrucken Germany and then the next weekend in Brussels. I was objecting to having to do both. Pat and I travelled with the main group of hairdressers plus Chris and Phillip to Saarbrucken. It meant us flying to Frankfurt and then a short flight to Saarbrucken.

Well, when we got on this commuter plane in Frankfurt, the plane was a turbo prop plane, but the underside of the wings were corrugated, and I swear there was a very faint swastika sign that had been painted over on the underside of the wings. We both looked at each other thinking what are we doing here? Flying on some war relic!

None of that group of hairdressers gave me and Pat the time of day, they just saw me as a barber, full stop. We did okay in the competitions, nobody won anything, not then nor in Paris before. I hated being looked down on, particularly when none of them were doing anything special in the competitions.

The following weekend, we were expected to compete in Brussels, again flying over on Friday, staying in an expensive hotel, and flying back on Monday. It was breaking the bank, two weekends running. Pat couldn't make it, and Sue was very unhappy about the costs and more time away.

I had a practice model named Melanie, her hair wasn't really suitable for the type of hairstyles we were doing in these competitions, but Mel was a good model, particularly in stage shows we were involved in. She was experienced in local theatre groups and knew how to pose and sell it to an audience, or in this case a jury. What I didn't tell Chris Mann, the team manager, nor Melanie, was that we would compete in Brussels, but I would make my own way there. Little did Melanie know that you needed army training for this trip. In my early years competing in Brussels, I'd travel overnight on the

John Belfield M.I.T.

Saturday night, do the competitions, and then travel straight back without staying in a hotel. So, that's what we did. Down to Dover, got the midnight crossing, which was nearly a four hour crossing, so there was a chance for a kip, into Ostend and on to Brussels.

For the ladies' events, the organizers always made a salon available to prep your model and set their hair. Yes, for these events, everything was from a roller set, so when we both arrived at the competition venue, the other British hairdressers, including Chris Mann, were questioning how we got there and where we'd stayed. I was feeling quite good with myself. I'd finally got one over on the others, or so I though, until we were ready to start the first event, which was an eight-minute day style from a roller set. The hairstyle was to look like it had been blow dried. Believe me, eight minutes is nothing, it's the most difficult test to do.

So, we were getting ready to start, and Melanie turned to me and said, "I feel sick!" and got up and ran to the toilets as the organizer said START!

Everyone bar me was frantically brushing away at their models' hair, and there I was, standing behind an empty chair! Melanie came rushing back with four minutes left.

I finished it, though not my best day style ever. My next event was converting her hair to an evening style. We did better at that one, at least Mel wasn't sick again, and I got my hair look finished.

You know when it's not your day. I should have been wise enough not to have bothered going, but as all the other squad members were going, I didn't have much choice. So, when I'd cleared all my gear off where I was working and had gotten Mel sitting/posing really well, I gave her hair one last look before leaving the competition floor, and there I saw it. I'd left the little price tag stuck on the leaf of her hair ornament. There was no going back to it, no touching the model's hair at the end of the competition, it was mandatory disqualification.

No, it wasn't my day, that's for sure. The rest of the British competitors were pleasant enough with me, but it wasn't rocket science to see my face didn't fit, but I wasn't there with empty pockets, not like some of them. Two weekends in a row was financially stretching it, and I wasn't desperate enough going for broke just to keep manager Chris Mann happy. He had his favorites, and I wasn't camp enough to fit some of his criteria. That's how I saw it anyway.

So, without any farewell to the rest of the squad, or from them to me, Mel and I started back to Ostend.

In fairness, it had been a long day/weekend with the travel the night before. We got back to Ostend about eight in the evening, Mel was exhausted, and I suppose I was too. It wasn't in my plan to stay over in Ostend, but that's what I decided to do. It seemed the most sensible, so I found a small seafront restaurant with rooms facing the harbor, there was a whole row of them, any one would do, just a couple of cheap Sunday night tariff single rooms and a meal.

We decided on one, it was owner run, and he would do us a meal too. We hadn't eaten all day, so we sorted our rooms out, and we sat in the window of what was the owner's restaurant. There was only Mel and I eating, as the place was empty, and to be fair, she wasn't that bothered about having anything to eat, it was me who was starving hungry. She went along with what I wanted, and I was concerned her having been sick earlier the she really needed to eat something.

The place had a recessed front door area as you walked in, and we sat at the first window table, and served our much needed meal.

As our eating progressed Mel took a turn for the worse and felt sick again. Well, she made it as far as the porch doorway and threw up, right outside the owner's front doorway. He wasn't a happy bunny.

Mel decided to go up to her room, and I was left with a irate owner and a half-eaten meal. The angry owner came back with a mop and bucket, and insisted I cleaned the mess up. There I was mopping up the sickly mess, thinking how my day had gone, what shit day, and the owner took my half eaten steak away, refusing to serve any more food. After I'd finished cleaning the owner's doorway and shop fronts, I too retired to my room with the thought's that it could only get better tomorrow.

We got back home without any more incidents. Mel was shattered. I thought after the weekend we'd had that she wouldn't fancy modelling for me again, but to her credit, she wasn't put off, and did, on quite a few occasions, model for me, but not in any hair competitions, more on the show side. With her drama and acting experience, Mel was a good stage model.

The European Championships were in Gothenburg Sweden. Not the easiest of places to get to, certainly not the way the management of the ladies' team was concerned. There was a song in the charts back then, "Trains and Boats and Planes," that's what it almost felt like. Heathrow to Copenhagen, then a flight to Malmo in Sweden, then the train to Gothenburg.

The Euros was mainly an individual event, both for the ladies team and the federation's men's team, so you could make your own travel plan's, but if you wanted to be a part of a team, and the big event the following year in Las Vegas, you did the team thing and all travelled together.

The Man in the Mirror

I'd continued joining in the training sessions, either at Stephen Way's salon in Bond Street London or Joshua Galvin's salon. This was an eye opener for me, two of the most famous names in the Hairdressing industry at that time, and two of the nicest people, too. They shared their salons, and their knowledge, too. It's my view that's what made Vidal Sassoon so well liked and known in hairdressing; that he shared his knowledge, a philosophy of The Fellowship of British Hairdressing, which is still carried on today. As a Fellow, it's something I'm very proud of; however, the fellow came much later; in 1982, I was just a member trying to get on, like so many fellowship members were and are doing even today.

Having said that, it wasn't going to happen for me just as a fellowship member.

This was 1982, with just my men's team success to my credit. Even though over sixty percent of my salon work was ladies' hairdressing, it didn't count for anything.

Trying to get selected for the ladies' squad to compete in the European Championships in Gothenburg, after my fiasco in Brussels, plus being from the men's team, just made my situation a lot harder. In the end, I got selected as reserve, so if one of the six chosen dropped out, I would replace them. However, there was an international event for team reserves to compete in the day after the championships, so there were two events for me to compete in, and I was going to give it everything.

Not one of those six chosen bothered with me, but to be fair, I didn't give them the time of day either.

We all flew out on Saturday. My model was a young lady named Francis, a school teacher and a regular client of our salons. She'd never done any modelling before, but she had a good look to her. My only problem was, I couldn't prepare her hair at the salon because her school had rules regarding extreme hair color (that's how it was back in the eighties) and Francis's hair was definitely going to be extreme.

So, Sue and I planned to prep her hair when we got over to Gothenburg in our hotel room on the Sunday whilst the main championships was taking place. It meant missing watching the championships, but with everyone else at the events, we had an uninterrupted day, coloring and cutting Francis's hair, and also for Sue to practice Francis's make-up for my event.

Christopher Mann, the team manager, had left me instructions that on his return from the championships that Sunday evening, he wanted see my model with her finished look to check my standards were good enough for my events. In fairness, he hadn't seen any of my work because I'd not had the opportunity to prepare my model and practice the two looks I needed to perform in my events, not only checking my hair looks but also my model's makeup and clothes I which would complement my total looks. Little did he know, or even ask for that matter, but Francis, my model, sat next to him on the flight out to Gothenburg.

Chris was very impressed with Francis' hair make-up and clothing presentation. He turned to Sue and I and asked us when my model had travelled over, seeing as we were all booked on a total package trip for both men's and ladies' teams and supporters.

At that, I couldn't resist and responded, "She sat next to you, Chris, on the plane, but we didn't prep and prepare her until today because of her working restrictions regarding hair color."

I won some brownie points with him as to my ideas on Francis's hair and total look, so did Sue over her make-up. He was well impressed how Sue had achieved her make-up from day wear to evening gala. I also got a strong impression he wasn't too happy as how the championships had gone during the day. It wasn't what he said, it was what he didn't say which made me wonder.

Well, it only took till the next day for Sue and I to find out.

My first event was day wear. We presented Francis as an English cricketer, dressed in all the full white, including a cricket bat as a prop, even down to some artificial grass on the floor around our styling chair, as for her hair, bearing in mind retro looks were coming back in fashion, I did a casual retro look with very in your face, extreme hair color.

If you look at women's cricket today, I'm boldly claiming I was one of the first to see it coming!

We certainly got a lot of attention from the judges and spectators. None of the ladies' team bothered to come over to the auditorium to watch me.

As for my gala, I stayed with the retro conversion, using a hair piece through the crown into the nape, using a high, Elvis, brushed-up front. This too was very modern for that time. Sue and I felt really good how we got Francis looking amazing, and I'd not practice either look before doing her hair on the day. It was unheard of in the competition world, to "not practice before."

The icing on the cake was at the results evening later that day. The ladies' team had their models with them with their hair done in their competition looks, as did Sue and I with Francis. We hadn't long come off the competition floor from my events, so we didn't have much choice.

The results evening unfolded with the main two events for the European Championships. Neither the ladies' team nor the men's team placed. Then it came to my Reserve International Event. In my first event, my name was called out 3rd overall. Up to the stage Francis and I went and proudly walked up to the podium for our 3rd place prize. In the next event, the gala, my name was called out again, for an International Diploma prize. Fourth place. Up Francis and I went again to the podium for our international prize.

Then came the cream on the cake. The overall winners were announced, "And in 2nd Place, John Belfield, Great Britain!"

And up Francis, Sue and I walked again to the podium for our Second Overall prize (in case you're wondering, there is never a monitory prize, purely prestige). Yes, we were the only Brits to make it to the podium, with the ladies' team just sitting there looking at a barber winning something they couldn't. No chance of a congratulations from any of them, but for me, my biggest moment out of it all. I felt recognition. Yes, I'd arrived, and this hopefully was the beginning of my chance of making the ladies' team. Boy, did we feel good!

Chris Mann congratulated us. He had no choice, really, but the next day, getting ready to return home, remember, "Trains and Boats and Planes," what a journey. Phillip Hodgkinson, the ladies' team trainer, approached Sue and I during the journey. He noticed that Sue had a video recorder, which we had hired for the competition. Sue recorded all our work, and Phillip asked if he could borrow the tapes. When we got back home, we sent the tapes to him to borrow so he could view my/our work.

The Man in the Mirror

You guessed it—we never got them back.

To our surprise, the following year for the World Championship in Las Vegas, USA, 1984, our two retro looks from the '83 Euro's formed the foundation of the looks he and Chris Mann wanted the ladies' team to work on for Vegas, and there was not one word mentioned about it being my hair ideas from Gothenburg.

Well none of the ladies' team had watched my events, the only two who did was Chris Mann and Phillip Hodgkinson and here they were, taking credit for it.

I was still the reserve for the team at that stage, and all I could do was to keep my mouth shut and go along with it all, otherwise I'd no chance of making the team. You live and learn in those circles. Keep your head down, your mouth shut, and don't expect anything else.

The next nine months was a big learning curve for me. The day wear conversion to gala (evening wear) was a traditional set on very smooth rollers, which I had already mastered, or so I thought. Colin Lewis was our trainer for these two events, along with Phillip Hodgkinson and manager Chris Mann. My work was on par with everyone else, but their models were very experienced on the competition circuit. I needed a new model, and pretty quick, too! My current group of models had been really good for me, but if I was going to make the team, and more importantly win something, I needed an exceptional model. Not necessarily stunning looking but with good, workable hair, five feet eight inches tall, with a long neck and could work with me as a team.

To add more stress to it, Chris and Phillip were scoring each training session with a view of making the final selection over in Las Vegas two days before the World Championships, which was also going to be Televised on BBC2 in a new series called Real Lives. The producer Ruth Jackson and her crew would be with us at the last few training sessions before we flew out to Vegas. No pressure!

Phillip Hodgkinson was from Wigan, and he and I were the only Northerners in the squad. I got on with then quite well.

Phillip knew of a girl from Blackpool who would make an ideal model for me, her mother owned a B & B/Hotel in Blackpool and was a client of Phillips. Her daughter, Kim, was only sixteen years old, but the attraction of a trip to Las Vegas was too good to turn down. What she didn't realize was the big commitment that went with it. I paid her a fee each time she sat for me, plus all her travel expenses from Blackpool to Stoke. I'd practice at the salon, then we'd travel down to London for squad training. We had a spare bedroom, so Kim would stay over with Sue and I. Kim wasn't the tidiest of people, which really annoyed Sue, who was left to clear up after we left early for the trip to London. But I was up and running, and beginning to feel more on par with the rest of the squad. Kim's youthfulness was an advantage for me. Although she had no modelling experience, she had a good look to her, and with Sue's make-up experience, she was able to bring Kim's youthfulness out in a natural way.

We used to meet a Stephen Way's salon on Bond Street, London, and I could still pinch myself even now, me, a Stokie, hairdressing in the most fashionable and expensive streets in Europe. This was no one off; we trained every other weekend, all day Sunday and Monday. Chris Mann used to have us stay over on the Sunday evening, which was very expensive, with two single rooms for Kim and I plus dinner together as a group. I could understand Chris's thinking, but after a few weeks, I was skint. I can't speak for the others, but for me, if I was going to carry on, I needed to cut down on my spending, so Kim and I drove home Sunday evening, then back on an early train down to London on Monday morning, and only occasionally did we stop over.

The squad was managed by Chris Mann, with Phillip Hodgkinson as trainer, and a guest trainer named Colin Lewis was also involved. Colin won the World Championships in Stuttgart in 1970, he was an outstanding hairdresser with all the traditional techniques in ladies' hairdressing. And it was Colin who taught me all those bygone techniques you'll never see or be able to learn again. Hairdressing today, standard-wise, is nothing compared with the skills of yesteryear.

CHAPTER THIRTY-NINE

Las Vegas World Championships 1984

Training for Vegas became very competitive between each squad member. Each time we met for training, we were marked/scored by the coaches. There was no togetherness.

We all wanted to make the team no matter what, so there was no sharing each other's knowledge, and we had to rely on the coaches for correcting the looks they wanted us to produce.

Colin Lewis was an exception. As for Chris Mann and Phillip Hodgkinson, it was very formal. Phillip, away from these training sessions, did give me feedback and some insight as to where I stood in achieving my goals, though most of it was, "If you don't start improving, you're not going to make the team." Very encouraging!

I didn't dare ask for my video tapes back from the Euros in Sweden. You know, the ones where you've got us all working toward but not one mention of credit to me, as now the day wear and gala hairstyles are based on my work. I would go as far to say if you wanted to create a bitchy, backbiting creep-up to the manager type of atmosphere, Chris and Phillip certainly achieved it. In case I'm not making it crystal clear—it wasn't an enjoyable experience.

The Man in the Mirror

Squad members Paul Garratt and Christopher Dove were definitely favorites in the eyes of the coaches. Paul because he played on his London working in Harrods background, and with Jan Rodgers as one of his models (the wife of Brian Rodgers, whose dancers were regular on the Paladium). and Chris Dove was the shining light of the squad; he couldn't put a comb wrong. His name was on the plane to Vegas for sure.

That left just me and Andrew Hill.

Andrew was and still is a very good hairdresser. I had the impression that, financially, Andrew could afford the challenging costs that Chris Mann threw at us, and he was young and good looking, too! Having said that, Andrew was and still is a nice guy, we still keep in touch.

Back home, the salon was doing well, we probably were the largest employer and individual salon of that era, with over fifteen staff.

I was lucky to be able to chase my dreams of making the British Ladies Hairdressing Team, and we were the salon to have an apprenticeship with. And there was very little staff movement, too. Lucky me! It's not like that today. Yes, people want the standard of training we give and a column of clients it creates, then off they go with as many clients they can get their hands on through networking social media, and the one constant—I was trained by John Belfield is said every time by all of them.

I do also think that in the seventies and eighties, leaving school and having the opportunity of an apprenticeship was something. I know in those days, a local salon group charged a fee to take an apprentice on, but working toward an apprenticeship qualification was worth having. The bonus at our salon was my World Cup Team connection. The trade shows I was involved in, my Teach-ins around the UK,

Europe, and beyond were all a big attraction. I would invite trainees to join me, and this was a big incentive. I could be in Edinburgh on a Sunday, Southampton on a Monday, and back working in the salon on Tuesday, but to be behind the scenes and working as my assistant on stage was a massive incentive and learning opportunity that no other salon in North Staffs could match. My salon was where the magic of hairdressing was, and I provided it.

Having said that, I loved it, which was more than I could say for my British Ladies Squad involvement.

The squad was finally narrowed down to four of us, Chris Dove, Andrew Hill, Paul Garratt, and myself. Three would make the team, and the fourth would be reserve.

Training was under competition rules, and Chris and Phillip would walk around and secretly mark everyone's finished hairstyle, then, with four weeks to go, BBC joined our training sessions, filming anything and everything, and they would be flying out to Las Vegas with us, covering the entire World Hairdressing Championships and our performances in it.

The final three hairdressers would not be announced until we got out to Las Vegas, two days before the start of the Championships, so with four weeks to go before we flew out, the training was now every week.

I've never been in such a cold, unfriendly atmosphere in my life. We were four individuals competing against each other for two reasons, one was to make the team, the other turned into who made the best television. Yes we all wanted to be on TV! So, the sucking up began.

The Man in the Mirror

I was way behind Chris Dove and Paul Garratt when it came to pleasing Chris Mann and Phillip Hodgkinson. It wasn't rocket science to see the amount of attention both Chris and Paul got from them, also the BBC were showing the same interest in them, too. What makes good television? You could tell that those two had been singled out as "interesting." I was hardly getting a look in. Being on TV was taking over the whole training days, the bigger the fuss you got from the managers and coach, the most likely you would be the one making the team, hence my view "sucking up" was definitely the order of the day. I hardly got a smell in. I'd go home after the end of each training day thinking, *I'm not going to make the team, nobodies said a word to me, it's all about being on TV and I'm hardly in it!*

Sue was very supportive, doing my model Kim's make-up. On each session, in fact, it was here that we got noticed. Chris Mann liked the way Sue was doing Kim's make-up, he even suggested that the other three models should have their make-up the same as what Sue had done on Kim, maybe I/we are getting noticed, if only for all the right reasons. Yes, we had a World Championship to compete in, and it was only a week or two away, and I wanted to be in it, sod the TV program. If I had a choice between the two, I'd pick the World Championships every time.

What a journey. We flew out from Heathrow to New York, where we had to clear immigration, as there wasn't any in Las Vegas. it took ages. flying BA meant most people on our flight were not American; four hundred plus people queuing! and we were only halfway there.

We made it to Vegas, our hotel was the Flamingo Hilton, which was right opposite Cesar's Palace. The team had to share rooms, Andrew and Chris in one and Paul Garratt and myself in the other.

John Belfield M.I.T.

Sue and Jonathan obviously had their own room, the same applied to the models. Dinner was organized for the first night for all of the team, models, and coaches. Sue had to settle on a table behind, as we were told that the final three in the team would be announced at this dinner and recorded by the BBC TV crew.

Chris Mann stood and made his speech for TV, then he announced the team. Starting with Andrew Hill, Then Chris Dove, and the final team member would be John Belfield, with Paul Garratt as reserve, you could of heard a pin drop. PG was not a happy bunny, and I'd got him sharing a room with me. There wasn't much food eaten after that. Sue was happy for me, but now we knew the team.

This was Friday evening, so we had Saturday to prepare, then the championships was over two days, Sunday and Monday. I wanted to get to bed, ready for practice the next day. Well, I didn't get much sleep. At One a.m., Paul was waking me up. "Give me some money, he said." Oh dear, he'd been drinking and had blown $500 in the casino downstairs, and he wanted more money, I obliged him a loan, and off he went back down to the casino, this went on for most of the night.

At the end of it, he was going to murder Chris Mann.

So much for sucking up, I thought.

The next morning, well, what was left of the night, I sleepily prepared for my run through practice day, only, with everything that had gone on the night before, I lost track of my model Kim. She'd hit the town the night before and was missing, she wasn't anywhere to be found. Chris Man was not a happy chap.

She finally turned up that afternoon, but I'd missed my mornings run through, she was worse for wear, she'd been up al night partying, and I was livid. Sue was ready to have a go at her, but it wasn't going to achieve anything. I got a couple of hours practice in, and we got her to bed early, with Chris Man checking her room every couple of hours. I certainly didn't want a repeat of the night before. I felt Chris Mann was ready to put Paul Garratt back in the team because of me missing the morning's practice, but he was in a worse state after his antics the night before than my model, so I breathed a sigh of relief.

Chris kept it as it was, and I decided to leave my anger with Kim until after the championships were over.

We travelled up to the competition hall with the men's team. I had to listen to the Constantinou Brothers Simon and Tino bragging on how they'd been allocated a "High Rollers Suite," one of the best rooms in the hotel. *How did they managed that?* I thought to myself, although I had more important things to think about than their bloody hotel room. For one, I was wondering how I was going to keep Kim awake all day. She wasn't looking her best. Well, it was only six-thirty a.m., we all looked a bit jet-lagged, I suppose it was to be expected.

Our day went well. The two events were day wear from a roller set, then converted to a Gala/evening style with postiche. Great just the cut and blow dry the next day.

I felt good.

Back in my hotel room, Paul was trying to sort out his gala style. I could see now why I made the team and not him. He was so un prepared that in the end, he borrowed Andrew Hill's hair piece because his was a complete disaster, and through all of the day, we had the BBC in the background to contend with.

I went to bed hoping that the following day went as well as today. Paul was near on chain smoking now. He hadn't recovered from his disappointment. Back down to the casino he went. God knows how much he'd blown in the casinos. His international event for the reserved followed the main event on Monday. The team's event was in the morning, then Paul's followed in the afternoon. The men's team's timetable was also different to ours, so we didn't travel to the arena with the men's team like we'd done the day before.

Because of my history with the men's team, I knew just about everyone who was involved from the federation. I got the impression that there wasn't a warmth toward me coming from the federation officials, and a few of the men's team too.

Well, someone got brave enough to say, "You've been training the American Team." So what, none of you have bothered with me, and I have friends in the American Team from my time living in New York, so let me guess the Americans are doing well and you lot need some excuse as to why you can't match them. Don't blame me, I love my hairdressing, both men's and ladies'. You didn't think I was good enough to be training you, so what's your problem? I'm a free agent. the Americans felt I still had something to offer, and now you realize I have, don't blame me for your poor performance, blame yourselves, and your egos too.

You know the saying, what goes around comes around. Well, it did. At the end of the first day (Sunday), as we arrived back at our hotel, the Constantinou Brothers, Simon and Tino, were at the main entrance with all their bags.

"You going home early, guys?" I said.

"We're been chucked out."

"Really?" Trying hard to keep a straight face."

"We messed up the bathroom with black hair dye, and apparently in the "High Roller" suites, your assumed to be big gamblers."

"I get it, you're more the Barry Island type (Their salon was in Cardiff) and not Vegas. The limo's gone as well, then? Shame! It's not quite going to plan then," I said as I walked into the hotel. That was the last I saw of them until the awards evening. Back in my smoke-filled room, Paul was hard at it, fag in one hand comb in the other. I guessed what was coming next.

"John, can ya just give us a hand with this!"

To be honest, I liked Paul. He was very London in his character, which fascinated me. He had some great stories to tell, which were a commodity to pass on—One of my hairdressing friends who works in Harrods was telling me the other day—you get the idea! When you're a Stokie, you have to work it as best ya can. most of our clients had never been to London, in their eye's anything that had London attached to it had to be better than Stoke!

We got the last event finished, and all three of us performed well. I helped Paul for his events, as we had a free day before the Parade of Nations and the results.

Ruth Jackson was busy filming her program for the BBC, and Paul was in his element. I'll give him his due—he didn't make the team, but he was sure as hell going to feature strongly in the Real Lives program with the BBC. I could see the draw it created, everyone wanted to be on TV. In that department, I did feel on the outside. I spent the rest of the day with Sue and Jonathan, plus playing tennis over at Cesar's Palace with Trevor Mitchell. Well, that was until the temperature reached 106 degrees. That was enough for both of us.

Liberace was the main entertaining star for the awards evening. None of us made it on the podium, nor did the men's team. We came 5th overall, though we were hoping for at least 4th. I'd never been below 4th place in all the teams I'd been in, but Chris Mann and Phillip were happy. Let me put it another way; we got noticed.

Liberace was amazing, absolutely outstanding, but there was something else; the American's won the overall winning team in the men's events, Sal Fodera, the American men's manager was on cloud nine. He came over to me, we were good friends, not just from my spell of living in New York, we'd connected at many events during the 70s and 80s, mainly in Europe. I suppose the language helped too.

The problem I had was the coldness I was getting from officials of the NHF. I'd been left in the cold since the men's team success in 1980 in Holland. Okay, I was asked to judge in Paris, what some would call the graveyard slot, and I fell for thinking I was the first to be asked, but in hindsight, with the UK being at war with Argentina, it was a judging job nobody wanted, and I fell for it. If the results came out badly, I would be getting the blame.

The Constantinou Brothers were bad losers at the best of times. If they didn't do well, it was always someone else's fault, and the World Champs in Paris was down to my judging.

We left Liberace and Vegas, the main party flying back to the UK. I had my family with me and a much needed family holiday to enjoy, plus making up for lost time being away in London almost every weekend. Even our vicar John Porter paid us a visit to see if I still lived at home!

CHAPTER FORTY

Well-Earned Vacation Gone Sideways

So, where would you go on holiday from Las Vegas? Bearing in mind Jonathan was not quite four years old? The clue is with Dean Martin singing "Come Fly with Me—down to Acapulco Way!"

We flew down to Acapulco, and booked one of the best hotels on the strip. But when we checked in and opened the door to our room, there were cockroaches on the bedroom walls and in the bathroom, too. I was not a happy bunny.

Our hotel belonged to an American group, and I told Sue we were not staying there. I'd get us transferred to one of their hotels in Florida. I'd also noticed that the hotel grounds was fenced off from the beach, obviously for security reasons. The general manager attended to me, and pleaded with me to accept a different room. I was insistent that we wouldn't stay; however, it was going to take a couple of days to re organize our booking and flights to Florida, the changed room was a suite on the top floor. Okay, things were improving, but we didn't like the hotel, so I was insistent that we were going to Florida.

We settled ourselves in, and the first couple of days were very enjoyable. I remember Jonathan swimming for the first time without his armbands on. I was really made up, he wasn't even four years old yet. We were getting over the madness of Las Vegas, and *Playboy Magazine* was doing a photo shoot on the grounds of our hotel one afternoon. They were well away from where the main guests were, but I was starting to think it wasn't such a bad hotel. Our suite was top drawer, too.

Well, our transfer was now arranged, and we would be flying out to Florida the next day, then the unbelievable happened. I'd heard noises in the night, and the telephone rang. It was reception asking us to assemble in the hotel ballroom. We'd been hit by a Hurricane. The corridors were awash with water, the rain washed in horizontally, palm trees were blowing over and touching the ground, and out front, the water was up to the rooftops of the cars outside.

Everyone in the hotel was assembled in the hotel's ballroom, what a bloody state. Our flight and hotel transfer was cancelled, as the road to the airport had collapsed.

Acapulco Bay was nice, a typical resort, but the rest of Acapulco was a dump, and it was on a hill above the bay, so the flood water that washed down from the town of Acapulco higher up, flooding all the bay area was unbelievably filthy, including sewage. We were looking at around five to six feet of water right outside the hotel, the whole hotel was flooded out. Heavy rain was hitting the windows and frames sideways , it came in through every nook and cranny.

It took a couple of days to make the hotel safe to move around in. fortunately, being in a suite which was on the top floor, we were one of the first to be allowed back in our room. Those people with rooms on the lowest floor were the last to be allowed back in their rooms. We gave up on trying to get to Florida, our main priority was getting a flight home.

Five days later, we got one of the first flights out of Acapulco to Chicago and then changed to a flight to London. With the main road to the airport washed away, we had to take a taxi detour over two hours inland. When we arrived at the airport, it was underwater. There was no check in, and we had to wade through a couple of feet of water with our bags out to the plane on the runway where there was no water flooding, then check in at the bottom of the stairs to the plane.

When we finally took off, there was a huge round of applause from everyone on board.

At Chicago, we had to change terminals, which involved baggage handlers. We had less than an hour, and technically our bags were still in transit, hence the handler, who asked me for $50. I argued with him and settled for $25. Yeah, you pay to learn in this world.

When we finally arrived at Heathrow, you guessed it! No bags. I should have known. all my hairdressing gear, our competitions show gowns, some worth hundreds of pounds, even back then. What a bloody holiday. Whenever anyone mentions Acapulco thinking it's a nice place, they don't when I tell them our story.

We got our bags back three weeks later.

Just to round off this Las Vegas trip, there was a good bit to end it all with. The BBC program on BBC2 gave us forty-five minutes with 10.5 million viewers. Almost as many as Coronation St.

All's well that ends well!

John Belfield M.I.T.

CHAPTER FORTY-ONE

A Move from Hanley

Whenever I've been competing in major Hairdressing Championships such as the World & European, the build-up to these championships is incredible. It takes over your life, every blinking minute of it. The problem is, when it's all over, with good or bad results, it leaves an emptiness in your life. Just having a holiday doesn't do it. It takes weeks to settle back down into a normal working life, and home life again, too.

I had some local projects which we as a business were committed to, one was a hair & fashion show for the heart foundation, the other was for the NSPCC. We did more than our fair share of fundraising for local charities, and we never said no, when it came to raising money for whichever charity asked. Every single penny the was raised went to the cause. We never ever took a penny out for so-called expenses. I learnt from experience never to trust people with fundraising money. I got involved once, and only once, with a third party on a fundraiser for our local Theatre Royal. It was fronted by Diddy David Hamilton. When the show was over, there was a full house at the theatre! I asked how much was raised, only to be told that after expenses, NOTHING! I'm not suggesting David Hamilton had done anything wrong, but the organizer never produced any expenses paperwork, which I'd requested to see where the money had gone. What was the point of doing the show if it didn't produce a sum of money for the cause you're doing it for?

I learnt my lesson, and never again, if I was asked to do something for charity; don't get involved with anyone, do it yourself.

Fashion shows were the thing in those days, but I would only agree to if the cause was local to the community I lived in so that I could feel my community benefited and our staff and models who were involved with the show could see that they too had made their contribution by giving their time in doing it. I would add that our shows were very entertaining. Gordon Alcock, a well-known local actor always choreographed my shows, and BBC radio Stoke always helped with my music arrangements. Yes, our shows were well supported both behind the scenes and those who came to watch.

Having done trade shows up and down the country with the World Cup squad, I was able to use that experience when we did our shows locally. Looking back, we must have raised tens of thousands of pounds during the 70s, 80s, and 90s. I never kept a tally, it wasn't my priority. I think there was a much bigger community spirit than what I see today, though maybe I'm not looking in the right direction.

Shopping has changed too. Gone are the individual "boutique" fashion shops. They always had a style and a following of regular customers who jumped at the opportunity to attend a Hair & Fashion show, no matter what the fund raising cause was.

I remember our first hair bonanza show was down in the basement at The Place discotheque in Hanley. Anybody and everybody went to The Place. Kevin Donavan brought the big city, i.e., Manchester, music scene to the potteries. Nearly all of the biggest name in the pop scene played there in their early years. The likes of Rod Stewart, The Stones, Bowie, you name it. It was a big privilege for me to grace the stage of those superstars.

After that night in '69, my hair boutique over my Dad's barber shop on Liverpool Road Stoke had a queue of clients wanting to get their hair cut by me. Without any exaggeration, it put my name on the social music scene and was the beginning of a sincere friendship with Kevin Donavan, which over the years has grown stronger and stronger. We catch up with each other every week, our friendship lasting over fifty years.

I'd always felt that the Market Square at some point would be unsustainable. By any standards it was a brilliantly designed salon, certainly the best salon in Stoke-on-Trent and North Staffs area; however, the hairdressing industry was changing. Big salons were for the likes of Manchester and Birmingham, and the city centre of Stoke-on-Trent was getting a new shopping centre, and with it higher rents. There was a knock-on effect with rent rises for all the town centre. The arcade where our salon was located was owned by an insurance group called Standard Life, based up north, and their only interest was money and a return on their property investment. Almost overnight, our rent increased to £400 per week. when we moved into Market Square in 1979/80, our rent had been £60 per week.

It was time to move on and out.

Staff started to take advantage of their popularity that we had created by being trained by us and having a client following, which we had developed in house for our business. Stoke-on-Trent was made up of six towns, and all had small low rent locations, which over a period of time I began to realise senior staff were leaving us, taking enough clients with them to open up their own salon in the cheaper rents offered in the other town centres nearer to where the staff lived. They had a ready-made business on the back of working for John Belfield.

Parking was naff in Hanley, not enough of it and too expensive. the end of the sole trader, and it was the same all over the country. From my perspective, it was also the end of the larger salons. Stoke-on-Trent became flooded with small salons with just one or two staff. Our salon employed fifteen.

I needed a new business model, and it wasn't going to be in Stoke-on-Trent.

Newcastle-under-Lyme, which was joined to Stoke-on-Trent to the west, was always the up market town of the area, with a residential population to match. But I didn't want another salon bang in the middle of Newcastle town centre. It was only a matter of time before the same that was happening in Hanley would also happen to Newcastle. So, my business model was finding a secondary trading location in a classy/character building with potential to rent the upper floor space.

We settled on moving out of Hanley to outskirts of Newcastle in a listed building with car parking at no. 9 King St., King Street, which was the main road from Newcastle to Hanley. This was to be the home of the salon business, with us renting the two upper floors off. The salon had a garden area with fountain and conservatory space for a beauty salon.

The property's ground floor gave us a nice, Georgian themed style salon. The front room with a three position men's hair salon, the rest to the rear was a ladies' salon with reception and joint waiting area, a styling space, a traditional dryer bank area, tinting space, and toward the back a staffroom and toilet.

This was a completely different direction from my previous salons, but none of the salons I've had or owned have ever felt like home.

Some of the fellowship who were responsible for the running of the ladies' team criticized my moving in the middle of a team selection period for the World Championships in Verona Italy. I played the comments down, as telling me how and when to open my business was nothing to do with any of them. So, the big move was on.

The salon was very successful, and I had no trouble letting the two upper floors, and having a large car park was a bonus. The big bonus, though, was the land that came with it, which we also sold off for an apartment development overlooking an area called station walks. The money from the land sale enabled us to fit out the salon and renovate all the building, which dated back to 1824. It was also just a short walk into Newcastle town center.

I thought it would be emotional and upsetting, making such a big move and gamble from what, for me, was my perfectly designed Salon. It had a European style layout with salon styling furniture to match. There was nothing like it in the area, and our reputation was huge—we were the number one salon to go to in the whole area of North Staffs and South Cheshire. Would our client base follow us to a converted Georgian House on the perimeter of Newcastle under Lyme? This was a big gamble, and I'd no idea how it would pan out. The majority of our staff were okay with it, and as for the clients, well, we would soon find out.

The Man in the Mirror

There was no such thing as social media, so we had to rely on making sure our existing loyal client base knew. By this I mean those clients who come every six to eight weeks. There were many who only came to us every three to six months and others once in a blue moon.

I began to recognize how insular some of the potteries community were. I remember two sisters who were regular clients who came together on a Saturday. When I told them that their next appointment would be at our new location in Newcastle under Lyme, which is less than two miles from Hanley (Stoke City Center), I was shocked when both of them replied, "We've never been to Newcastle. We only come to Hanley when our husbands bring us for our hair."

I asked where they both lived, expecting to hear them say somewhere quite a distance away, only to be to hear, "We live in Biddulph." Now, Biddulph is on the northern end of the Potteries, no more than four maybe five miles from the city center of Hanley. You might think this an extreme example of how Potteries people back then lived, but trust me, it wasn't!

In the end, one of their husbands brought them by car. This lasted maybe two or three visits, then it ended, it was too much trouble for the husband. We even had apprentices decline travelling from where they lived on the outskirts of Hanley to Newcastle. It sounds crazy saying this in today's age, but that was how it was back then. Having said that, I'm sure this mindset still exists in some areas of the Potteries.

There was no looking back. A portion of those Hanley clients came and gave us a try. Remember, we had no social media, our local paper the *Evening Sentinel* gave us some editorial along with two pages of adverts from ourselves and most of the businesses who worked on the building and salon interior. As a family, we were always loyal to

John Belfield M.I.T.

the people and businesses who did work for us, though there were the odd one or two who we'd spent hundreds of pounds with, not only on this current project but also on many maintenance things you need running a business in the past, who when asked to have a £50 supporting ad with our feature declined. Needless to say, we never used them again. We believe in loyalty; with our suppliers, our staff, and most importantly our clients, friends, and family.

CHAPTER FORTY-TWO
A Haunted Salon and Challenging Clients

Well, it didn't take long before we realized we weren't alone in the building. We only occupied the ground floor area with the Salon; the upper floors and the rear annex building we had left unrenovated, we hadn't the money to do the entire building in one go.

It was on a Friday morning early, before the salon was fully open at nine a.m., though I always started at eight. I was shampooing a lady's hair in the middle room toward the rear of the salon, when we both heard footsteps walking in the room above us.

My client said to me, "Have you got the upstairs rented now then?" I said, "No, there's no one upstairs."

My immediate thought was that we had an intruder on the premises. I stopped shampooing and ran upstairs, but there was no one there. *Weird*, I thought, and just passed it off as nothing, just one of those old building noises. Until it became a regular Early Friday Morning thing. Yes, we had a visitor! Or should I say resident and we were the visitors.

It didn't stop at just Friday mornings, we had staff when at the rear of the premises saying they felt as if there was a presence there.

One even went as far as saying she felt someone/something touch her on her shoulder from behind, but when turning around, there was no one there. It scared the life out of her. She came running up to the main salon area saying there was a ghost in the staffroom. Well at least it stopped staff spending time in the staff area when they should have been up in the main salon area.

The strange thing about it was that I never felt frightened of whatever it was. To me, it was friendly.

During these early years of occupying the ground floor area of no. 9 King Street, we as a family lived on Manor Road near Baldwin's Gate. It was Sue and I's family home in the early years for Jonathan and later our twins Harrison and Hannah.

Our business model had changed from how it was in the city center. Not all our clients followed us from Hanley, some came for a while but for whatever reason stopped coming, but at the same time, we had new clients from and around Newcastle, even as far as Market Drayton, Nantwich, Crewe, Leek, Stone and Stafford. With many beyond those areas. Most of those clients wouldn't have travelled to Hanley (city center), I could never figure it out, only to say that's how people were when it came to shopping. What I can say is we had a car park at the rear of the premises and on street parking at the front, and for me, looking at shopping patterns now, parking can make or break a business. Maybe I didn't recognize it back then, but it's paramount today.

We had an excellent clientele, born from that move from Hanley to Newcastle, but for whatever reason, you can't please everyone all the time, as they say. In time, my people skills developed, which, to be honest, took ages because I'd never had much experience dealing with certain clients who were continually difficult and upsetting to deal with. We never had many, hardly one a year, and I'm talking about those who continually found fault with something or other, and whatever you did to try and please them it wasn't enough, and believe me, we had the client who would reduce a staff member to tears for no justifiable reason, and that did on one occasion included me!

I was at home one Friday evening, and I said to Sue, "I've got that bloody woman in first thing in the morning, she's never ever happy with her hair, she comes to me every Saturday morning at eight-thirty in the morning and has for ten years, and I can honestly say, not once did she ever say she liked her hair!"

When I did my consultation with her every week, there was always, "Just look at my hair, I nearly called you on Thursday, just look at the state of it!" She expected her blow dry to last all week from one Saturday morning to the next. It was never considered that everyday wear and sleeping on it would be taken into consideration, it was always my fault if her blow dry didn't last all week.

Well, this particular Saturday morning, something else kicked her off, on top of the usual complaining. Our receptionist had double booked her appointment with another lady, and she picked up on the mistake, so did her husband, who always brought her and waited for her. I explained to the other lady I would keep her waiting, and she was fine about it, not a problem, or so I thought. However, having usual moaning dissatisfaction with her hair, when I'd finished her hair, and her and her husband stood at the reception to pay, he took me to one side.

Now, he was a big bloke with a loud Yorkshire accent, and just to piss me off that bit more, he FINGER WAGGED me and in a load voice said, "This is just not good enough."

Now his wife had not been inconvenienced, the other lady had. But he was a Hat West Bank Manager, so I said to him, "Don't you ever get it wrong with appointments? Is your appointment system so bloody perfect? Your wife has never been kept waiting once in ten years, and she hasn't today."

Well, he kept on finger wagging at me, repeating, "This is just not good enough!"

That did it, so I off loaded on him, "In ten years, your bloody wife has not once complimented me about her hair, it's always every week, 'Just look at my hair!' So you can take your miserable Mrs. and that blood finger of yours and PISS OFF! Don't ever come back or anywhere near my salon again!"

Off they went, mumbling something like, "Well, I Never!"

When I turned to the rest of the salon, you could hear a pin drop. It was deadly silent!

Now, I'd always made a point to the staff that we all needed to be able to handle people like the client who I'd just chucked out, so our young junior stepped forward, saying, "John, you always said…"

"That's enough, just get on with what you were doing." But I could sense the amusement that everyone was experiencing, enjoying having their moment with me. I didn't feel anger, just a relief and annoyance with myself that I hadn't done it sooner.

When I got home and told Sue I'd taken her advice, she hammered it home with me, saying, "You should listen to me more often."

The Man in the Mirror

The Newcastle Salon soon became home. The salon worked well, and in the summertime, clients could wait outside if they wanted to. We served Rombouts filtered coffee, all five variants, including a wrapped biscuit and sealed milk.

By today's comparison we offered too much for the prices we charged. I think being in Hanley for so long, we stayed with a similar price structure instead of creating a new business plan. I was aware that other salons worked there prices off our pricelist, and there wasn't a week that went by that we didn't have a phone call enquiry asking, "how much." It soon dawned on me that the How Much wasn't a client but another hair salon wanting to know our charges. The internet resolves that today, but back then, there was no such thing, it was word and mouth and our local *Evening Sentinel* to get any messages out there.

Fortunately, the fashion editor Virginia Heath was a good friend and was always looking for new editorial news for her *Tuesday Evening Fashion Pages*. We certainly had plenty of news for her. We were doing makeovers, including Sue on the make-up side and me with the hairdressing and photography. We prided ourselves on advertising all our own work and not pictures of hairstyles copied from magazines. It went as far as local salons using photos from hairdressing magazines, not realizing they were using pictures of my work and my photography.

On one occasion, we had a client come in to have her hair done, saying, "Did you know that 'so and so's salon' has an enlarged photo of your wife Sue in their salon's front window?"

Yes, my wife Sue—*my* hairdressing my photography, inferring it was their hairdressing! Now, I get why they used the photo, because Sue modelled a lot for me; she was and still is very good looking with wonderful, workable hair, so her photo was in many trade magazines with many popular hairstyles and hair colors, so I sort of got it, except those photos had my credits attached to the magazine photograph, so no real excuses. Needless to say, I gave the salon twenty-four hours to remove my copyright photographs from their salon window.

My thought's then came down to being located in the Stoke/Newcastle area. With no national media, we had no connection to national newspapers, Magazines, and TV, even those running Radio Stoke in its early day's weren't local to the area. They are now and have been for many years and are connected to its local community, but not in its infancy.

My hairdressing friends in Manchester were well connected with the national media, although we did manage Peble Mill in Birmingham a couple of times through my National Hairdressing Federation friends, and to those I say thank you.

Eventually, the ghost upstairs had company. We let both the first and second floors to different companies, and we settled into having neighbors upstairs. We never had any complaints from either about the ghost; well, not upstairs, anyway, but we did have a regular presence at the rear of the salon. Several staff had, friendly issues, nothing scary.

CHAPTER FORTY-THREE

John Belfield Product Range

We established a new identity with moving out of Hanley. I was beginning to enjoy my hairdressing, though, don't get me wrong, financially it was still tough.

I was still keeping my mum and dad. They had relocated to a bungalow in Barlaston, a small village on the south side of Stoke-on-Trent. Mum always wanted to live in a Bungalow, and I was happy to provide it.

Dad kept up his routine of coming up to the salon and pottering around helping out. I gave him a free rein. He did the laundry and tinkered in the garden area of the patio. We were inundated with squirrels eating his plants, and this went on for ages, then suddenly stopped almost overnight. I said to Dad one day, "It's funny, I haven't seen any squirrels for some time." He didn't comment, and then I read an article in our local paper that people had seen a number of dead squirrels over on Station Walks, which was the land behind the salon. Oh dear! What's he gone and done?

"Dad why are there dead squirrels over in Station Walks?" I asked.

"Oh! I've put some stuff down to stop them eating the plants."

"What stuff? There's an article in the local paper about dead squirrels over in Station Walks, I don't suppose you'd know anything about that, would you?"

Dead silence!

Oh shit, he's killed the bloody squirrels!

It's amazing what a medicated shampoo can do! We had a lovely garden that year!

It was a memorable year for a number of reasons, and no, the squirrels wasn't one of them. It was to be my last year for competing in the World Hairdressing Championships in Verona Italy. Was this to be our year?

I'd also started to try and create our identity through our own product range. We'd been Redken through and through up until then and had the exclusivity in our area. The product range was the Science of Hair, from acid balance shampoos and perms to liquid hair and volcanic ash. There was noting like it, we were ahead of the game!

Trevor Mitchell called me one day and asked if I knew anyone who could make some products up, as Redken was changing course in its exclusivity and was now going into any and every salon they could. It started a price war, particularly with their perms, which were considered the best in those days, and we were still doing a lot of perming. Mitch gave me something to think about, as we were experiencing the same aggressive approach in our area.

I began to realise I could make my own range of products. I did it back in the 60s, why not now? If we started in a small way, just a couple of shampoos and conditioners plus a leave in conditioner and see how we get on with it.

Body Shop started with a Trichologist helping with their range; I could do the same. A handmade, PH balanced product which was bio-degradable and not tested on animals, which was just what Body Shop was doing. Well! I could do that too!

I used my contacts through the Institute of Trichologists plus a few others I knew, and it wasn't long before I got samples made up, which, when finetuned, became the became the beginning of our product range. Ticking all the boxes that Body Shop did; a trichological prescription range by trichologist John Belfield, handmade, bio degradable, PH balanced, and not tested on animals. Thirty-five years later, and we've now got a professional range, including styling products and a trichology prescription range for hair thinning and scalp treatments, making up a product range of twenty-five products. Jonathan will take this product range and own it, as I believe it's where Jonathan's future is. Currently, he's working in the salon ten to twelve hours a day on clients, as that's where our current business model is, but with the right guidance and investment in online sales, it's where a new business model needs to be. We both believe our products are as good, if not better, than what's currently out there. However, we haven't told anyone outside our salon, except what activity we are getting from our new website.

I hope I'm still around to see this happen!

I look at how the hair cosmetic industry has gone and how gullible people are when hard advertising convinces the purchaser that anything else put up against that particular product is inferior.

When organic started to become popular, it wasn't long before a certain hair color manufacturer introduced a professional organic permanent hair dye, it was packaged in a white box with green leaves on it, this more or less made the organic statement without saying anything else. We were key accounts with this company, and the key accounts manager was really excited about their launch. I was too, as having an organic permanent hair dye on our coloring service was just where my philosophy was and should be, all through my hairdressing career I wanted to be the first, and in my eye's, that's who I am. I produced my first blow dry lotion on a female client for a cut and blow dry, then at the beginning of 1970s, we were one of the very first UK Salons to take Redken acid balanced products, a PH balanced shampoo, and an acid wave perm. This was unheard of back then, and clients took a lot of convincing. We even used henna mixed with black coffee as a permanent color product; our drains were regularly blocked with the amount of mud going down the drains.

So, there I was, the salesman made his pitch on his company's new organic hair dye, so, as a trichologist, I was curious as to what the active ingredients were. I read it's ingredient list, and it was exactly the same as a normal PPD hair dye but with one exception; beeswax! I'm looking at him, and he's got half a smile on his face. You've got to be kidding me! Just one organic ingredient in it? If you only need on ingredient for the product to be organic, on that basis at least half of our hair products qualify as organic!

No, we didn't go with it. There was no way we as a family would sell a product that coned our clients and staff, saying something it really wasn't.

Following that, we had ammonia free, so a hair dye which was ammonia free must be better than a hair dye with ammonia in it, but the performance of the hair dye without ammonia was inferior to that with ammonia in it!

In addition, we are firmly against animal testing. This is a classic statement on products, but it doesn't mean that the product ingredients haven't been tested on animals, it just means that the manufacturer is against it. It's true to say that all hair cosmetics at some point will have been tested on animals; however, this is not the case today. Yes, things have moved on, and for the better, too!

CHAPTER FORTY-FOUR

1986 - My Last World Championship in Verona Italy

Well, every dog has its day, and I was no exception. After how the team had performed in Las Vegas, we had one last shot at the Championship. I think we all had just one more hairdo in us, as they say.

Christopher Dove from the '84 La Vegas Team decided to make a career in the States. He was an excellent hairdresser, and though I didn't connect too well with his reserved Southern type of personality, as we Northerners say, I did respect his ability and could see him becoming a big stage name in the arena of hairdressing in the States. Once he left, I never heard from him again, which didn't surprise me one little bit. Team manager Christopher Mann lost his little "favorite."

There was no BBC this time, no distractions, and as much as I enjoyed the experience of TV following us during the run into the Las Vegas World Championships and the forty-five minute program that came from it, I felt it became a competition as to who could get the most screen time from it. Which one of us was the quirkiest character made the program more interesting to watch, even if they weren't the best hairdresser! I would have to say a hundred percent; Paul Garret won the TV screen time with the BBC, even though he was only the reserve in Las Vegas. Paul was a great character, I warmed to his personality and admired him as a hairdresser, too. He saw it for what it was; good publicity.

So, the team was selected early: Paul M'Cullock, Andrew Hill, and myself made the final cut. Christopher Mann was still the team manager, with Colin Lewis as Trainer, Philip Hodgkinson, our trainer in Las Vegas, stayed on in the States, touring with comedian Joan Rivers. Sadly, by the time we were competing in Verona, Philip had passed away.

The three of us gelled as a team. We worked as hard as we could to do better than we did in Vegas, having come in fifth place. And I had a new model, Sam. She was focused on us doing well and was just the right sort of person for me. She understood the need for us to have a professional understanding between each other and was a hundred percent focused.

Sue did a brilliant job with her make-up, and whenever Sue made her up, Sam radiated. She looked and felt good. This made a big difference sitting on the competition floor with 130-odd other glamorous models. Sam even enjoyed Jonathan, riding his little bike around the salon whilst we practiced

Yes, I was very happy. My team was me, Sue, Sam, and Jonty. It made a big difference to my practice sessions at home, as I could focus on my work and the standard I needed to get to. It was noticeable when we all trained together, too, I felt that for the first time, Chris Mann actually took me seriously as a team contender, having been in the Men's Team before. I was never his favorite, and I didn't creep up to him, either, so he didn't really know what to make of me, but before these championships were through, he most certainly would!

John Belfield M.I.T.

Everything was going well, all those little details, from the flight to the hotel, and the early morning run through at three-thirty a.m. just to get our models' hair working well from a roller set (it made the next all-important set work better).

So, we were at the start of the championships, it was eight a.m., our models were set and under the dryer for an hour, and the eight-minute day style was the first event.

I was collecting my thoughts of the day in front of me whilst Sam was under the dryer, and Chris Mann walked over to me, asking, "Are you ready for this, do you feel nervous?"

I looked up at him in amazement. What a stupid Bloody Question to ask me. So, he got an even more Stupid Reply. "Chris! I've just given up the last two years of my life since Vegas to be here right now. Nothing, and I mean nothing is more important right now than this, of course I'm bloody nervous! Any more questions like that, and I'll be angry, too!"

He walked away and said nothing more to me for the rest of the day. YES, I was ready, he got the message!

The championships went perfectly. Sue did the bizo on Sam's makeup, and she looked stunning. Each event went like clockwork, and on the night of the awards, we'd gotten through the parade of Nations. There were now a couple of hour's entertainment of extracts from the opera's that were staged at the amphitheater, Aida and Carmen. It was going to be a long night.

I managed to go and sit with Sue and Jonathan during these Operas. One of the American Team who I knew well, Sal Fodera from New York, came up and joined us.

The Man in the Mirror

There was Jonathan, sitting with his Union Jack t-shirt on, the whole area was candle/or mob phone-lit, and Jonathan turned to me and said, "Have all these people come to watch you win a medal, Dad?"

Sal Fodera turned to me and said in his strongest Brooklyn accent, JARNN, if ya don't win a medal this evening, ya better go out and buy one, cus ya boy is going to be very disappointed!"

Fortunately, I won a Silver Medal. Our British ladies' team came second overall, the best result ever. No need to tell you which country won Gold. Yes, you got it—Italy!

Friends I knew from other countries came over to congratulate us, they all made the same comment, "Second in Italy is as good as first John!"

I knew what they meant. My Friend from Sweden, Life Olyne, gave his usual comment, "That's Life, John!"

I'd been in or involved in a British Hairdressing Team since 1969. Both men's and ladies' teams, and still hold the accolade of the only UK hairdresser to win medals in a World Championship in both men's and ladies' hairdressing.

It was now time for me to move on. Enough was enough. I have to say, I was around in one team or another longer than anyone else. For most, not all, just one championship was enough, win or not. They took something special back to their salons that meant a lot against their competitors who didn't have that extra to say about themselves or their working standard.

I was hoping to stay on the edge of the teams that followed, give something back, as they say. I felt I had a lot to give back, but I also had a lot to give back to my business and my family. Yes, it was a way of life in a family business, even if the business was only one family member. I did and always would keep up the family image, and Mum and Dad's way of life as they knew it and wanted it. I'd no reason to change it. This included my Dad's sister "Aunty Doris," although a Bootherstone by marriage to my Uncle Eric, after he passed and with no children, Doris was a Belfield, born at the same shop as my Dad, No 58 Liverpool Rd.

Doris and Eric lived in the back bedroom upstairs, the front bedroom was for my Nan and Grandad, so apart from the salon at the front, the rest of the ground floor was communal. Thinking about it now, it was very cozy. The middle room had a large fireplace, which was used for cooking. The back kitchen was a wash room with a mangle, an outside dolly (wash) tub, and a gas stove for boiling a kettle. Every time we had a customer in for a shave, I'd be back and forth filling shaving mugs with boiling water from the kettle. The used slops went in a bucket under the sink in the shop, and at the weekend, that needed carrying through and emptying in the grid in the back yard a dozen times a day. The toilet was further up at the top of the yard. The whole scenario of how we all lived and existed was, now that I'm looking back, embedded in our way of life. It certainly was for me, and Mum and Dad, after they retired, they couldn't stay away. Same for Doris, and the same for me. Where will I be in the morning? You guessed it; "up the Shop." I must admit it annoys Jonathan, but after sixty-two years, I just can't stay away!

CHAPTER FORTY-FIVE

Hannah & Harrison Arrive

So, After Verona, we were back. It was 1986, and I knuckled under, getting on with working in the salon, doing my teachings on Sunday and Mondays, trying to make some money out of my reputation within the hairdressing industry, in the UK, Europe, Japan, and the States.

My family life was getting a better balance, and holidays happened more often. June and October, school holidays we would drive down to the South of France for a couple of weeks, staying either in an apartment or caravan. It was cheaper on those dates, just out of season.

We had an outdoor forty-eight-foot swimming pool at home, five feet in the deep end and four feet in the shallow end. It was perfect for swimming in, especially after a long day in the Salon. Jonathan was well on his way to becoming a good swimmer, and the one thing back then we didn't do was use the pool for entertaining. In fact, we made a point of not telling anyone. When you've spent your life on a council estate, it felt a bit awkward saying we had a swimming pool, it just wasn't us, that side of our family life we liked to keep private.

By '89, our twins were born. I remember working in the salon, and Sue was in the early stages of her pregnancy. She'd just been to see her consultant, and I was setting a lady's hair when she came in and walked up to me.

I said, "How'd it go, is everything okay?"

She said, "The Consultant says, either you're having the biggest baby I've ever delivered or your having TWO!"

"What! Two?"

"Well, I've got to have a scan before he can confirm it…"

"Bloody'ell, two!"

A few months later, Hannah and Harrison were born. We were over the MOON!

It was hard for Sue in those early days. She went months without leaving the house. I'd come home from the Salon, and Sue would still be in her dressing gown. It was eight in the evening, and before I could get out of my car, Sue would put the twin's in the car, hand me a pack of sandwiches, and say, "Go and drive around for a couple of hours, I'm knackered!"

Friends and family all offered to come over and help for an hour or two, but as soon as we asked, "Any chance you could come over next Wednesday evening?"

"Oh! I can't do that evening."

There was always a reason why not, and we just got on with it in the end.

In 1990, we started to holiday again in the South of France, half term in May and again half term in October. I would drive down in our Ford Granada Estate car the day before, with a Tandem Bike on the roof for me and Jonathan to get around on whilst we were there.

I'd have the car packed to the rafters, portable TV, children's videos, you name it, I had it.

Sue and the children would fly down to Nice, "hand baggage only" the day after, and I'd have everything unpacked and sorted. we'd usually have an apartment and later a caravan when the children were older to cope with the heat, I'd be at the airport to pick them up, and our holiday was up and running. The same applied at the end of the holiday; I'd take them to the airport for a flight to Manchester and then drive back with the kitchen sink and all.

It was a twelve-hour drive on a good day from Cannes to Calais, only, on this particular October, it wasn't to be such a good day. Back then, you needed to take the periferique ring road around Paris. It was a nightmare of a road to be on at any time of the day or night, but on this occasion, the heaven's opened, the road flooded, and I got stuck on that bloody road for over two hours just crawling at a snail's pace.

I didn't get to Calais until midnight, and I was knackered. I'd missed my ferry by three hours, and the next sailing on my cheap ticket was six a.m. the next morning. I decided to stay in one of the cheap dockside hotels, no problem. The next morning, I got the ferry and sailed through customs in Dover and drove nonstop back to Newcastle under Lyme, straight to the salon, having been away for two weeks. It was a Monday, and I had a full day of clients booked in on Tuesday. I liked to sort the post out and get my head around how things had been whilst we were away.

My holiday routine was to call the salon every day, normally from a pay phone, as mobile phones weren't around back then. I'm talking telex messages and pigeon post, but without fail, I'd find a phone somewhere to call the Salon. Sue hated me doing it, but I'd make an excuse, saying I was just going to get am English paper. She knew what I was up to, but I preferred knowing rather than walking into a load of trouble at the shop and having a shit load of sorting to do.

Well, all my phone calls to the salon didn't flag up any issues, nothing to worry about, then. I parked my fully loaded car outside the salon, and in I went. Just two weeks of post and a scan of my week's appointments, what could go wrong?

"John, we didn't like to tell you and spoil your holiday, but Joe, a stylist, he waited for you to go on holiday, then served his two weeks' notice."

He'd spent the two weeks giving his business cards out to all our customer's, explaining where his shop was and how clients could go to him with a discounted rate, all behind my back whilst I was away. The little SHIT!

My holiday went out of the window pretty quick.

Joe was a guy who stood on the doorstep of my salon one Saturday afternoon, begging me not only to give him a job but to finish his training off, which wasn't happening at the salon he was currently at. I remember saying to him that Saturday, because he'd just turned up in the middle of a busy day, "You've got three minutes to convince me why I should give you a job and retrain you to my way of hairdressing." I always was a soft touch; he got the job.

I showed him the door that Monday afternoon with my father's words of wisdom ringing in my ears. 'Just remember, you're on your own in this world.' Never a truer word said.

Loyalty was always a big thing with me, and I suppose still is. I never learned from that incident, because it happened every time someone left us. I used to make a point with all our staff, "If ever you decide to move on and open your own business, I'll help you if you need anything, ie., chairs, basins, or stock, anything, just ask, but when you go, LEAVE MY BUSINESS ALONE!"

Needless to say, that never happened. Their focus every time was to take as many clients as they could from me, and I never heard from them again. Not one, neither then nor now, ever said thank you for my training and all you have done for me. Not one of them. But the words "Trained by John Belfield" featured in their promotions, from handouts to social media. I never got a Christmas card from any of them ever.

CHAPTER FORTY-SIX

Suspicious Times

Back at the salon, having shown Joe the door, I needed to get home, unpack my car, and get ready for work the next day. At home, I've got the tandem off the roof of my car, and I'd started getting the rest of our things out of the car, I'd had the back seats down flat so it was like a van, everything packed flat with just a small gap so that I could see through the rear view mirror. I'd gotten some of our belongings out, when I came across what looked like a bar of brown soap wrapped in cling film, I show it to Sue, asking, "What have ya packed this for?" thinking *why didn't you just bin it rather than bringing it back?*

She said, "I didn't put that in the car."

"Well, I certainly didn't, it must have been you."

So, we both had words, not giving in to the fact that neither of us had put this odd looking brown stuff in the car.

So, what is it, and how did it get there?" I was beginning to get concerned. It was now about eight p.m., I'd had enough, what with the drive back from Dover and chucking Joe out of my shop. I was tired, I still had a fair bit to unpack, and I had a full day on at the salon the next day. I had the mindset just to chuck it in the bin, yes I came close to doing that, but something didn't feel right.

I called a close friend, Phil Maskery, he lived nearby and was head of staffs "Scene of the crime" dept at Stafford. He suggested we meet for a pint down at the Sheet Anchor pub in Baldwin's Gate village.

I turned up at the pub, Phil was already having a pint at the bar, and I walked up to him and put my package on the bar, saying hello at the same time.

"What the bloody hell are ya doing with a block of cannabis! That's cannabis," he said. "Where did you get that from?"

"I found it whilst unpacking my car. We've just got back from holidaying in the South of France, and it was tucked in amongst our things in the back of my car."

A typical copper response followed, "You'd be looking at a few years inside if customs had stopped you with that amount of cannabis in your car. Its street value would be about a grand!"

"Come on, Phil, I don't do drugs. In fact, I'm dead against them, you know that."

To which he said, "If you had been stopped by customs with that amount of cannabis in your car, I would have questioned how well I know you!"

"Thanks, Phil!"

With that, he suggested he call out the drug squad team. I went back home, not even consuming a pint, and waited for the drug squad to turn up. Four of em arrived, and it was all very amicable, but there were undertones which I felt; it could turn if they weren't sure I was telling the truth.

Four hours went by with me having the go through my entire holiday from start to the drive back, which was eventually their main focus. By two in the morning, they felt satisfied with my statement, and we called it a night. I hadn't even finished unpacking the car, and my first client was in at eight a.m. the next day.

So, into to the Salon I went after a few hours of disturbed sleep, dwelling on what had happened over the last five or six hours. I always park my car in the same place at the rear of the salon, we had a car park for around ten cars. The salon was busy, me especially, with being away for two weeks, and now having to try and keep Joe's clients, who were asking for him. It was about ten-thirty a.m., and I was cutting Evira's hair. She had a handbag and accessory business in the town of Newcastle.

An employee walked in and asked, "Where's your car?"

I said, "Where I always park it."

"It's not there," he said.

I rushed out back to look, and my bloody car was gone!

What the hell was going on?

I finished Elvira as quick as I could, then called Phil, and the guy who led the interview last night called. He said to go home, call your wife, and don't answer the door or phone. we will get a squad car out to you.

Sue was in a panic, she was there on her own with the children. I left the salon, and it was chaos when I got home. The police had secured our property, Sue was very upset, Dad sorted Jonathan out, he was at school, and the police asked me to attend an interview down at Newcastle Police Station. So, there I was, and this wasn't so friendly this time.

The Man in the Mirror

"So, which of your drug dealing friends have you pissed off to cause yourself this situation?"

Oh Dear! This wasn't what I expected. "Are you arresting me?" "Well, prove to us why we shouldn't be."

"Hang on a minute, do I need a solicitor before this goes any further?"

"That depends on what your reply is to the questions we put to you."

I refused to answer any without consulting a solicitor. Phil, my friend turn up, and he was highly respected within in the force. I soon saw how high a ranking officer he was. He suggested they wait until my car is found, and I should go and sort my family circumstances. So, I left the station and went home, still trying to get my head around what was happening.

At home the police had installed a special device on our telephone, should we have an emergency, the phone would call directly to the nearest squad car to respond straight to our house. I got a phone call from the police at three a.m. telling me that my car had been found on the Medway car park in Newcastle town center. It had all the door panels ripped out of it and had been taken to a special unit in Birmingham for forensic analysis. I was required to attend a police interview later that morning to continue where they had left off the day before.

I still couldn't believe it was happening, one minute down on the beach, now this! Where will it end?

At the Police Station, it was more of the same as the day before, except they explained to me that my car had been packed with cannabis. All the door panels, even the boot door, had cannabis packed in it. I couldn't understand how that could have happened, then the question's started. "Who are you involved with, why did the drug delivery go wrong?" Enough was enough. I was getting angry. "You're not seeing what I'm seeing. If you're going to carry on this line of investigation, I want my solicitor present, and I had you guy's around my house for over four hours until two a.m. in the morning, and not one of you thought about looking at my car, which still had most of our holiday belongings in it.

So, at that point, apart from the one piece of cannabis I found in my luggage, the car was sitting full of cannabis at my house, and not one of you ever suggested taking my car for analysis, how would that read in the PRESS about you lot! Either you back off me, or that's what I'm going to do as soon as I leave this police station."

Well, that did it. They calmed down and had a more friendly tack with me. The big question was, how did the drugs end up in my car without me having a clue about it?

Phil turned to me and said, "You had about £20,000 worth of cannabis in your car. Had customs stopped you, you'd be looking at a seriously long prison sentence."

I repeated had I'd said to him in the Sheet Anchor, I'm dead against any form of drug use and always will be. The law doesn't deal with drug dealers strong enough, not then and certainly not now!

The police then explained their theory as to how they thought it had happened. I'd said that our holiday routine had been the same for a number of years, driving down to the South of France late May and again October half term, so they called the salon, can I booked an appointment with John? He's on holiday until this weekend, so they have a pretty good idea when I'd be crossing the Channel at Calais. So, they waited for me to arrive at the docks, then followed me on the ferry, I had the tandem on the roof of my car, so I was in the lane with the caravans and campers. The police suggested that when they followed me onto the ferry, the car deck is sealed, there's no staff in the car deck at all, so they hid in their caravan or camper, then opened my car's central locking using half a tennis ball over the lock and hitting it with air pressure, which would trigger the central locking to open. Then they filled all the panels but had one block of cannabis over, so instead of risking having it in their vehicle at Dover, they hid it in amongst my luggage with the intension of robbing me on the roadside when I stopped on your my way home. All my personal details and address would have been in my vehicle with my travel documents should they not get the chance on my journey back from Dover. They would get the drug's at my home, but because I stopped and parked outside my salon with the tandem on top, they also had my business address too.

Well, I didn't stop at all on my journey back, and my home wasn't that easy to find. Remember, there wasn't Sat Nav nor mobile phones, even the drug squad couldn't find our house when Phil called them out. I had to stand at the bottom of our shared drive on the lane so the police could find us. I guess the same thing applied to the drug dealers.

One thing I do clearly remember about the crossing was, when the boat was preparing to dock at Dover and we were instructed to return to our cars, I was one of the first back to my car, and the campervan which was behind me I noticed already had people sitting in it. Not family-looking people, more the young beach type travelers. It did occur to me then that they were quick getting in their vehicle, because I really was one of the first on the deck. Usually you'd be opening the doors, putting your duty-free in the boot, taking your coat off, preparing to have a big drive ahead, but these guys were already sitting there ready to go. I could be wrong, but I don't think I was.

After that meeting, things calmed down a bit. Sue and I were concerned about our security, even though we had the police direct to car device. I wanted to get rid of my car, and at the salon, the alarm was rear entry. I was concerned going out through the back door right by where I parked my car.

About a week went by, and the salon had settled from my situation, and then one day I opened the post, and this came anonymously in the mail.

"You cost us a lot of money,
we don't think that's very funny.
When you double cross Jack,
always look behind your back.
Psychology is a science,
psychopaths like a little violence.
Avaricious men who value finance
keep their mouths shut in silence."

If I wasn't before, after reading this, I most certainly was very concerned that something might happen either to me or, worse still, my family. The post mark was Crewe. The police did have the view that those who were responsible were local people. This was thirty years ago, and it still bothers me!

The Man in the Mirror

We were on alert for weeks/months after, both at home and at work. Then, one day, I got a phone call from Phil Maskery.

"I need to see you on official business."

"What business, Phil?"

"Why don't we meet at the Sheet Anchor for a pint or two and I'll explain everything to you."

So, there we were, having a couple of pints, which, after three or four hours, I was drunk. What got me into that state was what Phil said.

"This has come from the very top. We'd like you to go back and do the same try again."

"You must be bloody joking! Go back and do it again? You can bloody forget that, I haven't got over the last time yet let alone repeat the same! No, deffo NO!" I've never been that drunk before and never since. Phil could take his drink, but me, no. I stupidly drove home, and when Sue opened the front door, I was confined to the front room with a bucket. Boy was I sick, and the room was spinning around. No, never again. I've been merry, but not never as drunk as that!

I still see Phil, he'd say fancy a pint later? Not with you, no, NEVER! He'd laugh, and it's been a joke between us ever since.

I sold my Granada Estate. I was conscious that whoever was involved must have been local to our salon. It was too risky being seen driving around in that car, even though I loved my Granny Estate. The car was perfect for us as a family, but it had to go.

CHAPTER FORTY-SEVEN

From Bad to Worse

We got through Christmas, and the salon was busy, as you would expect it to be. Christmas Eve and the week leading up to it was mental! Twelve hour days, and I always worked the two Sundays before Christmas, too. There was always someone who'd left it late trying to get an appointment. I'd work til midnight before I'd turn anyone away. You know what they say; "Look after your customers and they will look after you."

It was the same with New Year's Eve. It was over the top hairdos and long dresses, all the main hospitality venues had traditional dinner & dance parties. Those days are long gone, and since lockdown, we close between Christmas and New Year. How times have changed!

We'd changed accountants from Neil Bradley to Richard Nadin at Dean Statham. Their offices were just up the road on King Street, and Neil was a very likeable character, but his drinking was getting too much. I never had any real control of our accounts, Neil was very much, "Don't worry, Ducky, I'll sort it," but it left me wondering.

It was January 1991, and I got a call from Richard Nadin, he'd had our accounts off Neil before Christmas.

"I've gone through your accounts for the last three years. Neil Bradley has messed up. You've got around 30K of back tax to pay."

"What! That can't be, surely!"

"Well, I'm afraid it is. He's not done your accounts correctly."

"How are we going to bloody pay that back?"

Whilst I was in the middle of trying to sort out a way of repaying this money, my dad ended up in hospital with "Endocarditis." It was serious, he had an infection of the heart muscles, and my brother Stuart called me to say they couldn't accommodate having our mother, who was beginning to show signs of dementia. So, he was arranging to place our mother in council care.

"What! You can't do that, what will Dad say?"

"Well, he's likely to die from his condition, the hospital have said his condition is causing concern."

"We should wait until Dad's situation is clearer, we can't just dump Mum in council care, Dad would go mental!"

"Well, we can't have her," he said.

"Right, give me a couple of hours, I'll come and pick her up."

Now, I'm not going to explain my brother's reasons for his decision, but from my perspective, his home circumstances were far better than mine! With two-year-old twins and an eight year old at home, we could and should have been able to compromise having Mum between us until it was clearer what was going to happen with Dad. After all, he was still alive!

So, I went and picked up Mum from his house. Needless to say, my reception wasn't friendly. Having said that, it wasn't before, so this was just going to make his attitude toward me even worse.

Sod Em! We ain't dumping my mother!

So, I took her home. Yes, it was chaotic. We had Mum for around six weeks. No, Dad didn't die, he slowly began to improve, though the situation didn't help Mum's dementia, if fact it made it worse, but we managed.

I used to take Mum to the Salon each day, where she had her hair done every day, then in the afternoon, either me or one of our staff took Mum to the hospital where she'd sit with Dad, then I'd go and pick her up in the evening after work and visit Dad and take Mum back home with me. It wasn't ideal but better than my brother's alternative.

After a few weeks had gone by, I bumped in to my brother in the car park at the hospital. He was going to visit Dad. I had Mum with me, so I asked him if he would help me for just one weekend and have Mum for two days to give me and Sue a break.

To which he replied right in front of Mum, "You wanted her, you've got her," and started to walk away from me.

I called out to him, "So you're saying the welfare of your mother is down to me?"

"YEP!" was his reply. Mum and I just stood there, not one little bit of friendliness from him whatsoever. "Come on, Mum, take no notice, let's go home."

That was the last time my brother saw his mother alive. She died suddenly two weeks later. The night before Dad was due out of hospital.

The day before Mum's funeral (March '91) I had a sharp, acute pain in my right shoulder, just like I had been stabbed with a knife right in the joint and my right hand was feeling funny. I put it down

The Man in the Mirror

to all the stress I'd been through. We the drugs incident, a huge back tax to pay, then Mum passing suddenly, but I'd never experienced pain like it. My doctor gave me a painkilling injection into the shoulder joint to help me through the funeral the next morning, which it did.

But the pain got worse, and my fingers on my right hand were going numb. I couldn't work, and my doctor wasn't sure what was causing such pain. I called two private physios I knew, hoping a bit of treatment would do the trick. They put a harness around my neck and literally tightened it to the point where I was almost being HUNG! The pain left instantly, and I thought, *Great, they've solved it at the first attempt.*

Then the bad news came. "You've got a collapsed disk in your neck, and its trapped a nerve, hence the pain, when we let you down from the neck harness, the pain will return."

And Boy did the pain return!

They were able to get me a private appointment with a Consultant neurologist, Dr Donald Campbell, and during the next few days, I was admitted into the Nuffield Private Hospital on Clayton Road Newcastle under Lyme. I was positioned flat on my back with with a neck harness back on with weights hanging down the back of my bed and my neck stretched, it was the only way I felt pain free.

Mr Campbell arranged an MRI scan, which showed my 5th & 6th discs had collapsed and the 8th & 9th almost closed too. He went on to say that I'd had whiplash, which had caused this type of injury, which can take four or five years to appear. It's almost like a broken neck in slow motion. You will need surgery to prop and hold the disks apart, without it you will permanently lose the use of two or three of your fingers on your right hand and also lose the control of your bladder."

It was beginning to look like my hairdressing career was over.

Mr. Campbell went on to say that he was one of the front runners in the most up-to-date method of surgery which included "buffalo bone" being grafted between the two disks, which would hold the disks open. I would be pain free, but it would restrict my movement in lifting my head when looking upward, and because the damaged nerve can only repair its self at 1 millimeter a day, it would take two years for the nerve repair to reach my fingers.

Brilliant! What else could go wrong? Was this the end of my ability to do the only work I knew?

My income ended there and then. I was still keeping my dad in way he was accustomed to, even though my mum had gone. We had the twins, aged two, Jonathan, aged eight, a country property with a swimming pool, 30k of tax to pay back, and some undesirable drug dealers giving me the heebie geebies since that bloody threatening note turned up.

Oh, and after surgery, I couldn't speak for three months.

Anything else? Yeah, the business was £68k overdrawn!

My Bank Manager Ken Shakespeare came to see me. That time had come. The bank was going to close me down unless I could give them something to get them off my back, at least in the short term.

What could I do? Having a young family needing me to provide, as well as my Dad, I'd funded his and Mum's lifestyle for almost twenty years. And the salon, our staff, some had worked for us for years. I felt a huge responsibility to all of them, what was about to happen would change the lives of all in one way or another, but my family's life more than anything else.

We sat and talked with Ken Shakespeare, my accountant Richard Nadin, plus Sue and Dad about what options we had. Richard felt my best option was bankruptcy. I was facing a future of not being able to work, not for just a few weeks but months. Ken said he could hold off having the bank foreclose, at least for a couple of months. Richard wasn't happy with this, arguing knowing you'd no ability to pay was fraudulent.

Dad suggested if we pooled all our assests we could get through it. He decided to sell his and Mum's holiday bungalow in Rhyl. On the grand scale of things, it wasn't a lot. I remember him buying it, mainly from the sweat I'd put into the business, with the profit the shop was making. It wasn't the time to start bringing up the past, but with Mum passing and Dad's health in question, it was the right thing to do. I was adamant he kept living in my bungalow in Barlaston. They both loved living there, and Sue and I put our home up for sale. All in all, this was enough to get the bank off my back and buy us some time financially.

We got through it together, the bank took our house proceeds, plus Dad's bungalow money, and he stayed in Barlaston. I sold part of the business to a staff member, and Sue and I bought a semi detached house on Queen's Park Avenue by Longton Park in the southeast of the Potteries.

It was a further nine months before I was able to work again.

Little did I know what else was about to happen.

The staff member who bought twenty-five percent of the business had visions of grandeur. He used a section in our agreement to serve notice on me should I not return to work within an agreed time. That's friends for you. Why only have a quarter of the business when I can kick him out un take it all for nothing?

John Belfield M.I.T.

Yes, my dad's words were ringing in my ears. *Don't forget, you're on your own in this world!*

I have to say from experience, I'm too trusting with people, particularly staff. No, he didn't succeed. What's the phrase used in these sort of circumstances? *Over my dead body!* Enough said on the subject—he's gone.

CHAPTER FORTY-EIGHT

Ireland, Here I Come

What I thought was two relative minor car accidents ended up changing the course of my international career. I was in line to be one of the ladies' team trainers for the World Championships in London in 1994 at Wembley, but my inability to be able to do any form of hairdressing for over a year, I got overlooked. In fact, I ended up demonstrating how to cut hair using Electric Clippers only on the WHAL hair clipper stand in the exhibition area. I used members of the audience who were watching me for models. Actually, during each day, I cut the hair of fifteen people, each from a different country around the world. Could that be a world record I wonder? Well, I'm gonna claim it.

Well, if the English didn't want me, there were always the Irish. No, it wasn't quite like that. I got a phone call from Trevor Mitchell, he'd been over to Dublin doing some teach-ins with the men's team. Ireland hadn't put a ladies' team out in a championship in twenty years. They wanted to start a new team or squad and needed someone to get them started. There was no money in it apart from travel to Dublin once a month. And after the snub from the Brits, I was up to giving it a go.

John Belfield M.I.T.

My first time over to Dublin was a bit of a red carpet affair. I drove from Newcastle under Lyme at six on a Sunday morning to Holyhead, parked my car at the docks, and crossed on the HSS Fast Ferry to Dun Laoghaire, just on the south edge on Dublin. I was collected at the docks and taken to a Peter Marks (flag ship) salon on Grafton Street, one of two main shopping streets in Dublin. It was a fabulous salon, and there was around twenty to twenty-five hairdressers with models waiting for my arrival. A lady named Irene Devereaux, who had a salon in Dublin was the team leader, and Maeve O'Leary-Hart from Athlone was the team manager and also editor of *Irish Hairdressing Magazine*. So, I made a short speech, talking a bit about my background and my ambition to put Irish Hairdressing on the map again. How hard could it be, there must be four good hairdressers amongst this lot, surly.

I started them off doing a commercial day style, so as they all started, and I wandered around, introducing myself and casually observing each one's approach. That is, who'd done a competition day style before. As it turned out, none of them!

My expectations were a little high, half of the sets would have stood out in a Sweaty Betty Salon, but, *What am I doing here?* went through my mind. Then, as I approached one hairdresser, who's model was very pretty model, until she spoke, "My fucking eyelash is falling off," in a hard Irish accent. Irene, who was walking around with me, turned and said, "We all use the "F" word in Ireland, you'll get used to it."

That's easy enough. How about, "What the fuck are you trying to do?" was a sentence I used with every single one of them, not once, not twice, all the fucking time!

None of them had any experience in hairdressing competitions, certainly not at international level. Most had come just for free tuition to improve their basic skills and also make the claim," Member of the Irish Hairdressing Squad."

Four weeks later, there was another twenty odd hairdressers, all just turning up for free tuition and the title! I wasn't a happy bunny, each trip from start at six a.m. to getting back home was around twenty hours, and I had nothing to show for it.

I was determined to make a go of it if I could, I'm no quitter, but I don't believe in flogging a dead horse either. It was early days, and in the back of my mind, I was thinking some of these hairdressers would maybe give my products a go, that would make the whole thing doable, if only!

I kept going over each month, sometimes taking a model over for Irene to use, although managing the team she wanted to compete too, and I needed to move it along as well. After many months of trying, eventually I had a core of eight or ten hairdressers who regularly turned up, including two from Galway on the west coast, their day would start as early as mine. The locations for training varied in the Dublin area, and on occasions centrally in Athlone at Maeve's Salon.

I can't say I didn't enjoy my time with the Irish, what I did enjoy was seeing progress for my efforts and evidence that some had actually been practicing back in their own salons; now that I found rewarding, progress at last!

So I had my core of ladies' hairdressers, and I stuck with it. Occasionally, the odd new person would join or one would leave, and from this we planned on doing an international competition in Paris, something to work toward, and I was hoping that once they had the experience of competing at that level, it would give them the desire to continue and really achieve, then my mission was finished; they were up and running, plus being self-trained together.

It was a usual Sunday afternoon, and everyone was practicing their looks. We were in a salon on the edge of Dublin, and I was wandering around between each of them, when out of the blue a voice from behind me called out, " Hello there Luvver!"

I turned, and standing there was my old friend and Minder Charlie!

"What the fuck are you doing here?"

"I heard you were in town, and I've brought my family to meet you."

There beside him was his wife and two sons. They'd driven over from Limerick, which was about a three hour drive for them to Dublin just to see me. I hadn't seen Charlie in over twenty years. I'd got him a job in Koln with Wolfgang Steinbach, but that was years ago, we'd lost touch with each other.

I decided to finish up earlier than planned with the training, leaving Irene to carry on, and I joined Charlie and his family for a late lunch and a big catchup on the lost twenty odd years since we last spoke.

"To everyone in Ireland, I'm now known as Charles," he said. "Okay, Charlie!" I replied. "Just kidding! So what are you doing back in Ireland?"

"Well, it's not such a long story. My Wife and two boys are German, we were happily married, living in Germany, Wolfgang was a good employer to me until they took the Berlin Wall down, then, suddenly, people like myself was occupying a job of a German. Tens of thousands of people like me lost their jobs, so we came back to Ireland. We're living in a small town on the outskirts of Limerick called Newcastle."

"I heard that, Charles, I know a couple of teachers who fell on the same sword!"

It was great catching up on the last twenty-odd years, and I was pleased to see he'd settle down with his family and he was training the Irish men's team. We talked about working and bringing the two teams together, and agreed on having both teams compete in Paris in their international event in the autumn at the Palais de Congress exhibition center.

So, all that summer, we worked on the international in Paris events for overseas hairdressers. We made reasonable progress getting the teams to an acceptable standard, everyone was doing as well as they could. Hopefully we were setting the groundwork for a future Irish International squad/group of hairdressers who would be self-sufficient.

I arranged my own travel from Manchester on the day before the event. I would meet them at the team's hotel, chosen by the Irish federation because it was right across the road from the exhibition center, perfect for everyone taking part. I arranged for the ladies' team to have one last run through that Saturday evening, so when I arrived I could check everyone's hairstyles and hair color, which I did until two in the morning, correcting faults which shouldn't have been in their work had they practiced enough back home. So, with that done, I arranged for us all to be down for breakfast at seven a.m., ready to cross the road to the exhibition by eight-thirty a.m. For some of the team, meeting for breakfast at seven meant coming in at seven. There was an Irish bar right next door to the hotel, and most had spent what was left of the night drinking in the bar until morning. Now I realized why this hotel was their first choice for somewhere close to the competition venue! Or was it the other way round—most likely!

But with it came a problem—most, not all, were hammered. Drunk! I was not happy.

"If this was your main priority, you could have stayed in Dublin to get drunk, not in Paris on the eve of our first major international event. During this upsetting situation, which I clearly wasn't happy about, one of the men's team, Eddie Walsh, a guy who'd I'd helped on many occasions, turned to me in a drunken state and said, "We don't need you bloody English coming to Ireland telling us what to do." Yes, many a true word said in drink. I left Charles to sort his team out, and those who were in an okay state to compete, I took over to the exhibition center to get them sort of organized to compete in the championships. My roll was to register as the Irish Judge for the championships.

I didn't see them again until back at the hotel that evening, where there was a group dinner arranged for all of us. I learned from Charles that Eddie Walsh actually went over and competed in his event, it was an embarrassing day for everyone concerned. Eddie Walsh that evening, still under the influence, tried to apologize to me, as did some others too, but the damage was done and my mind made up. I announced over dinner that I would return one last time to Ireland to hand over to someone else for the ladies' team training responsibility, after that I was finished.

I was very disappointed to see, not from all but from enough, that there was still resentment toward the English for all that happened many years ago. Even though I wasn't doing the training for any personal gain, in fact just the opposite, I was well out of pocket financially, but for me, hairdressing was a worldwide community of likeminded people, of which I was one who had benefited in so many ways in my life's journey .

I kept a lose connection with Maeve and Irene for a while, but for some reason not Charles. We never kept in touch after the Paris episode, I'm sad to say. Maybe I should have tried harder, having reconnected our friendship after such a long time, I do feel some guilt in the way it ended. All in all, I do have good memories of my time in Dublin.

John Belfield M.I.T.

CHAPTER FORTY-NINE

Delivering an NVQ to a Fourteen-Year-Old Still at School

In some ways it's perhaps as well. I was still recovering from nearly losing the business, yet our salon product range was growing, and so was our apprenticeship training through in-house on the job NVQs. There was lots to do to keep the uniqueness which our brand locally was known for.

We started in the late 90s with a training company owned by a Lady named Annetta Talbot and her partner, David. This was an era when we would get a couple hundred applications for apprenticeships, usually between January and Easter. We used Saturdays and holidays, giving trials to the most likely ones we thought really really wanted to do hairdressing.

Over time, we gave work experience on Saturdays to fourteen-year-olds who we thought would make it with us. We needed parent/guardian approval to do this. The system worked very well for both parties. The government through the schools introduced an NVQ level 1, which students could work toward on a Friday afternoon. This lay the foundation for a modern apprenticeship in a number of vocational industries for when the student left school. We even delivered an NVQ level 2 in customer service to a fourteen-year-old.

We were the first salon to deliver such a qualification in our area, maybe even in the UK! In my view, this system benefited the student and the employer. How I wish that was the case today. Back then, there was less rules in the workplace, and there was more give and take with freedom to encourage genuine enthusiasm. Hairdressing is a way of life, it's now a job with so many rules and regulations, there's no chance of chasing your dream in the workplace these days, it's like a prison for both the employee and the employer. The main outcome: get the qualification regardless of the standard, so long it ticks the right box, that's all the trainee is interested in.

As employers, both Jonathan and I would always go the extra mile for our employees, giving them a standard that stands out from the rest. But finding like-minded apprentices isn't easy. Salon times have changed. Having Saturday staff was always our main option for school leaver recruitment, but Saturdays are now a short day; we close at two. This is the norm throughout the hairdressing industry; in fact, some salons I know don't even open on a Saturday anymore.

Our ethos has always been: we recruit and train apprentices because they are our future team of qualified stylists. That's how we've always looked at building our future stylists, its something we are very proud of when a client walks into our Salon, that every person working in the salon started as an apprentice with us, as training builds a loyalty. It's the foundation to build a business's future on. This has always been one of the reasons for our continuous success; however, I have to say it's not the norm in hairdressing anymore. The majority of hairdressing salons today don't employ apprentices anymore. It speaks volumes of an industry that fractured in many ways.

Completing an apprenticeship, whether in hairdressing or in other industries, should mean something; have a value comparable with other qualifications and a standard for the person who has completed it. In my mind, I believe we achieved this standard. Our salon certainly had a huge demand from people applying for our apprenticeship training. Against our competitors, our salon was the number one place to train. Colleges were well down the pecking order; you might get a qualification at a college but the hairdressing industry looked on it with having little value against an apprentice who had achieved their qualification at a salon in the workplace.

Dad had been living with us in an annex flat on the ground floor at the rear of the property since my mum had passed, he had the best of both worlds; puttering around the salon each day, still connecting with our most regular clients, until one day, I was planning a weeks holiday in the Lake District, and I explained this to him, that we'd be away but there was always someone in the salon from eight a.m. and the cleaner after work, so he'd have company almost up to his bedtime.

Why I thought this was okay, I don't know, but with four days to go before this holiday, he started acting weird.

I was in the staffroom area with him, it was a Tuesday morning, our holiday wasn't until Sunday, and I asked, "What's up, Dad?"

"Don't you worry about me," he said, "Diane (one of our staff), shes going to stay with me whilst your away."

"What! Oh no she isn't, I'm not having staff staying with you, it's not right, and there's going to be people on the premises from eight a.m. to eight p.m., you've only got to get yourself ready for bed and up the next morning." I wasn't getting anywhere with him, and I began thinking by the time we left for the Lake District on Sunday, he'd have us coming back before we'd opened our suitcases.

In desperation, I called a residential home on Sandy Lane, just a few blocks up the road from the salon, I put my situation with my dad to Christine the manager, asking, "Would you be able to have my dad for a week whilst we go on holiday?"

She would have him for a week, they had a room, too, saying to bring him up later because they would need to assess him first to see if he was suitable for the level of care they provide.

So, on our way up to the home after work, I said, "Look, Dad, we're going away for a week, so can you at St Quinton Care Home." (It sounds like a prison, St Quinton! But it's not, it's very nice).

So, in we went, and the first thing he noticed was the menu on the wall by the dining room, then a couple of residents said hello, they knew him from church.

So there we were with the manager Christine, standing it the room that was available, and she turned to my dad and said, "Well, Joe, we'll have you here for a week."

He looked up at me and said, "Go get my things, I'll stay now."

"We're not going away until Sunday, its only Tuesday evening."

"I'll stay now," he said again.

I looked at Christine, and she said, "Okay, Joe, you can stay now." Off I went back to the salon to get his things.

Sue said, "What's going on?"

"Now he's saying he wants to stay there now, unbelievable! He sworw he'd never go in a home, now he doesn't want to come out."

And that was the beginning of life in a home for Dad. I went to see him a couple of days later, and he said to me, "I know my flat is nice, but can you sort it for me to stay here."

"If that's what you want, Dad."

It ended up working out well, apart from me have to cough up the topping up money. Each day after his breakfast, he'd come down to the shop and spend the morning with us every day, then he'd go back for his lunch, and I'd visit him with the twins some evenings.

Dad developed a fear of dying on his own, so he'd sit in with the staff during the night for company rather than be in his room on his own.

He died on Friday 13th September 1996 at nine-thirty a.m. in the middle of the dining room with all the residents.

On the day of his Funeral, having my last private moments with him, I realized I was nobody's child anymore.

CHAPTER FIFTY

Celebrating Ninety Years in Business with Boxer Frank Bruno

1998 Was our 90th year as a family business. We had two of our staff take on a hairdressing franchise in a new health and fitness club on the outskirts of Stoke-on-Trent's city center called Esporta. This was, I hoped, a new opportunity of expanding into franchising my hairdressing brand. The club manager was keen to have a big name to do the opening for him. Well, at that time, I knew a guy named Trevor Vale who lived next door to Frank Bruno. Trevor had a group of salons in the Essex area, with a well-known collection of celebrities as clients to go with it.

Together, we came up a plan that Frank Bruno would come up and do the opening of Esporta, and Frank would come to our salon afterward to join us and our many clients in celebrating our ninety years.

Obviously, there was money involved in securing Frank doing this opening, and Esporta had left me the job of negotiating Frank's fee of £5000. The difficulty was that Frank's wife Laura was the person I had to deal with and not Frank himself. That might seem straight forward enough, except Laura was a hard character to deal with, and she had a dialogue of four letter words to go with it! Esporta would only offer £3000, so this was my bottom line fee to secure Frank coming up and doing the opening, Trevor had already agreed to bring him up to us from Essex.

Just to give you an idea as to what my negotiating was like with Laura, when I called her and put this £3K offer to her, the response was he ain't EFFIN going EEFIN anywhere for EFFIN three grand, in a very load voice down the phone. She wouldn't budge on the £5 grand fee she was wanting! I had several phone calls with her, all had the same number of four letter superlatives in her responses to the fee. In the end, Epsorta increased their offer to 4K, and I put 1K to it to make up the £5K needed.

There was an added bonus in the end, as Kevin Donavan, a good friend and well-known business man in our area, came up with an even better idea. He knew the head of sport at Central Television in Birmingham, we ended up with TV covering Frank's visit to our salon's celebration. It was a perfect day for us, and the publicity it created for the salon, especially when he turned up in his red Rolls Royce convertible, with its reg no FB1.

Frank was brilliant, mixing with all our clients and friends, chatting and having his photo taken with all of them during the two hours he was with us. Before he left, I had him sign five pairs of Red boxing shorts (red was Frank's fighting color) and five pairs of Boxing gloves. Over the following couple of years, through us donating these items for local fundraising events including "Children in Need" on the air auction at BBC Radio Stoke, they raised over £5K for local causes.

After the opening of our franchise in Esporta Health Club, I was given the opportunity of taking other salons. Esporta was a new group of health clubs, and being offered other sites at their Clubs was a good business prospect for me and my family. In most cases, the clubs were in the building stages, and I was asked by their architects to advise them on the layout and workability of these salons, because having readjusted the layout of ours in Stoke, Esporta realized their architects hadn't a clue about hair salons and if they had continued it would have been costly redesigning all their new clubs with salons in them.

I ended up doing the working drawing for twelve salons up and down the UK as these Esporta Clubs were being built.

Because I was involved with finding suitable franchisees for these salons, I was never offered a fee for this extra design work. In most cases, I don't think Esporta were even aware of my involvement with the architects.

I did have a good working relationship with Holly Smallman, who was Esporta's estates director, and within three to four years, we had franchises within Esporta's health clubs in Leeds city center, Cookridge North Leeds, Bolton, Stoke-on-Trent, Litchfield, Stafford, Wolverhampton, Gloucester, Oxford, Chelmsford, Romford Harlow, and Northwood (London)

Each franchisee had a three year contract with Esporta and myself, and apart from a franchise fee, each salon was contracted to using John Belfield International Brand name and products.

As each contract came up for renewal, Holly Smallman dealt with each franchise and myself, which meant that I dealt with any ongoing issues. It made her job easier and kept me with an ongoing franchise business with over a dozen salons buying our products. Jonathan, my eldest son, having just finished school, was showing an interest with our product range, so it was only natural that he took on this side of our business.

Having Jonathan make his decision to become part of our family business is very special to me. It's given me a new energy with a more youthful outlook on our future together.

With no previous experience in dealing with such a large company like Esporta, I trusted the people who I was dealing with, which turned out to be a big mistake. My first warning sign came when I was invited to join a meeting at the Wolverhampton Club. There was Esporta's commercial director, their regional manager, and the club manager where the meeting was held. Having listened to the regional manager make his presentation to the commercial director, this presentation included graph after graph showing percentages for this and that. There were more graphs on foot fall, peak and low times of the day, and our salons were located in the beauty areas of each club. I had no interest in getting involved running a group of beauty salons, although over time, a couple of franchisees did. So, after the regional manager finished his presentation, the club manager did the exact same presentation on his Wolverhampton club, with more graphs and percentages for this and that. I began to realize that the commercial director's presentation would be more of the same at board level, and this left me with one question to ask, having sat there for a couple of hours

Is your club making any money?

NO was the answer. I didn't go as far as to say, well, what was that all about that I've just sat through for the last two hours? The word profit never got mentioned once.

I'd put my heart and soul into this franchise business. I was working full time in the salon then on a Sunday and Monday I'd be driving around either salons in the north one week, then salons in the south another week. Seven days a week every week. Having had the experience of nearly going under, I was determined to make a go of this franchise business for my family's future and for Jonathan's future, too.

But that meeting presented a very different picture, and I was right to be concerned, because what happened later made our franchise business unworkable. Esporta restructured each level of management, the estates director Holly Smallman lost her job, and all future franchise contracts went through each club manager.

Having our franchise business in the hands of each club manager was a disaster. When the Chelmsford salons contract came up for renewal, the club manager cancelled all negotiations for us to renew. My franchisee had been there six years. He'd never given the club a problem, his rent was paid on time, why wouldn't the club manager not renew? It didn't take me long to find out. He had a sister who was a hairdresser, and she had a salon on Molsham Street in Chelmsford. Now she had another salon to move into with a ready-made business, and I had nobody at Esporta to turn to now that they had cancelled their estates dept. It also meant that if they wanted to, my franchisee could go directly to the club manager when their contract came up for renewal.

That was it. I sold some of them back to the franchisee and got out of the rest. Ten years later, Esporta went under. No surprise there.

John Belfield M.I.T.

We had enjoyed working and successfully running our Salon in the environment of a Georgian building dating to 1824. With rear parking for clients and staff, it was ideal in many ways, and the character of the building gave the Salon an ambiance which clients enjoyed being in, with our living accommodation upstairs just as interesting. But with a growing family, it was time for us to consider relocating our home and once more our Salon too.

Number 9 was a lovely building, full of character, but expensive to maintain. I also understood my family having to run up and down stairs a dozen times a day, though I only came down in the morning and upstairs once at the end of the day.

I had overcome a downturn in our finances, and we were reasonably back on our feet to make a move. Owning a listed building with a lot of local history also gave us a financial platform to enter the domestic property market for a family home. It did mean finding a premises to move the salon to, though.

A property on King Street became available at no. 52. it was a phone shop and before that a hair salon. It had two other floors over it, with the top floor being a flat. It was ideal, as we had a better street location and potential for other options with the upper floors. The down side was it was a rental property, but this was as good as we could expect.

I was able to design a really nice, modern Salon with my tec drawing knowledge, and I soon had a 1:20 scaled working drawing, with plans for the electric and plumbing too. In another life, I could have been an architect.

Twenty-three years later, we are still in the same property. We now own it, and it has expanded into a hair and beauty salon with

The Man in the Mirror

a Trichology Consulting room on the first floor. I've never stayed in one place as long as I have in this salon, and I've no desire to move. It's home.

CHAPTER FIFTY-ONE

Diagnosed with Advanced Prostate Cancer

Jonathan decided to take up hairdressing, and we did have one franchise business in Hanley (Stoke city center), which was independent from Esporta. When this became available to us, Jonathan worked and ran that salon very successfully until my cancer diagnosis in 2017.

At first we both carried on working both Salons, and the cancer was treated with Abiraterone and Enzalutamide for two years. Both are testosterone inhibiters. Prostate cancer feeds on testosterone, so, in principle, remove the testosterone and the cancer can't feed or grow.

Following this was thirty-seven radio therapy daily sessions to target not only my prostate but also my lymph nodes beyond the prostate where the cancer had spread to. For this expensive treatment, I had a private health policy to claim, which enabled me to avoid chemother- apy, and during this period, I was still able to work on reduced hours, which I still wanted to do. It was costing my insurance policy ninety-six thousand dollars a year. Eventually, after two years, the premiums went up to £300 per week, I had to end it there and use the NHS. I was then moved on to Zoladex injections every three months.

Fortunately, at the salon, I was at in Newcastle under Lyme, which was the original salon, although, having had different locations over a hundred and ten years, it's where our most loyal and long-standing staff were working. the Hanley salon in comparison was a relatively new add-on to our business.

It's important to say that the success of our family business is also down to our long-term loyal staff, especially Christine McDonnell, who has worked for us for over forty-five years. Also the late Liz Harper, who worked with us for thirty-five years before she sadly passed away. Chris and I have fond memories of our time together with Liz. Another very special mention is Julianne Wantling and Chelsea Davies, who both started with us from leaving school and doing their apprenticeship with us. They are an experienced team of hairdressers. I should also add our beautician Camille. She didn't train with us, but she's run our beauty salon successfully for over twenty years.

From myself, Jonathan, and Sue, too, a big thank you to everyone. Having said that, I should also say on behalf of Jonathan and myself that we've been incredibly fortunate to have a long list of loyal clients. Too many to mention all by name. Some have been clients over forty and fifty years. They have had their first haircut with us. This is the backbone of our business—grandparents, parents, and their children, too. Thank you for keeping us in business, which at the time of writing this book is a hundred and sixteen years!

Because of my health and prostate cancer, Jonathan and I decided to close our Hanley salon. The city center had changed significantly from how it used to be, becoming a no-go zone in places. Many of the more traditional, sole trader type of businesses were closing and moving out. We made the decision to relocate as best we could all our staff and as many clients as possible to our Newcastle salon. We were still in the middle of getting everyone adjusted to the move, and to say it was work in progress in hindsight would probably be an understatement—and then Lockdown!

Everything was affected by lockdown and Covid. This was completely lifechanging for everyone. From a business and employer and employee's perspective, the workplace changed forever. So many people lost their lives to Covid, and for those family and friends we know who did, our condolences go out to everyone.

It was around Monday the 16th of March, the week before Lockdown on the 23rd in 2020, and I was travelling back from London. I'd been work in Southampton and London doing a couple of Trichology Personal Injury Reports for an agency I was working for. Mid-afternoon, I got a call from Harrison, Jonathan's younger brother, who's now grown up and working as a dentist.

"Dad , I think Mum has got Covid, you can't go back home, I've booked you in a local hotel for the next few days, stay away, Mum needs to be isolating."

I spoke with Sue, and she sounded awful, but these were the government's instructions at that time.

Within a week, we were locked down, and I was still isolating in a local hotel at Trentham Gardens, one of the few that was still open. I was due to do a reading at a dear friend's funeral, Gwen Jones, on the 24th of March. This was reduced to a graveside reading of less than ten people the day after my hotel closed, so I returned home, having completed my isolation. Sue was still very unwell for a couple more weeks.

We re-opened on the 4th July and had a brainstorming meeting with all our staff. Some didn't want to return to work, saying it was still unsafe, others were wanting their holiday entitlement, which they had booked during lockdown but couldn't go. Every member of staff was paid furlough at eighty percent of their wages, but for some it still wasn't enough.

Jonathan had organized screens between each styling station, at the back wash area, and at reception. He had a one-way system—in at our rear salon entrance and out through the front. BBC TV featured our salon on their national website as the safest salon in Britain. The French news agency picked up on the same story, yet for some, this still wasn't enough.

We finally agreed on a six hour shift system, eight a.m. to two p.m. and two p.m. to eight p.m., half working alternatively early one week and late the next. It worked throughout that period until things started getting back to normal. Some staff didn't want to work the hours they did before lockdown and got used to being at home, so those staff moved on to renting chairs or working from home, so long as they could take as many clients of our with them, they didn't care. Our loyal staff stayed, and they are still here working with us today.

By 2022, we had recovered from the Covid lockdown, which lasted on and off for a year. Our business model has changed, and all our senior staff work the hours that suit them, which has helped us maintain our business, although not how it was. Appointments are now hourly, which gives that extra bit to the client and more enjoyment and job satisfaction for our staff. We still offer apprenticeships with on the job qualifications from NVQ level 2 and up to NVQ level 3&4. Very few salons today take on apprentices, we are one of the few salons in our area that still does. The difference between the two is fundamental. Toward the end of 2022, I was having trouble swallowing, I was sent for an endoscopy (a camera down my throat) at my local hospital.

After it was done, the doctor came to Sue and I and said, "You have an ulcerated area in your esophagus, which I'm fifty percent certain is likely to be cancer. It might only be ulcerated, but it's possibly esophageal cancer. We'll do a CT scan whilst you're here." After which, we were sent home, very upset, wondering what the future might bring. This was just before Christmas.

During the holiday, I had another appointment for another endoscopy, scheduled for early January. Sue came with me again for this one, and after the procedure I mistook a comment from one of the nursing staff, saying everything was fine and you can go home. We both did very happily.

At the end of January, I had a phone call from one of the nursing staff asking me to come in. I was at the salon working and agreed to the appointment on Thursday the 2nd of February.

It was all very casual until the nurse said, "Can you bring your wife or someone else with you?" Then the penny dropped. This wasn't going to be good news. And it wasn't.

After an introduction by a senior cancer nurse and two other staff attending, she said, "I'm sorry to inform you, but you have Oesophageal cancer."

Both Sue and I were upset by this news.

We scheduled an appointment for Monday morning with a senior surgical consultant followed by a senior oncologist

The Man in the Mirror

My hairdressing career ended on Saturday, the 4th of Feebruary 2023. My last full time working day.

My surgeon, Mr. Bouras, explained that I had a forty-five percent chance of survival with surgery, and the operation took ten to twelve hours was the biggest operation performed at this hospital. But my age might be a problem, and I would need chemotherapy before and after surgery. This was confirmed by Dr Kier at his appointment with me. Without surgery, he gave my survival rate of six to twelve months maximum. I needed the surgery.

I started thirteen weeks of chemotherapy at the beginning of March, each session lasting approximately five hours, with another drug connected for a further twenty-four hours before being removed. Each was administered through a pic line, which was fitted through my arm for the duration of the treatment before surgery. My prostate cancer treatment was suspended during this period.

I was given steroids before, during, and after chemo to help the side-effects, plus anti-sickness tablets too. Believe me it was shit. For days after chemo, you feel like crap, and just when you improve, it's time to go again. My cycle was every fifteen days. It finished at the end of April, then they gave me May to recover before surgery on the sixth of June, subject to me passing a fitness test.

Well, I failed the fitness test—they put me on a bike, but I've got two hips and a knee replacement. However, I can swim further than I can walk! my surgeon was concerned I wouldn't survive the surgery. Twelve hours is along time to be under anesthetic, and anything could happen; a stroke or heart attack, it was a big risk. He said I would need further heart tests before he made his decision to proceed or not.

I decided to go back to the swimming pool, having not swam for twelve weeks, and try and get myself fit for the tests my consultant needed for his final decision whether to do my surgery or not.

There was a guy swimming in the next lane to me, he was already into his swim, and I remember speaking with him about four years ago. He had told me he also coached at Stafford Triathlon Club. I'd not seen him since that first time we talked at the end of the pool. So there he was, already swimming, and he was still swimming when I left the pool to get changed. As I was getting dressed, he entered the changing room and spoke to me.

"I know an awful lot about you," he said to me.

I looked quizzically at him, "Sorry, what do you mean?"

"I'm one of the four surgical team that's going to do your operation, and after seeing you swim, I'll tell my boss you're the fittest seventy-seven year old we're ever likely to have on the operating table for your type of surgery."

And that's how I got my surgery. Yes, somebody up there was looking down on me, because without the surgery, I wouldn't be writing this book.

2023 finished with me having more chemotherapy than before surgery. During the three weeks in hospital, I had a questionable CT scan result with my hip bone. The surgeon felt there was something for concern, and during my recovery at home my GP arranged to see me and Sue. He told me the scan results showed bone cancer, and he took me through the process of palliative care and advice on how to approach taking more time with my family whilst I could.

We both returned home very upset, I decided to re-look at my will, and I also wrote details of my funeral.

I had an appointment later the same day in oncology, and my consultant wasn't prepared to go as far as my GP, but he said he was concerned with the CT scan results. I had an emergency MRI scan the next day, and the following day, my doctor called me in to see him.

He said, "I've got your MRI scan results here. "It's not bone cancer."

You can imagine my relief at those few words.

Yes, I'm through it all. I'm still connected to the hospital for five years, and I'm in a group of patients who've all had the same surgery called "Swallow," which is a side-effect from having your stomach moved up toward your throat.

I was told recovery from this level of surgery, coupled with my age, would take twelve to eighteen months for me to feel something. Well, it's been just over twelve months now, and I feel so lucky to of have such an incredible team doctors and nurses. Mr. Bouras my surgeon and his team, oncologist Dr Keir and his team, and the four senior cancer nurses, Debbie, Sarah, Laura, and Lisa—a big thank you. And all staff at the Royal Stoke and Stafford Hospitals and my GP Dr. Sullivan, who made it all happen, thank you.

To my wife Susan, I got though it because of all the love, understanding, and care you showed me every hour of every day. Without you, I wouldn't be where I am today. And Jonathan, Harrison, and Hannah too! I Love you all!

John Belfield M.I.T.

I'm now back with my prostate cancer oncologist, and where that will take me, I've no idea, but I can say this: Cancer isn't about death, it's learning to live with it."

I'm never going to be able to pick my life up where it was before all this, but I'm getting there. I'm back doing some trichology consultations, and clients, too. Not every day, but it's a new beginning. Jonathan is now running the business, and for years he's stood and worked in my shadow. Now it's his time to take our family business of a hundred and sixteen years forward into the future. He has a great team of staff supporting him, and now I'm standing in his shadow.

I leave these pages for my family to be completed when my story is finally over.

John Belfield M.I.T.

14th August 2024

O! if for honour, fame, yet sigh
While noble ardour fires the eye,
Yet let the midnight lamp behold,
Studious of what these themes unfold;
'Til old experience do attain
'To something of prophetic strain;'
Then shall ye live, and drink with me
The draft of immortality;
And, in the historian's future page
Shine forth the Coiffeur of the age!

J.B.M.D. Lafoy, 1817

www.ingramcontent.com/pod-product-compliance
Lightning Source LLC
Chambersburg PA
CBHW072046110526
44590CB00018B/3054